C000198368

READING THE GAELIC LANDSCAPE
Leughadh Aghaidh na Tìre

John Murray / Iain Moireach

Whittles Publishing

Published by
Whittles Publishing Ltd.,
Dunbeath,
Caithness, KW6 6EG,
Scotland, UK

www.whittlespublishing.com

© 2014 John Murray/ Iain Moireach

reprinted 2014 (twice, second with corrections)

All rights reserved.
No part of this publication may be reproduced,
stored in a retrieval system, or transmitted,
in any form or by any means, electronic,
mechanical, recording or otherwise
without prior permission of the publishers.

ISBN 978-184995-100-5

Printed & Bound by MBM Print SCS Ltd, Glasgow

CONTENTS

ACKNOWLEDGEMENTS

In memory of my father, Ian, with whom I first climbed *Meall nam Fuaran,* Hill of the Springs (**Plate 12**) near Amulree, for my mother, who tackled *Meall a' Mhadaidh,* Hill of the Dog, behind my grandmother's home in Lochearnhead and for my wife who fell asleep in the snow upon the Shee of Ardtalnaig.

Thanks go to Robert Gray (Chartered Forester), Quentin McLaren (formerly Scottish Natural Heritage and Cairngorms National Park), Dr. Greg Kenicer (Royal Botanic Garden Edinburgh), and Ann Paterson (Gaelic tutor), for their encouragement and guidance. Special thanks go to Ian MacDonald (formerly of the Gaelic Books Council), Charlie Withers (Professor of Historical Geography at the University of Edinburgh), Ian Fraser (formerly of the Scottish School of Studies) and Dr. Jake King (Ainmean Àite na h-Alba, Place-names of Scotland) for their detailed and substantive editing and suggestions, which have improved both text and argument immeasurably. All plates and figures are by the author except the back cover. The book was made possible by research leave from the University of Edinburgh.

'The names people give to places imbue them with a symbolic significance that unnamed places lack ... Naming is ... endemic to the perceptions and shaping of a locality, for names alone create a mental image that has special significance for local people - and names can be the means by which an outsider begins to perceive a place's unique qualities.'

(Hough 1990,18)

*Plate 1: 'A Little Place' - Creagan nam Plaoisg – Little Rock of
the Husks, Brig o' Turk, Trossachs (also in colour section)*

'... for local people with a knowledge of Gaelic, and especially
with knowledge and memories of past events, the landscape
is a living landscape and place names are mnemonic devices
that trigger recollection of particular activities ... by naming
places after people or by commemorating an event with a
name, people are located in the landscape.'

(Jedrej and Nuttall, 1996, 123)

'... I know every corner of this land, every little burn and
stream, and even the boulders in the stream. And I know
the moors and every little lochan on them. And I know the
hills, and the passes, and the ruins, and I know of things that
happened here on our land long, long ago ... Every little place,
every hillock, every hill and slope, has its own name.'

(Gunn 1976, 250)

There is a series of black and white photographs illustrating the landscape throughout the text.
A selection has been repeated in a colour section. These versions are referred to in the captions
to black and white illustrations, where applicable.

PREFACE

Whilst fishing below Quinag (NC203283) in Sutherland *(A' Chuinneag – The Milking Pail)*, I met an English fisherman. Pointing west into the heart of the mountain (**Plates 2 and 26**), he said that he had given up fishing at the black loch, as gales gusting in the corrie *(coire)* had made casting impossible. Surely I said, the black loch lay to the east, high on the northern flanks of *Glas Bheinn - Grey Mountain* (NO254265), on the other side of the glen. What he was talking about, is called *Lochan Bealach an Còrnaidh - Small Loch of the Pass of the Folding of Cloth* (NO207282 whose spelling should be *Bealach a' Chòrnaidh)*. Two thoughts came from our conversation. We could not communicate precisely about the location of large things, which are self-evident parts of the landscape. Secondly, since my fellow angler could neither read nor understand what was written on the map, he had invented his own English place-name, unique to himself, whose meaning he had confused with older Gaelic names.

Later that week on a visit to a shop near Drumbeg, (NO125267 *An Druim Beag - The Small Ridge)*, I saw a notice at a road end saying that the owner's family had stayed on the croft for over 150 years. I talked with the proprietor about the walk we had just finished and how the old peat roads passed *Poll nam Muc - Pool of the Pigs* (NO123315) and *Loch Bad an Òig - Loch of the Spot / Thicket of Youth* (NO117314) and how these engaging names spoke eloquently of some forgotten history. The owner said that she had neither heard nor understood them. Though the first language of her parents had been Gaelic, as was usual in Assynt forty years ago, they had not passed on their native tongue to their daughter, which was commonplace amongst the generation of that time. Despite 150 years of family

Plate 2: A' Chuinneag - Sàil Gharbh, Bealach Cuinneige and Sàil Ghorm

history rooted in one place, she had lost touch with the landscape as it had been expressed in the language of her immediate ancestors.

In these two exchanges, an insider and an outsider to the landscape were both unaware of the richness recorded on the map. Such brief conversations persuaded me to write this book.

PART 1

I: INTRODUCTION

How many people have looked at a map of the Highlands and been intrigued and yet, at the same time, felt excluded by the wealth and strangeness of the place-names recorded? Most of us, like the English fisherman mentioned in the preface, can neither understand nor pronounce the unfamiliar combinations of letters and syllables of this language painstakingly printed on folded paper. Sometimes we consult a Gaelic dictionary or Ordnance Survey's comprehensive *Guide to Gaelic origins of place names in Britain*. As a result, we are drawn into the diverse and extensive alphabetical glossaries provided. Often, however, little remains for long in our memory. This may be because we have no framework on which to organise our new and hard-won Gaelic vocabulary. Perhaps our short-term memory evaporates because there is little chance to apply, and so reinforce our knowledge. There are, after all, few opportunities to practise the language on the Highland mainland. Given the history of Gaelic, many native speakers are hesitant to converse with strangers, in what has sometimes become a private means of communication. Ordnance Survey (OS) maps may be the sole contact non-speakers have with the language.

This can happen when we use any one of the 46 of the 72 Scottish 1:50,000 scale OS Landranger maps, which together cover the area where Gaelic was spoken until the late nineteenth century, known as the Gàidhealtachd *(GEHLaltuchk)*. On these sheets most place-names are recorded in a reasonably correct and contemporary spelling with a recognisable and fairly consistent grammar. They are easy, therefore, to translate without recourse to complex toponymic or etymological research, which can prove a step too far for even the most ardent enthusiast. Names are not so easy to remember however, without some understanding of Gaelic grammar.

This book aims to build a framework for organising such knowledge, which should help the better recall of Gaelic place-names. It is intended that readers will learn about diverse aspects of place and how these have been recorded, through a deeper understanding of a language specific to the landscape of the Scottish Highlands and unique in its perception of that landscape. Landscape will become more legible through an appreciation of Gaelic place-names.

Name elements and qualifying adjectives, which are common to many features, are here organised into types. Categories include: the physical, the biological, the visual and the cultural. Knowledge of other name types, like those associated with agriculture, settlement and history, will encourage a more connected understanding of Highland landscape and culture than what it is possible to learn from place-name inventories alone. Categories also cover areas of specific interest to hill-walkers, sailors, anglers, botanists and ornithologists, which will enrich their understanding of the landscape and appreciation of place. Instead of merely denoting a place, the aim is to connote a name with its meaning in the context of the specific landscape to which it applies.

The book will explore the following questions. Why are place-name distributions often uneven for no apparent geographical reason? What happens to place-names at the edge of their cultural range? Why is the Gaelic vocabulary of place so different to English or Scots? How can Gaelic generic place words be related to geographical terms? What kind of landscape do Gaelic names portray? What kind of plants and animals were present when the landscape was named? What might be the reasons why certain words are preferred in naming? When there are no exact translations, how can we understand meanings? How have poets and song writers used place-names in the Highland landscape?

A brief guide to pronunciation, which does not involve having to learn the International Phonetic Alphabet, will also be introduced, so that outdoor enthusiasts will be able to apply and communicate their understanding through practice. Capitals indicate stress on the first syllable. Since place-names usually consist of modified noun groupings, no comprehensive knowledge of Gaelic grammar will be necessary, beyond an awareness of definite and indefinite articles, plurals and genitives. Actual place-names will be used as vehicles for understanding the few simple rules which exist. Brief guides about the history of Gaelic, cartography and the study of place-names are also included, as there are several reasons why care has to be taken in the interpretation of mapped names.

The book is intended to appeal to serious enthusiasts who seek a deeper understanding of what they study and enjoy in the Highlands of Scotland. There are sections on landform, ecology, land use, water and cultural landscapes, which will interest walkers, naturalists, geographers, anglers and sailors. In the emptiness of much of the mainland Gàidhealtachd, such people may now be more knowledgeable in their use of landscape than anybody else, but not necessarily about the meanings place-names embody. In a sense, outsiders to the Highlands have become the new insiders. Given the decline in rural life, which has taken place in many areas, the book may also appeal to young native speakers, whose vocabulary may no longer include words which describe the landscape in Gaelic. What is being attempted is a semantic reclamation of a lost domain. An attempt to recapture a poetry of place, enshrined in the identifying labels which have been given to the landscape by Gaelic-speakers.

In the past, Gaelic place-name publications have tended to emphasise the needs of climbers and walkers and concentrated on hills and mountains. This book intends to cover a wider territory and attract a more diverse readership and so enable a more comprehensive reading of the landscape. Munro bagging may be accompanied by a new sport of name spotting in future.

Readers should note that place-names, which are shown on OS sheets, current at the time of writing, have been quoted largely as they have been spelled on maps. Some spellings are incorrect or inconsistent with modern orthography. Accents and single missing letters have been added where these are missing and the correction is simple and obvious. Correct and contemporary spellings of generic Gaelic place-name elements can be found in the two indexes at the end of the book.

2: A BRIEF HISTORY OF GAELIC IN SCOTLAND

After nearly a millennium of expansion, where it superseded Pictish on the Mainland and Norse in the Hebrides and western seaboard, Gaelic experienced two periods of significant decline. The first affected the whole of Scotland and the second was confined to what we now know as the Highlands or *Gàidhealtachd*. It is broadly defined along its southern and eastern boundary by the Highland Fault (**Figure 1**), except along its northern boundary with north-east Caithness, where Scots superseded Norse.

As a result of these periods of decline, Gaelic is now no longer spoken widely in either Scotland or, indeed, the Highlands. This is particularly evident on the Mainland. Only in the Western Isles and parts of Skye is the language spoken by the majority. When visitors to the Highlands try to interpret place-names from Ordnance Survey maps, they are often not in a Gaelic-speaking area. There are usually no native speakers to advise about a map's accuracy, or the local pronunciation and meaning of place-names. Paradoxically, in the Outer Hebrides, where Gaelic is most widely spoken, place-names, particularly for settlements, are often likely to be Norse rather than Gaelic. Given the extent of the Highlands and the high frequency of Gaelic place-names distributed widely over most of the area, what explains the rarity of the spoken language? Why is a landscape so richly named so empty of the people who named it? What has happened to them and to their language, which is distributed so widely over the map?

Strangers are sometimes confused about the identity of the two languages unique to Scotland, Scots and Gaelic. Neither appears to be *the Scottish Language*. Scots has its origins in Northumbrian English, one of the three dialects of Old English. Whilst Irish is the language of Ireland, Scottish Gaelic, to which it is closely related and whence it sprang, is not *the Language of Scotland*. Such confusion has not always existed.

Writing from Jarrow Abbey, Bede the eighth century Northumbrian monk cites the language of the Scots people as Gaelic. For the Scottish historian Fordun, at the end of the fourteenth century, Gaelic was still perceived as the Scottish language. Even at the beginning of the sixteenth century, John Major, another Scottish chronicler, records that most Scots until recently, spoke Irish, by which he meant Scottish Gaelic.

The speech, which had been previously confined to the Lowlands of Scotland now became known as Scots. The use of the word 'Irish' by Major is significant, as it shows that a Lowland writer perceived Gaelic as a language of another nation. In other words, he distanced it from mainstream Scottish identity, Lowland values and its lifestyle, which were developing in the Central Belt. Terming Gaelic as Irish also distanced the Highlands from the Reformation and sometimes encouraged an anti-Catholic focus to be directed at Highlanders. Later still, in the mid-eighteenth century, Dr Johnson spoke of Gaelic as 'Erse,' another form of the word Irish.

In 1609, the Privy Council of Scotland passed laws, which became known as 'the Statutes of Iona,' requiring, amongst other measures, that Highland chiefs send their heirs to Lowland Scotland to be taught in English-speaking and Protestant schools. At the court held on Iona, some Highland chiefs put their signature to the statutes. The Statutes of Iona are often considered as the first in a series of Scottish Government measures aimed at the break-up of traditional Gaelic culture and tradition. Nine chiefs signed the agreement: 'Angus Macdonald of Dunivaig in Islay, Hector Maclean of Duart in Mull, Donald Gorm Macdonald of Sleat in Skye, Rory Macleod of Harris, Rory MacKinnon of Strathordaill in Skye, Lauchlan MacLean of Coll, Donald Macdonald of Ylanterim (Eilean Tioram) in Moydart (Captain of Clanranald), Lauchlan Maclean of Lochbuy in Mull, and Gillespie MacQuharrie of Ulva.' The other MacDonald clans of Clanranald, Keppoch, Glengarry and Glencoe did not sign and continued to adhere to the Catholic faith. Two clauses of the Statutes relate to bardic tradition and education.

The chiefs not to entertain wandering bards, or other vagabonds
of the sort 'pretending libertie to baird and flattir,' and all such
'vagaboundis, bairdis (poets), juglouris (jugglers), or suche lyke' to
be apprehended, put in the stocks, and expelled the Islands.

(Why jugglng presented such risks, apart from obvious physical ones, is unknown?).

Every gentleman or yeoman in the Islands possessing 'thriescore
kye (cows),' and having children, to send at least his eldest son, or,
failing sons, his eldest daughter, to some school in the Lowlands,
there to be kept and brought up 'quhill they may be found able
sufficientlie to speik, reid, and wryte Inglische!'

Seven years later, in its continuing drive to promote education in English, the Scottish Privy Council stated amongst its objectives in passing the Act for the Settling of Parochial Schools:

that the vulgar Inglische toung be universallie plantit, and the
Irische language, whilk is one of the chief and principall causis of the
continewance of barbaritie and incivilitie amongis the inhabitants
of the Ilis and Heylandis, may be abolisheit and removeit …

In 1709 spelling had improved, but the policy of the Society in Scotland for the Propagation of Christian Knowledge (SSPCK) for education and Gaelic continued in the same vein.

Nothing can be more effectual for reducing these Countries to order
and making them usefull to the Commonwealth, than teaching
them their duty to God, their King and Countrey, and rooting out
their Irish language, and this has been the care of the Society so far
as it could, for all the Schollars are taught in English.

To be fair to the Society, this was revised substantially in later years. (The Statutes of Iona are online at: http://www.ambaile.org.uk/en/item/item_page.jsp?item_id=118765)

Not surprisingly, the distancing of the Gàidhealtachd from much of Lowland life sometimes provided a seedbed for political action, culminating in the Jacobite risings of 1689, 1715, 1719 and 1745. The last uprising ending ignominiously at the infamous Battle of Culloden, and finally resulted in the 1747 Act of Proscription, which banned the wearing of Highland dress and the bagpipes, and marked the end of the clan system.

Clan chiefs soon came to see people on their land as tenants rather than as a source of recruits for their private armies. Their priority turned to the maximisation of income from their estates. This often led to the introduction of industrial scale sheep farming run by Lowlanders and the consequent clearance of small-scale agricultural tenants from the hinterland and their forced resettlement on the coast, or their emigration. For toponymists, such narratives can help explain why the fertile and distinctive landscapes of Strathnaver and Kildonan in Sutherland and Loch Tayside show a paucity of mapped names, whilst coastal areas in Assynt often display a much more diverse collection of place-names.

On Loch Tayside, the farms of Morenish (NN597351), Kiltyrie (NN629367) and Cloichran (NN618343) were cleared by the Marquis of Breadalbane's factor in the middle of the nineteenth century. These areas do not include many place-names. The few present are either in English or anglicised. The edge of the loch, despite its many bays, points and confluences, and despite the site of the old settlement of Lawers at the water's edge, is almost entirely void of names. It is as if the new sheep farming society had cut the link between the water and the hill. Toponymic emptiness can also be seen in nearby Glen Quaich, which was cleared by the Marquis's factor at the same time. Duncan MacGregor Crerar of Glen Quaich wrote from Ontario, Canada:

> 'Evicted thus were Albyn's sons of fame,
> Their lands are teeming now with sheep and game,
> How sad and lonesome this once happy glen,
> Where, Oh Glen Quaich, have gone thy gallant men?
> Doomed on whom falls the heartless factor's frown,
> Oh God, arise and crush such tyrants down.'
>
> (in Gillies 1938, 212)

Although within the area shown in **Figure 1**, after the Clearances, and in some counties like Sutherland, some communities were forcibly moved from the hinterland to the coast, the southern and north-eastern boundaries of the Gàidhealtachd roughly paralleled the geological fault, over much of its length. To this day place-names

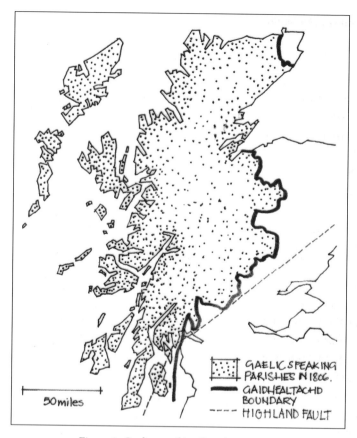

Figure 1: Gaelic-speaking Parishes in 1806

show a marked difference in conformity with Gaelic spelling and grammar within a short distance of the line.

North-west of Crieff is Easter Knockbae (NN837254) and slightly further north lies *Cnoc Beithe – Birch Knowe* (NN864268). *Bae* is a phonetic rendering of *beithe* close enough to suggest some understanding of Gaelic amongst English or Scots speakers. Nearby lies *Meall Tarsuinn – Rounded Crossing Hill* (NN877297), with an outlying spur to its south-west called *Mull Hill* (NN883284). *Mull* is a rough attempt at the sound of *meall*. These instances suggest the existence of bilingual English and Gaelic communities in close proximity. Similarly, in Reay Parish, in the north of Caithness, *Cnoc Dachow* (NC965645), whose meaning is obscure, lies close to *The*

Knowes (NC965643). *Knowe* is a good translation into Scots of *cnoc*. Within three kilometres either side, correct Gaelic orthography is found at *Cnoc na Mòine* (NC940652), Knowe of the Peat, and *Cnoc an t-Samhraidh* (NC977620), Knowe of the Summer. In the south-east of that county, near Lybster, lies *Airigh Hill* (ND212381), where Gaelic is combined with English in the name. Whilst six kilometres to the north lie *Àirigh Bheag* (ND213438) and *Àirigh Mhòr* (ND220442), the small and the large sheilings, in pure and correct Gaelic. A line drawn between Reay and Lybster limits the Gàidhealtachd boundary, which can be traced by the distribution of the generic name for field, *achadh*.

Despite this first period of linguistic retreat and government retributions after Culloden, from the early sixteenth century until almost the end of the nineteenth century, the Gàidhealtachd or Gaelic speaking area remained reasonably constant. Various reasons have been advanced for the first period of Gaelic decline in the Lowlands.

The relocation of the Scottish capital of what was still a Gaelic-speaking kingdom from Perth and Dunfermline to the English-speaking Lothians; the introduction of feudalism to Scotland and its use of Norman French; and the establishment of English as the language of trade and commerce may all have contributed to a decrease in the use of Gaelic. To add to the decline, compensating infusions of Celtic culture would have been weakened with the severing of links with Catholic Ireland, its literary culture and bardic traditions, after plantations of Lowland, Protestant Scots had been established in Ulster.

The second period of decline happened after the passing of the Education Act in 1872, when primary schooling was brought under the control of central Government and made compulsory. Previously, education had been organised by the Kirk and the SSPCK, which had by now come to encourage the use of Gaelic to some extent. Centralisation occurred just nine years before the 1881 census, which was the first survey of its kind to pose questions about Gaelic. Whilst earlier church organised schools had sometimes allowed for some education in the language, the 1872 act completely ignored Gaelic. Thus ideas of advancement through learning were dissociated from Gaelic language and culture. A wooden board *(maide-crochaidh)* was hung around the necks of pupils if they were caught speaking the language.

Consequences of this policy in action can be seen in a letter written in 1901 by the Duke of Atholl, who was trying to encourage Gaelic on his estate, to Lord Balfour, the Secretary of State for Scotland, complaining about the local school inspector.

> *I find that this Mr Thomson, who has inspected*
> *the schools in this neighbourhood ... does all he*
> *can to oppose and cry down the Gaelic ...*

(in Ó Murchú 1989, 56)

In a memorandum to the Secretary of State from the Secretary for the Education In Department in Scotland, Sir Henry Craik attempted to explain the situation.

> *To encourage the children at the elementary school*
> *to waste time that might be better spent, on fantastic*
> *nonsense such as this, is about as pernicious a way of*
> *spending money as his Grace could devise.*

(in Ó Murchú 1989, 57)

The timing of the Act, can be examined in parallel with census data, which had begun to record information about Gaelic from almost the same time.

Year of Census

In 1881 and 1891, Gaelic was spoken throughout the Highlands. Only in Caithness, in towns bordering the Moray Firth, along the south-eastern edge of the Grampians, in south Kintyre, on the east coasts of Arran and Bute, was the language spoken by less than 50% of the population. Nearly a quarter of a million Scots spoke Gaelic in Scotland in 1891, over 6% of the population. Between 1901 and 1931 the number of Gaelic speakers declined from 230,806 or 4.5% of the Scottish population to 136,135 (2.8%). By 1951, only in the Hebrides (except in the north and east of Mull), Morar, Sunart and the western margins of mainland Inverness-shire, Ross and Sutherland did a majority of people speak the language. Fewer than 2% of the nation's population were now Gaelic speakers. Of the four core counties in the Gàidhealtachd, Argyll and Sutherland proved the least resilient to linguistic erosion. Given the policy of the education authorities, it

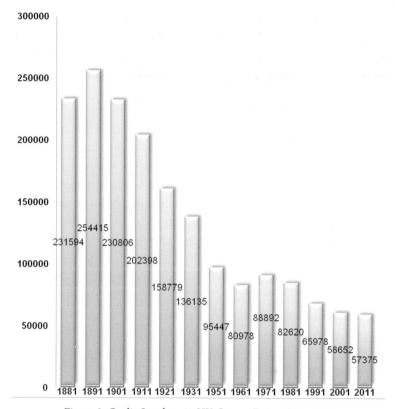

Figure 2: Gaelic Speakers in UK Census Data 1881 - 2011

is not surprising that parents did not think it worthwhile to pass on their language to their children.

The rate of decline in Gaelic speakers appears to have decelerated in recent years. The 2001 census reported 58,652 people, having fallen by 11.1% from 65,597 in 1991. In 2011, the decline had slowed to 2.2% to 57,375. This represented 1.1% of the Scottish population recorded as having some ability in the language. Half of these lived in the Outer Hebrides, Highland Region or in Argyll and Bute. Gaelic has continued to decline in these core indigenous areas, but this has been masked in part by an increased number of speakers in the Lowlands. In 2001, nearly 50% of Gaelic speakers lived in the cities of the Central Belt. Kenneth MacKinnon compared this new distribution to 'a Gaelic archipelago in a Lowland sea.' The 2011 census also recorded the positive result that the number of speakers under twenty years in age had increased by 0.1% - presumably as a result of the growth in Gaelic medium education. In 2005, the language was officially recognised by the Scottish Government, but unlike Welsh, Gaelic is not recognised as an official language of the United Kingdom.

Perhaps the most noticeable visible difference for the visitor to the Highlands, which has accompanied the recent Gaelic revival is the erection of bilingual road and rail signs throughout much of the Highlands. To the place-name enthusiast this is a welcome and useful initiative. Many names have now had their Gaelic origins revealed. What was obscure and meaningless has become transparent to those non-Gaelic speakers with some knowledge and curiosity. The meaning of place-names now helps to inform and strengthen a sense of place and cultural identity, coming from the past and extending to the present Gàidhealtachd. If we did not know the Gaelic spelling of Acharacle, for example, which is Àth Tharracail, we might mistake a field *(achadh)* for a ford *(àth)*, and misunderstand the reason for the siting of the settlement near the outflow of Loch Shiel *(Loch Seile)* and the significance of the fact that it commemorates a man with the Norse name of Torcuil.

Most of the verification of the names on the bilingual signs has been undertaken by Ainmean-Àite na h-Alba (AÀA) - Gaelic Place-names of Scotland, the national advisory partnership for Gaelic place-names, based at Sabhal Mòr Ostaig (SMO) on the Isle of Skye *(An t-Eilean Sgitheanach)*. SMO, which is now part of the University of the Highlands and Islands, was begun in the humble setting of an old stone barn by Sir Iain Noble in 1973. He had bought the estate of *Fearann Eilean Iarmain* in Sleat *(Slèite)* from the impoverished Lord MacDonald. What started as a Further Education establishment is now the Centre for Gaelic Language and Culture in Scotland. As Noble said at the time, this was the first new institution of this kind since Columba founded Iona Abbey.

About the same time, Sir Iain provoked the beginnings of a bilingual policy on road signs. The then County of Invernesshire wished to carry out road improvements to the south of Portree, which required the purchase of land from *Fearann Eilean Iarmain*. Sir Iain agreed to this on condition that three bilingual signs were erected for Broadford, Portree and Viewfield Road. These were *An t-Àth Leathann, Port Rìgh* and *Goirtean na Creige*. This last name means the arable enclosure of the rock, and bears no resemblance to meaning of the English version. After a long struggle with the Council, signs were eventually erected. Upon local government reorganisation in the 1970s, Comhairle nan Eilean rapidly replaced anglicised road signs with Gaelic versions - often with no translation supplied. Bilingual signs are now commonplace on roads in the Highlands, but less so at the time of writing in the Highlands of the former Counties of Stirling and Perth. Where possible Gaelic station names have also been introduced throughout the rail network in Scotland. The results of such policies has propelled Gaelic into the mainstream world of maps and mapping. Such patterns are mirrored elsewhere. Citing Mount Egmont, Mt McKinley and Mount Everest, which are also known as Taranaki, Denali and Chomolungma in the native languages of New Zealand, Alaska and Nepal, Ruairidh MacIlleathain argues that Ben Lomond, Ben Nevis, Braeriach, Cairn Toul and the Pap of Glen Coe (*Gleann Comhann*) should, in the Gàidhealtachd, be recorded on maps with their dual identities. In Gaelic these would be: *Beinn Laomainn, Beinn Nibheis, Bràigh Riabhach, Càrn an t-Sabhail and Sgòrr na Ciche*.

The following table of well-known Scottish mountains, adapted from MacIlleathain's 2010 lecture to the Islands Books Trust, clearly shows how correct Gaelic renderings provide a rich and informative resource for those trying to read the landscape through place-names.

Table 1: Anglicisation of well-known Mountains and their Original Gaelic

Anglicised form	Original Gaelic form	Meaning
Ben Alder (NN496718)	Beinn Eallair *byn YOWLehr*	water flowing over rock
Ben Chonzie (NN773308)	Beinn na Còinnich *byn nuh CAWNyeech*	Mountain of Moss
Ben Lawers (NN634415)	Beinn Labhair (Plate 3 and 19) *byn LAHvir*	Noise Mountain
Ben Lui (NN266264)	Beinn Laoigh *byn loeu-ee*	Calf Mountain

Anglicised form	Original Gaelic form	Meaning
Ben Vorlich (NN628188) & (NN296124)	Beinn Mhùrlag (Plate 4) *byn VOORlak*	bag-shaped mountain
Ben Starav (NN126427)	Beinn Starbh *byn STAHrav*	blocks of rock
Derry Cairngorm (NJ017980)	Càrn Gorm an Doire *caarn GAWrom un DAWruh*	blue hill of the copse
Dreish (NO273736)	Dris *dreesh*	bramble
Mam Sodhail	Màm Sabhail *maam SOWehl*	barn
Morven (ND004286)	Mòr Bheinn *mawr vyn*	big mountain
Mount Keen (NO408869)	Am Monadh Caoin *um MONugh coo-win*	the gentle high country
Quinag (NC203283)	A' Chuinneag (Plate 2 and 26) *uh CHOONyak*	the milking pail
Schiehallion (NN714547)	Sìth Chailleann *shee CHYLyun*	fairy hill of the Caledonians
The Black Mount (NN275468)	Am Monadh Dubh *um MONugh doo*	the dark high country
The Cairnwell (NO135774)	An Càrn Bhalg *un caarn valak*	the hill of peatbanks

Correct renderings in Gaelic also enable correct pronunciation and familiarity with the language through usage. Cairn Toul is an interesting case. To the Lowland Scot, who pronounces *dour* as 'do-er,' it is tempting to pronounce -toul as 'tool.' Paradoxically, the Southern English speaker who may pronounce *dour* as 'dower,' is more likely to voice the Gaelic correctly, as Cairn Towel. Similarly and mistakenly, Tomintoul (*Tom an t-Sabhail - the hillock of the barn*) in the northern Cairngorms is often pronounced Tomintool.

Correct pronunciation can also help the understanding of meaning in the landscape. How do we know what Balloch, near Loch Lomond, means, if we do not know that the original Gaelic form is *Bealach*, meaning pass and pronounced BYAHluch, with stress on

Plate 3: Ardeonaig - Beinn Ghlas and Beinn Labhair, Tom a' Bhuachaille is on the left middle ground of the picture

Plate 4: Glen Beith - Beinn Mhùrlag, Stùc a' Chroin and Beinn Odhar, Tom Cadalach is on the right middle ground of the picture behind the sheep

the first syllable? If we did not know the sound of the name, we could conclude that Balloch had the quite different meaning of Town of the Loch, or *Baile an LOCH*, near Inverness, which is pronounced with the stress on loch, and confusingly, also anglicised as Balloch.

If the spelling of Gaelic names is incorrect on maps and in guides, how can we be sure if the anglicised prefix kil means a church (*cill*), a wood (*coille*) or the back of something (*cùl*), which are completely different landscape elements? If Auchtertyre is spelled thus, or as Ochtertyre, how do we know if the name refers to a field, *ach(adh),* or the upper part, *uachdar,* of the land - possibly quite different kinds of place? The problem with anglicisations is that they are inconsistent. Throughout the text this book will identify many common corruptions of Gaelic spelling and their correct forms. Like the introduction of bilingual road signs, it is hoped that this will redress the imbalance in how Highland landscape is interpreted through place-names, in favour of a more grounded and deeper understanding.

3: MAPPING THE SCOTTISH HIGHLANDS

In 1984, four groups of students taking part in a hydrology field course were asked to make a sketch map of the same short stretch of river in northern Manitoba. Their subjects were biology, engineering, landscape architecture and technology. The biologists saw the stream as habitats grouped around a sinuous flow. They mapped areas of deposition, erosion and former water channels. The engineers drew a straight watercourse, which they thought was causing problems for the land either side. They mapped areas of slumping and active bank erosion. Landscape architects produced a plan whose graphics (though rendered with beauty and clarity) communicated little about place, natural phenomena or landscape process. Technology students made a drawing, which communicated accurately, if crudely, what was there and what was really happening.

This contemporary student exercise showed how hard it is to represent the natural world even when it is drawn from life. What was omitted and included on the students' maps was strongly influenced by their background, what they wanted to see and what they valued. Despite the advanced techniques available to modern cartographers, maps remain selective about what they choose to include and how it is represented. Place-names are no exception, particularly when what is being mapped, and who is carrying out the mapping, may come from different cultures. This is especially true when there is an asymmetry of power and purpose between those providing information and those recording it. Maps are documents of both commission and omission.

The first person to map Scotland from a Scottish point of view was Timothy Pont, who worked between 1596 and 1614. Although coverage of Scotland was incomplete and some of his work has been lost, it formed the basis of Blaeu's Atlas, published in 1654. Pont was a graduate of St Andrews and a Lowlander and so had Gaelic-speaking assistants for at least some of his work in the Gàidhealtachd. It is thought that the motivation for his task was part of the general policy of the Scottish monarchy to bring the Highlands and the Borders under more effective central control. With this purpose in mind, the maps were intended as a study documenting how geography and society contributed to regional identities. Accompanying notes assessed the resources and productivity of the landscape. The focus was on how the rural economy of Scotland was organised. There was an emphasis on farms, mills, churches, bridges and roads, but much less notice was taken of natural features. Nevertheless, river systems are often used as an organising framework around which information on the mapped landscape was located.

Out of 20,000 place-names recorded by Pont, over three-quarters are settlement names. Pont must have consulted local Gaelic-speakers, since the language has been phonetically realised into Scots on the maps with reasonable accuracy. On Loch Maree, he records 16 islands named in Gaelic in more detail than on any later map, including the Ordnance Survey. Roy Wentworth discovered a small drawing in the margin of one map which showed that four island names appear on no other record.

Three island names which Pont sketched in the corner of this map have different names to those recorded by William Roy's military sur-vey of the mid-eighteenth century and those entered by the OS in their name books made in the second half of the nineteenth century. One island, in particular, changed its name twice in that journey through time. Pont records it as ylen or ella Gewish, which is probably *Eilean Giuthais - Scots Pine Island* (NG913730). The same place is recorded in Roy's *'Fair Copy'* as Id (island): na Feannaig and I Fainnig in his *'Origi-nal Protraction,'* which could mean either Island of the Crow or Crow Island. The OS Name Book records the place as *Eilean Loisgte*, Burnt Island – which is what is shown on the contemporary 1:25,000 sheet.

There is no reason why different people at different times should not have had different names for the same place. Toponymic options may express contrasting but not necessarily contradictory aspects of place. Places will also change over time. Vegetation can be subject to the most rapid alteration. A causal interpretation of the name changes might be as follows. We begin with an island wooded with mature pines, *Eilean Giuthais*. These are felled and deciduous trees and shrubs regenerate and fill the vacant space left in the canopy. Such species are more favourable to the roosting of crows than conifers. The island catches fire, perhaps because of the combustible nature of broom and gorse, which also have regenerated in the lighter conditions of the new woodland. The island becomes known as *Eilean Loisgte*. The writings of two travellers shed some light on the matter. Thomas Pennant, who journeyed through the Highlands in 1769, suggests that the island was wooded with 'firs,' the vernacular for Scots Pine, whereas the geologist John MacCulloch, over fifty years later mentions a scattering of trees and thickets of mixed species over the islands.

Pont's cartography is not conventional in the modern sense. He gives the general disposition of the land, but not with geometric accuracy. Some of his sketches of mountains seem almost like rough perspective drawings, and the spontaneous quality of their draftsmanship suggests that they were drawn in the field. This contrasts to William Roy's work in the eighteenth century, where mountain morphology tends towards a default symbolism of monochrome pen and ink hatching rendered by Paul Sandby. He later became well-known as a watercolour artist.

Before William Roy's survey, Blaeu's Atlas, based on Pont's work, was the best map available. Nevertheless, a month after the Battle of Culloden, Captain Frederick Scott, writing from the prominent landmark of Castle Stalker in Appin, noted '*this Place is not marked on any of our Maps*.' He also found out that place-names differed between those shown on his charts and those used by local people in their daily lives. The 1745 rising revealed the lack of, and illustrated the need for, an accurate map of the country. Cartographic accuracy, or the 'quantifying spirit' became an ideal for the Age of Reason.

William Roy, who later became a Major General, was commissioned in 1747 to undertake a military survey of the Scottish mainland, beginning in the Highlands. Roy used the routes of General Wade's military roads, constructed after the 1715 rising, as a basis for organising his work. Unlike previous maps, which were often little more than an amalgam of previous charts, Roy's survey used actual measurement and traverse survey along the length of the new road network.

After summers in the field and winters collating the results of their work in Edinburgh Castle, in 1755 Roy's team produced two versions, a sketch and a fair copy. The latter comprised 84 brown linen map rolls giving 38 folding sheets. The complete map measured 20 by 30 feet. This was an impressive achievement accomplished in so short a time. However, as the work was not related to longitude or latitude and the maps were not aligned to true North, mistakes, after many traverses and successive offset measurements, accumulated steadily. The east end of Loch Leven in Fife is shown twenty miles south of its true position. The maps are also deficient in features which had no strategic military value, and informed guesses were made about the nature of the landscapes remote from a Wade road. Most of the islands were also omitted. Roy himself thought the survey was more of a *'magnificent military sketch than a very accurate map of the country.'* Place-names were not recorded systematically, and where they were, this was not done with any apparent knowledge of Gaelic. Some phonetic renderings are shown, which do have a certain value, as they reflect local pronunciations of the time.

Roy's 'magnificent...sketch' was stored away in a cupboard and never seen until its rediscovery in the early nineteenth century. Maps were state secrets. Nevertheless, in this seminal work lay the origins of Ordnance Survey, formally established in 1791. OS mapping of Scotland continued fitfully from 1819 and at various scales until its completion at the end of that century. In Ireland matters were conducted more swiftly, motivated by the aim of maximising tax revenue.

As part of their work in Ireland, the OS established rules for collecting, recording and mapping place-names. These were subsequently applied to the Scottish Highlands. What follows is an extract from the 'Instructions for the Interior Mapping of Ireland' drafted by Thomas Colby Superintendent of the OS in 1825.

The names of each place is to be inserted as it is commonly spelt, in the first column of the name book: and the various modes of spelling it used in the books, writings ... are to be inserted in the second column, with the authority placed in the third column ...

(in Withers 2000, 535)

Rules were also laid down for choosing 'authorities' to authenticate the place-names collected.

> *For names generally the following are the best individual authorities and should be taken in the order given: Owners of property; estate agents; clergymen, postmasters and schoolmasters ... Small farmers and cottagers are not to be depended on, even for the names of the places they occupy ...'*
>
> (in Withers 2000, 535)

Such an exclusive approach, reliant on informants from the landowning and professional classes, meant that those who worked the land and were closest to its riches and rhythms were marginalised in the formal recording of place-names. As a result, local variants in naming were ignored. Subtleties of the spoken language were mistakenly represented as fixed and constant. What was not standard became accepted as standard. Parts of the map also remained blank for no other reason than an understandable reluctance of the informants to give freely of information, which the Government might use to their disadvantage. In some cases, settlements of native Irish were missed out. Those closest to the land itself were either mapped off or mis-mapped onto the paper landscape. Problems of representation were more complex still, since those collecting information had no influence over its final transcription in Ordnance Survey offices in Southampton, giving further scope for misrepresentation.

In the Scottish Highlands, mapping recommenced in earnest on Lewis in 1846, for no other reason than that the landowner, Sir James Matheson, wanted an update on the resources of his estate. Rules developed in Ireland about gathering place-names were extended to Lewis. Alexander Carmichael was one of the 'authorities' commissioned to ascertain the authenticity of names. He was a Gaelic-speaking historian and folklorist from Lismore and thus an exemplary 'authority.' Today he would be called an ethnologist. Carmichael wrote about what happened to his painstaking work, once it was beyond his control.

> *I have gone to the locality and in every instance corrected the place-name from the living voice on the spot. From these corrections I have written out each name in correct Gaelic*

*and have revised and re-revised my own work. I have adhered
strictly to the local sound and pronounciation of every word.
Well then fancy my mortification when Cap. MacPherson tells
me that he means to adopt neither Norse nor Gaelic theory in
spelling but to give the name in phonetic spelling.*

(in Withers 2000, 547)

In a subsequent letter he comments further on his 'translation' of
the living landscape onto paper:

*... I found that many ... place-names which I was at so much
pains and expense in collecting were entire left out ... that some
names on the old maps were left unaltered in form thus lending
the meaning different. I took the liberty of drawing the attention
of the Dir G of the OS to these alterations and the reply was that
the names were omitted to save expense that old names were left
out as they were obviously incorrect and that the final mode of
spelling rested with the Inspector General.*

(in Withers 2000, 547)

It is clear, therefore, that we must treat maps with caution, aware
that they reflect the society from which mapmakers originated and
the manner in which the landscape and its inhabitants have been
interrogated. Nevertheless, over the greater part of the Highlands,
now bereft of native speakers and in the absence of further
knowledge coming to light, today's mapped record is arguably
as close to the best as can now be obtained. This may remain true
even after consulting original name books, manuscripts of earlier
maps and charters. Within the confines of this study, it has not been
possible to substantiate through deeper research the authenticity of
the many thousands of names listed, even if that ambition could be
satisfactorily realised. The names in the mapped record at the current
OS 1:25,000 scale only represent a surface layer.

Later OS maps include information about landform, which aug-
ment spot heights with contours. These connect points of equal elevation. Before leaving this chapter it is worth recounting how an early
use of contours was employed during the 'Schiehallion experiment.'
After Newton's discourse on the universal theory of gravitation, there
was much scientific debate about the shape and mass of the earth.

Mountains could be used to test contrasting theories. Deflections of a weighted plumb line from the vertical could be measured and used by extrapolation to find the mass and volume of the earth. Schiehallion was deemed ideal for the experiment because of its isolation from other peaks, which would also exert a gravitational pull, and because its symmetrical shape meant that any declination from the vertical could be considered commensurate on both sides.

Accordingly, Charles Mason, later to be replaced by the British Astronomer Royal, Nevil Maskelyne, embarked upon an expedition to the mountain. They spent four months on the summit. A mathematician and surveyor called Charles Hutton realised that the numerous readings and measurements of deflections could be organised according to common values, meaning that they could be plotted along a line on the map, encircling the mountain. Hutton did not discover the contour or isopleth. Several other thinkers of the time had been developing similar ideas. Hutton did articulate the idea, however, in the context of Scotland and Schiehallion - the Fairy Hill of the Caledonians.

Roy, by now a Major General and renowned cartographer and scientist, visited the team at their mountain redoubt. He verified their measurement of Schiehallion's height barometrically, by relating air pressure to elevation. Though the scientists complained about the weather and how it interfered with their observations, they were also kept company by local people, who brought them gifts of food. A local boy, *Donncha Ruadh (red-haired Duncan)* entertained the party with fiddle music and songs. The farewell party in October, fuelled by local whisky, went so well that the observation hut was burnt down, with the loss of Donncha's cherished fiddle. Maskelyne sent Duncan a new Stradivarius a few weeks later, to which the young fiddler composed a song.

> *On the trip I took to Schiehallion,*
> *I lost my wealth and my darling,*
> *… Mr Maskelyne, the hero*
> *… did not leave me long a widower,*
> *He sent my choice treasure*
> *That will leave me thankful while I live.*

(in Hewitt 2010, 62)

The conjunction of enlightenment scientists and mapmakers with eighteenth century Perthshire Gaelic speakers, perhaps personifying rational and intuitive aspects of the human mind, on the summit of The Fairy Hill of the Caledonians is an unrepeatable amalgam. This meeting of science with Gaelic culture also produced a map with place-names. It is worth comparing this 1778 Schiehallion document of Hutton's with the current record.

There are twenty-three Gaelic names recorded near or on the measurement contour. Despite their irregular spelling, all can be tentatively translated. Names seem to have been collected from Gaelic speakers, as they have been rendered phonetically, with some accuracy by the English speaking team. However, only nine, fewer than half, can be directly related to the contemporary map. In a way, this small episode, occurring 100 years before formal OS mapping, encapsulates many of the issues, which impinge upon research into Gaelic place-names.

Table 2: Comparison of Schiehallion experiment Map with OS 1:25,000 sheet

OS grid ref.	Hutton's sketch	OS 1:25,000 map	Meaning
?	Aonachmore	No record but probably *Aonach Mòr?*	Big Ridge or Moor
NN699571	Faoirmail	An Fharmail	The Pitcher?
?	Malbirroch	No record but possibly *Meall Biorrach?*	Pointed Hill?
?	Derridnafanaig	No record but possibly *Doire na Feannaige?*	Wood of the Crow?
NN735557	Knocknanaine	Cnoc nan Aighean	Hillock of the Heifers
NN717573	Lochandumaig	Lochan an Daim(h)	Lochan of the Stag
?	Tomcluig	No record but probably *Tom na Cluig?*	Hill of the Bell?
NN729567 & 733568	Maldonglaikcharne	Meall Dubh & Glac Chairne	Black Rounded Hill & Hollow of the Cairn
?	Druimglackchairne	No record but possibly *Druim Glaic Chuirn?*	Ridge of the Hollow of the Cairn?
?	Tyntockich	No record but probably *Taigh an t-Socaich?*	House of the Snout or Pointed Land?
?	YNelrig	No record but probably *An Eilirig?*	The Deer-trap
?	Leadnabroilag	No record but probably *Leathad na Broighleig?*	Slope of the Blaeberry?

Table 2 (cont.)

OS grid ref.	Hutton's sketch	OS 1:25,000 map	Meaning
NN761536	Duncaoillich	Dùn Coillich	Fort of a Cockerel
?	Tomlea	No record but probably *Tom Liath?*	Grey Knowe?
?	Tomnaol	No record but probably *Tom an Aoil?*	Lime Knowe?
NN744527	Firroch	Am Fireach	The Moor
NN734528	Mulichnahaoidenmore	Aodann Mhòr	The Top of the Big (Hill) Face
?	Tomnauarren	No record but possibly *Tom an Fhuarain?*	Knowe of the Spring?
?	Malloist	No record but possibly *Meall Loisgte?*	Burnt Rounded Hill?
?	Crochdnamointich	No record but possibly *Cnoc na Mòintich?*	Hillock of the Peat Moss?
NN694528	Craigbhadd	No record but possibly *Creag a' Mhadaidh?*	Rock of the Dog?
NN697536	Creagnafarridh	Creag an Earra	Rock of the Watch - *Creag na Fàire?*
?	Malnanoirag	No record but possibly *Meall na h-Oighreig*	Rounded Hill of the Cloudberry?

(I am grateful to Ian Fraser, Jake King and Ian MacDonald who suggested many of the tentative translations listed in the table).

4: A BRIEF GUIDE TO GAELIC GRAMMAR AND PRONUNCIATION

There are several linguistic obstacles to the non-Gaelic speaker who tries to understand Highland landscape through an examination of how its place-names have been recorded and mapped. It is relatively easy to learn a basic vocabulary from the useful guides produced by Ordnance Survey, Scottish Natural Heritage and the two National Parks. Nevertheless, the construction of names, which usually comprise a noun or nouns with or without qualifying adjectives, and how these change in the genitive and the plural, can make understanding difficult.

The variety of forms for the definite article, such as *a', an, an t-, am, na, na h-, nan* and *nam* applied to the two genders of Gaelic nouns can impede accurate translation. Misunderstanding is commonplace. A well-known angling guide to the lochs and rivers of Scotland lists over five pages of entries under the definite article alphabetically, in its seven various forms. How absurd would it be if the book's English entries were also listed under *of, of the* and *the*. Such misunderstanding limits the usefulness of the guide and removes an area of potential interest from the reader. Pronouncing the written word is often cited as another difficulty in understanding Gaelic. In comparison to English, the language is both more logical and consistent in its orthography. Contrary to popular perception, it has very few sounds which are difficult to pronounce, once its spelling system is understood.

Instead, then, of trying to learn pronunciation through lists of vowel and consonant combinations, this chapter explores many common and recognisable place-names, some of which have been anglicised. These examples will also be used to illustrate some necessary points of grammar.

Several common Gaelic toponymic terms have come into English and Scots and need little translation. These include *ben/beinn* (byn), *cairn/càrn*, *corrie/coire* (CAWryuh), *craig/creag* (crayk), *dun/donn* (down), *glen/ gleann* (glown), *knock/cnoc* (crochk), *kyle/caol* (coeuhl), *machair* (MACHehr) and *strath/srath* (strah). Other words such as *pàirc* (perrk), like the Scots park meaning field, and *eilean* (EHlan) meaning island, are so close to English that they should be easily recognised. Pronunciation is dealt with during the exploration of grammar but the International Phonetic Alphabet, which many find obscure, is not used.

4.1: Definite Articles, Gender of Nouns and Agreement of Adjectives

Gaelic has only eighteen letters. It has no **J, K, Q, V, W, X, Y** or **Z**. As a result, consonants are often combined to make sounds for which the language has no single letter. This may contribute to what can make many mapped Gaelic place-names look impenetrable to English speakers. The letter combinations **Bh** and **Mh** are perhaps features of written Gaelic which seem most alien to non-speakers. They always sound at the beginning of words like **V** in English. *A' Bheinn Mhòr,* meaning the big mountain, is a very common occurrence. It can be found anglicised to Ben More, near Crianlarich (NN433244). Anglicisation loses the resonance given by the final letters **NN**. Doubling of the consonant makes a sound like *vyn* with the definite article, which aspirates or lenites the letter **B**; and *byn*, without the definite article.

Definite articles in Gaelic are much more varied than in English. There is no indefinite article. The definite article does vary for masculine and feminine nouns in both their genitive, singular and plural forms. In the case of nouns beginning with vowels and the letter **S**, its form also varies according to the first letter and the gender of the noun. Although this may appear challenging, the best solution is to learn nouns along with their articles and simple combinations in both the genitive and plural. Learning the noun alone does not save work over the long term. As a general rule nouns ending in *-ach*, *-an, -as, -ir* and *-iche* tend to be masculine, whilst those ending with *-ag, -achd* and *-id* are usually feminine. Memorising simple place-name examples, with their articles can also help. *An t-Allt Mòr,* The

Big Stream (masc.) in contrast to *An Abhainn Mhòr,* The Big River (fem.) is a useful mnemonic.

To return to our first example of Ben More: anglicisation of *Mhòr* to More also loses the indication that the word for mountain is feminine. This is represented by the aspirated or lenited form of *mòr,* which is *mhòr.* So the big mountain is: *A' Bheinn Mhòr* and pronounced as: *uh vyn vore.* When feminine nouns beginning with a **B, C, F, G, M,** or **P** are lenited, **H** becomes the second letter, which gives *a' chroit* (uh crotch), the croft, *an fhang* (un ang), the sheepfank, *a' ghlumag* (uh GHLOOmak), the puddle, *a' mhòine* (uh VAWNyuh), the peat moor, and *a' phàirc* (uh ferk), the enclosed field. In contrast, *an dail* (un daahl), the haugh, *an leac* (un lehchd), the flagstone, *an nathair* (un nah-hair), the snake, *an rèilig* (un RAYlik), the grave and *an tìr* (un cheer), the land, have no inserted **H** when lenited. The grave accent in modern Gaelic, which some of these examples show, results in a lengthening of the vowel as in other languages. The stress in Gaelic is usually on the first syllable, whether that is accented or not.

The article before masculine nouns beginning with a consonant is **an**, or if it occurs before **B, M, F** or **P**, it is **am**, simply because it is easier to say. This explains the way Dumbreck *(Dùn Breac)* in Glasgow has been anglicised. Therefore, *An Gleann Mòr* (un glown more), meaning the Great Glen and showing no lenition of either noun or adjective, is masculine. So is *am bràigh.* Neither noun, although **G** and **B** are both lenitable to **GH** and **BH** respectively in other circumstances, is lenited because both are masculine.

Loch is perhaps even more familiar than *Beinn.* It has entered both Scots and Scottish English vocabularies. It is usually masculine. So the small loch is *Loch Beag* (pronounced bake), with no lenition of the adjective. Another example of a commonplace name element, which has entered English and in this case is feminine, is *creag* (pronounced crayk). According to lenition rules for feminine nouns, the yellow crag is *A' Chreag Bhuidhe* (uh chrake VOOyuh).

Despite what appears to be an alien spelling system, Gaelic orthography adheres to its rules more often than English. Furthermore, there are not many sounds which are unique to the language. **CH** in Loch is probably the most well known - and exists in all other Germanic languages, but has been lost in contemporary English. This is always pronounced as a breathy abrasive in the rear of the mouth. Linguists must enjoy calling it the voiceless velar fricative. So *loch* never sounds like lock. *An cladach* (un clatuch), which is masculine and means the stony shore, or *a' chruach* (uh CHROOuch), which is feminine and means the heap, also both possess this terminal fricative, and in the case of *cruach*, with its definite article, an initial fricative as well.

However well the Scots voice the **CH** of *loch*, many will be unfamiliar with the need to pronounce the initial fricative of *a' chruach*. The Black Wood in Rannoch, *A' Choille Dhubh* (uh CHAWLyuh dhoo), is another example. Here we see the definite article leniting the **C** of a feminine noun to **CH** and also the subsequent adjective leniting in agreement with that noun from **D** to **DH**. The lenited adjective *dhubh* illustrates another consonant combination, which is unknown in both standard and Scottish English and makes a similar sound to **CH**. **GH** is pronounced in the same way as **DH**. Both are more guttural, voiced and nasal than **CH**; like a stronger version of **GH** in ghost. Think of how the Spanish say Girona or La Giralda, or how the Dutch pronounce the letter **G** in Den Haag. However, before the slender vowels **E** and **I**, both **DH** and **GH** are pronounced as a **Y**, a letter which is absent from Gaelic. So *Beinn Dhearg* sounds like byn YERrak. Notice too the softening of **G** to a **K** sound. This is similar to how **D** is often softened to **T**. The noun *bad* in *Bad an Òiq*, the place of youth, sounds for example, like baht un awk, with the **H** in baht representing a small puff of breath before the final letter. We have already experienced a similar softening of the final **G** of *creag* and *beag* to a **K** sound.

Returning to some further forms of the definite article: if a masculine noun begins with a vowel, then the article becomes **an t-** with its **T** making a tchuh sound. So, *An t-Eilean Beag* (the small island), is pronounced *un TCHAYlan bake*.

In contrast, when a feminine noun begins with a vowel then the definite article remains the same. *An abhainn bheag* (un AHvin vake), the small river, which is feminine and similar to the Welsh *afon* and gives us the anglicised avon, is an example. Where a masculine noun begins with an **S**, then the definite article remains as **an**. *An Srath Mòr* (un straah more) – Strathmore is an example.

In contrast, feminine nouns beginning with an **S** have the article *an t-*, which renders S silent. *An t-Sròn* (un trawn), meaning nose of the promontory, gives us Troon in Ayrshire.

In these examples so far, it can be seen that the adjective usually follows the noun in Gaelic, as in many other European languages, but unlike English. Where more emphasis is required, adjectives can precede the noun. *Geàrr Aonach* (gyar OEnuch) NN160555 in Glen Coe, meaning the short, steep ridge and *Garbh Bheinn* (garav vyn) in Ardgour (NM903623) are examples of emphatic abruptness and roughness respectively. Notice how the preceding adjective causes lenition of the noun following, but is not lenited itself. A less emphatically rough mountain is *Beinn Gharbh* (NC216224) in Assynt, where the adjective following is lenited in the usual way to agree with the feminine noun.

4.2: Plural Nouns and Adjectives, and the Gaelic Spelling Rule

The definite article changes for plural nouns, but for both genders it is identical. Before a vowel it is *na h-* and before a consonant it is *na*. Plurals rarely occur on their own in place-names. They are more usually associated with the possessive case, or genitive, which complicates matters for the learner. In most cases the plural is indicated by the suffix *an* or *ean* after the slender vowels **E** or **I** in the preceding syllable. So the plural of *a' chreag*, which is feminine, is *na creagan* (nuh CRAYkun), whilst for *an t-eas* (un ches), which is masculine and means the waterfall, it is *na h-easan* (nuh HESun). For *an taigh* (un tie), which is masculine and means the house, the plural is *na taighean* (nuh TYun), whilst for *an eaglais* (un EHGlish), which is feminine and means the church, it is *na h-eaglaisean* (nuh HEHGlishun).

Some common terms, such as *gleann* and *beinn,* add a **T** before the usual suffix to make plurals *gleanntan,* and in the case of *beinn* there is also an internal vowel change in the first syllable, giving *beanntan.* Similarly *baile* (BAHLuh), meaning farm or village, gives us *bailtean* (BALtchun). Sometimes the singular form of the noun is contracted when making a plural. So *machair* becomes *machraichean* (MACHreechun). Such irregularities may have occurred because they are just easier to say than regular forms.

In these examples of the plural, an important spelling rule can be seen at work. In Gaelic this is called *caol ri caol is leathann ri leathann* - narrow with narrow and broad with broad. (Both *caol* and *leathann* are common adjectives in place-names). When a slender vowel, like **E** or **I,** ends the first syllable of a word and the second syllable is separated from the first by a consonant or consonant combination, then the first vowel of this following syllable is also slender. Similarly, when a broad vowel like **A, O** or **U** ends the first syllable of a word and the second syllable is separated from the first by a consonant or consonants, then the first vowel of this latter syllable is also broad. This explains why *baile* becomes *bailtean* and *eas* becomes *easan* in the plural. Sometimes separating consonant(s) are silent. The Gaelic for field is *achadh* (ACHugh). Its plural is *achaidhean*, consistent with the spelling rule and pronounced ACHee-un, where the silent **DH** acts only to separate the penultimate and final syllables. *Achadh* provides the common, anglicised place-name prefix Ach or Auch.

Other forms of the plural, particularly for some monosyllabic nouns, are expressed as a slenderisation of the syllable. *An Cnoc* (un crochk) the hillock becomes *na cnuic* (nuh crooichk), for example. *Cnoc* also shows how the combination **CN** is pronounced in Gaelic, which is like a nasalised **CR** and unknown in English. *Cnap* (crahp), meaning lump or knob, is similar. Similarly the plural of *an t-allt* (un towlt), which is masculine and means the stream, is slenderised to *na h-uillt* (nuh hooiltch). However, to confuse matters somewhat, this is exactly the same as its genitive singular, which forms the next subject.

4.3: The Genitive Case - singular and plural

The possessive or genitive case is naturally very common in the construction of place-names, as with the action of adjectives it gives greater specificity to nouns. The effect of the genitive on noun form in both singular and plural is something the interpreter of place-names has to be familiar with, to see through what can obscure the appearance of familiar words in the nominative case. As before, consequences for articles are different for masculine and feminine words and according to what letter begins a noun and whether nouns are singular or plural. Plural nouns are the most simple in their genitive case.

Two earlier examples will be examined, as they show the most regular form of the genitive for each gender. These are *cladach*, which is masculine, and *cruach*, which is feminine. Their respective genitives with definitive articles and coupled with *ceann*, are *ceann a' chladaich* (cyown uh CHLAteech) and *ceann na cruaiche* (cyown nuh CROOeechuh). Notice how the masculine noun is aspirated by the article *a'*, and its final syllable is slenderised from **A** to **AI** with a consequent slenderisation of pronunciation. Notice also how the feminine article becomes **na**, which does not lenite, and how the second syllable is slenderised. *Cruach* also gains a third syllable forming an **E** ending. For feminine nouns beginning with a vowel the article becomes **na h-**. This is also the same for both genders in the nominative plural.

Generally articles applying to masculine nouns in the genitive become the same as those for feminine nouns in the nominative. So, *a'* applies to lenitable words like *cladach*, whilst **an** applies to non-lenitable nouns like *lochan* (small loch) and nouns beginning with a vowel like *allt*. The latter gives us *Taigh an Uillt* (Tie un Ooltch) or Taynuilt. **An t-** applies to nouns beginning with an **S**, like *sruth* (sroo), meaning a current or stream, giving *Creag an t-Sruith* at NN578139 (crayk un trooee), to the south of Strathyre. Here, after heavy rain, a jet of water runs down the face of a large boulder.

Slenderisation caused by the genitive case can also change whole syllables. So *binnean* (BINyun), masculine, meaning high conical hill, becomes *binnein* (BINyane) and *bidean* (BEEtchan), also masculine, meaning pinnacle or high, pointed hill becomes *bidein* (beetchane). The more common *ceann* becomes *cinn* (keen) in the genitive, identical to its plural. Similarly, *toll* (towl) meaning hole and giving *Clach Toll* in Assynt, becomes *tuill* (tooeel), the same as its plural, whilst *tom* (towm), meaning knoll, becomes *tuim* (TOOim). Its plural is different, however, as *toman* or *tomannan*.

There are many exceptions to the common rule. The genitive of *srath* is *sratha*, for example. Similarly, for *druim* (DROYim) it is *droma*, which gives *Taigh an Droma* or Tyndrum, the house of the ridge. The genitive of *am bràigh*, despite being masculine, can be *a' bhràighe* or *a' bhràghad* (uh VRAAut). Although *tràigh* (try), meaning beach, is feminine, it has a similar genitive to *bràigh*, which is *tràghad* (TRAut). *Càrn* can be *càirn* or *cùirn* in the genitive, which is the same as its plural, and which is also irregular.

Table 3: Summary of Gaelic Article - Nominative and Genitive Forms

	Singular		Plural
Case	**masculine**	**feminine**	**masculine & feminine**
Nominative	**An** before consonants, including s, except b, f, m and p **Am** before b, f, m and p **An t-** before vowels	**An** before vowels, fh, d, l, n, r and t **A'** before bh, ch, gh, mh and ph **An t-** before s followed by l, n, r or a vowel (the same as the masculine genitive)	**Na** **Na h-** before a vowel (the same as the feminine genitive)
Genitive	**An** before vowels, fh, d, l, n, r and t **A'** before bh, ch, gh, mh and ph **An t-** before s followed by l, n, r or a vowel (the same as the nominative feminine)	**Na** **Na h-** before a vowel	**Nan** **Nam** before b, f, m or p

Plural genitives, like plural nominatives, are easier, because nouns usually, but not always, remain in the singular form. For them, the article is either ***nan*** or ***nam***, if they come before a **B, F, M,** or **P**. Both masculine and feminine forms are also identical. *Bealach nan Corp* NN556109 (BYAluch nun corp), Pass of the Bodies, North of Ben Ledi, and *Sgùrr nan Gillean* at NG472253 (skoor nun GEELyun), the Peak of the Boys in the Cuillins of Skye, are masculine examples. *Coire nan Saighead* at NN606157 (CAWryuh nun SYut) The Corrie of the Arrows, *Sgiath nam Mucan Dubha* at NN497074 (SGEEuh num MOOchkun DOOah), The Wing-shaped Hill of the Little Black Pigs in the Trossachs are examples in the feminine. In this last example, we know that the suffix ***an*** applying to *muc* denotes the diminutive, little, for if it were the genitive of pig, *muc* would be in its singular form. So, *nam mucan* in this context means: 'of the little pigs.' *Àrd*, meaning high, and *mòr* behave in the same way as *dubha* in the plural, resulting in *beanntan àrda* and *gleanntan mòra*. Note also in Gaelic how it is not possible to distinguish the corrie of the arrows from corrie of the arrows.

Table 4: Examples of Nominative and Genitive Nouns in text order

Case	Singular		Plural
	masculine	feminine	masculine & feminine
Nominative without article	Gleann	Beinn	Gleanntan, beanntan
	Cladach	Creag	Cladaichean, creagan
	Coire	Cruach	Coireachan, cruachan
	Eilean	Abhainn	Eileanan, aibhnichean
	Srath	Sròn	Srathan, srònan
	Eas	Eaglais	Easan, eaglaisean
Nominative with definite article	An gleann	A' bheinn	Na gleanntan, na beanntan
	An cladach	A' chreag	Na cladaichean, na creagan
	An coire	A' chruach	Na coireachan, na cruachan
	An t-eilean	An abhainn	Na h-eileanan, na h-aibhnichean
	An srath	An t-sròn	Na srathan, na srònan
	An t-eas	An eaglais	Na h-easan, na h-eaglaisean
Genitive with definite article	A' ghlinne	Na beinne	Nan gleann, nam beann
	A' chladaich	Na creige	Nan cladach, nan creag
	A' choire	Na cruaiche	Nan coire, nan cruach
	An eilein	Na h-aibhne	Nan eilean, nan abhainn
	An t-sratha	Na sròine	Nan srath, nan sròn
	An easa	Na h-eaglaise	Nan eas, nan eaglais

There is no need to consider the dative case of nouns, as they do not appear in place-names.

5: PLACE-NAME CLASSIFICATIONS - REVEALING LAYERS IN THE LANDSCAPE

In the early twentieth century, Ordnance Survey published a brief booklet on the most common Gaelic words used on its one inch to the mile maps. This was enlarged in 1951 and 1968. The current 2005 Guide to Gaelic origins of place-names in Britain is much larger in scope, and runs to 36 pages of alphabetically listed names, with definitive examples and grid references. It is available online at: http://www.gaelicplace-names.org/index.php

As one of the authors of the guide states elsewhere:

> We have become such slaves to the alphabet that we frequently forget its very nature of mere convenience, and tend to look upon its sequence … as something which … classifies or categorises beyond the order which it imposes … Indeed this seemingly convenient tool is the enemy of all classification.
>
> (Nicolaisen 2001, 2)

With this caveat in mind, an expanded version of the 'Guide to Gaelic Origins of Place-names in Britain' has been compiled here and divided into seven categories and twenty three sub-categories. The system chosen is based on the teaching and practice of Meto Vroom, a Dutch academic, and will be familiar to many landscape architects. In this scheme, landscape is classified according to three interacting horizontal layers: the abiotic or the non-living at the bottom, the biotic or living in the middle and occupation or cultural layer at the top (see fig. 3). Place-name categories in Gaelic can easily be attached to such names such as: *creag* (rock), *darach* (oak) and *baile* (township). The top layer can be further developed by considering Patrick Geddes's trio of 'Place, Work, Folk' to generate categories of land use, occupation and people, which, in Gaelic, would give *àirigh* (shieling), *ceàrd* (smith) and *gille* (boy). These layers themselves can influence each other, often and literally from the ground up.

The siting of a summer shieling or temporary summer habitation will have been chosen because of the presence of running water and well drained and fertile soils which favour the growth of grasses palatable to grazing animals. Once shielings had been established, the long-term effects of pasturing animals and their manure will change vegetation patterns. Cutting of peats for fuel by shieling residents will alter drainage regimes and erosion patterns. These layers of landscape thus interact in a circular and continuous manner through time.

Processes of landscape change can also originate and be concluded within one layer. As humanity has moved from a hunter-gatherer to a global communications culture, with technology able to overcome many past constraints on development, it can be argued that the origins, relationships and consequences of landscape change now exist predominantly in the cultural top layer. On the other hand, more traditional societies, like shieling dwellers in the Highlands of the past, are more dependent on vertical processes of landscape change coming from abiotic and biotic layers. In the contemporary world, the dominant cultural layer can become increasingly disjointed, with modernist influences spreading virally from culture to culture through the mass media. This is sometimes expressed in the naming of streets after Hollywood movie stars, and the many squares and places commemorating African or American presidents, which exist throughout the world, and even earlier by British street names commemorating battles in the Napoleonic, Crimean and Boer wars.

We might think that early Celtic culture was exempt from the rapid spread of cultural influences. Some might suppose, for example, that the women of the shieling sang songs of love and loss in a purely local context. However, Donald Meek has argued that early Irish legend originating in Connacht and Sligo was transferred to the Perthshire Highlands. The Lay of Fraoch (*Laoidh Fhraoich*), where *Fraoch* means heather but is also the name of the hero involved, refers to the healing powers of rowan berries gathered

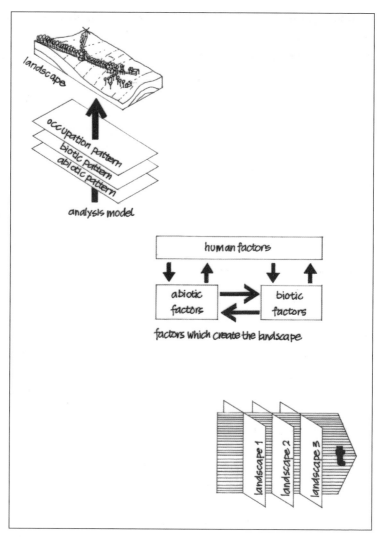

Figure 3: Layers in the Landscape

from a heathery island in a loch. In the eighteenth century the legend was associated with an island in Loch Freuchie, *Loch Fraochaidh* (NN864376), near Amulree, where berries abound on the hills. It is thought, before that, the *loch* was called after the Glen where it lies, *Gleann Cuaich*, Glen Quaich (NN797396). Both names were known in the eighteenth century.

Similarly, the Lay of Diarmaid (*Laoidh Dhiarmaid*) whose first origins can be traced to Ben Bulben (Irish: *Binn Ghulbain*) in Sligo, has been relocated on Ben Gulabin (*Beinn Ghulbhain*) at NO102722 in Perthshire's Glen Shee (*Gleann Siodh*). Both mountains have a snout shape, though the name may also derive from the personal name Gulban. Here is a place-name, which has been applied to a new locality to accompany a ballad moving from Irish to Scottish culture. Moreover, the new context has been carefully chosen to echo the formal landscape character of the original location and so sustain the narrative action. The previous name of *Beinn Ghulbhain* and what attribute of the mountain it described, snout-shape or otherwise, is not known. The process begs the question: when is a place-name not the name of a place? Is it when it represents a symbol on a cognitive or narrative map?

Walter Scott situated his long narrative poem, '*The Lady of the Lake*' on Loch Katrine in the Trossachs. In the text he renames *Eilean Molach*, the shaggy or rough island, as Ellen's Isle (NN487083) after the story's heroine. Such was the poem's popularity that the name has persisted, albeit with the original Gaelic name also included on the map, along with another name from the poem, the Silver Strand, where other parts of the plot take place. Such an overlay of place-names coming from a poem, subsequently recorded by Ordnance Survey is on a scale beyond earlier practice. Such was the all pervading influence of Scott's fictionally transmitted psycho-geography, in the nineteenth century there were widespread protests against the raising of the Loch's level to supply water to Glasgow, which in the process concealed most of the Silver Strand.

How does a layer of Gaelic place-names sit in the abiotic / biotic / culture model of landscape when there are no inheritors of those who transmitted their unique toponymic psycho-geography to mapmakers of the late nineteenth century? How do we perceive this toponymic layer, when the culture, language and the land uses, which created it have vanished from the greater part of the Highlands? In some ways the named inheritance points to an inadequacy in the model, which supposes a continuous cyclical interaction between the abiotic, the biotic and the cultural. It does not envisage an interruption of the vertical process of influence and counter influence

*Plate 5: Loch Katrine: Bealach nam Bò, Coire na(n) Ùruisgean and Eilean Molach.
(Bealach nam Bò is the break of slope in the left background below
the rock face, Coire na(n) Ùruisgean is above the steamboat and
Eilean Molach is at the bottom right) (also in colour section)*

in the process of landscape change. The model cannot accommodate the excision of Gaelic and its culture from most of the Gàidhealtachd. What remains is a toponymic layer representing a psycho-geography, which is frozen in time and detached from subsequent possible representations of the landscape. It is as if a chapter in the book of this landscape has been lost or erased. Such a notion is similar to the geological concept of non-conformity, where, though rock types may be physically contiguous, they are discontinuous in time.

It could be argued that the act of naming landscapes is in itself now dead, or at least no longer recognised by mapmakers. Loch Occasional in Balquidder appears and disappears when the River Balvaig floods. Whilst the name of this ephemeral water is known to local residents, it does not appear on any map. Similarly, there is an island of significant size, which has appeared in Loch Tay at the mouth of the River Dochart, as a result of siltation from forestry development further upstream in the catchment. It is mature enough to have developed riparian woodland in its own right. Although the island appears on the map, it is anonymous to both cartographers and most of the local community. Even the continual flux and dramatic results of fluvial processes do not necessarily lead to new names. In the contemporary Highlands, perhaps we are less mindful of abiotic and biotic processes and their outcomes than preceding Gaelic-speaking populations? Given the density of their naming where it has survived in full, it is difficult to imagine how such a prominent island could have remained anonymous a few hundred years ago.

Mountaineers may be an exception to this trend. Several peaks in the Cuillins are named in Gaelic after nineteenth century climbing pioneers: *Sgùrr Alasdair* - after Sheriff Alexander Nicolson, *Sgùrr MhicChoinnich* - after John MacKenzie, *Sgùrr Theàrlaich* - after Charles Pilkington and *Sgùrr Thormaid* - after Norman Collie, who was MacKenzie's great friend and climbing companion. Perhaps such active naming in Gaelic still occurred because the Cuillins were relatively unexplored, and guides and informants of the time were local Gaelic-speaking Sgitheanachs. Or perhaps earlier names have been lost.

In other places, where Gaelic has been less active in recent times, and in contrast to nineteenth century Skye, climbing names are more likely to be in English, such as Cat Gully (NN641431) and Raven's Gully (NN642425) beneath Ben Lawers. In both cases, however, the newer English names refer to the adjacent Gaelic names of *Lochan nan Cat* and *Creag an Fhithich*, so continuity with past naming is sustained in translation. Less consistently, other recent naming can be completely unrelated to Gaelic. On Arran, The Bastion (NS997439) and the Devil's Punchbowl (NS004438) are unconnected with the earlier language's *Cioche na h-Oighe* (*Cìoch na h-Òighe* -Maiden's Pap) and *Coire na Cìche* (Corrie of the Breast) although clearly a bowl and a corrie have some formal similarity.

Elsewhere amongst the granite tors of Arran, the names of Portcullis Buttress, Pagoda Ridge and Meadow Slabs can be found. The last is named after a patch of grass growing at its base, whilst the others all attempt to describe a visual quality. One name (Plate 8) which has a direct link to Gaelic is the Witch's Step (NS973443), translated, perhaps unfairly, from *Ceum na Caillich* (old woman). Naming activity amongst mountaineers and other outdoor enthusiasts reflects their position as new insiders to the landscape. With some knowledge of language, new naming could become more able to build on earlier precedent, which has often successfully captured the *genius loci* or spirit of place, in a unique Gaelic lens.

Place-name Classifications

Place-name examples have been drawn from across the Gàidhealtachd, but there is preponderance from the central and southern Highlands, and very few from the Cairngorms. The spelling of names is for the most part listed in the forms represented on OS maps, with the addition of missing accents and minor, single letter corrections. Generic words are shown in nominative, genitive and plural forms. Apologies must be made for any awkwardness in translation. The detail of Gaelic names and the resultant grammatical complexity sometimes escape the brevity of English couplets. *Slios Meall na Saobhaidhe*, in Torridon, NG880480, Slope of the Rounded Hill of the Den does not run easily off the tongue.

Commentaries offered before each section of examples within a category do not cover each name listed in the tables. Instead, the text focuses on examples with a significant hinterland of interest and reference. However, the section on mountain form is more comprehensive than others owing to an earlier study by the author. In the field, alphabetical indexes of generic nouns and adjectives in the book's appendices can be used to locate names in the relevant categories. Pronunciations are indicative. They do not attempt to capture the subtleties of Gaelic speech. It would be very hard for any phonetic system to render the four Gaelic sounds for **R,** a unique number in any language, and its three sounds for the letter **L,** with any accuracy. Map references should be read along with the National Grid layout of squares labeled with N-.

PART 2

6: LANDFORM AND HYDROLOGY

6.1: Mountains, Hills and Knolls

This section has been greatly informed by Peter Drummond's Scottish Mountaineering Club (SMC) book on Scottish hill names and also a detailed study made by the author in the Highland parts of the counties of Perthshire and Stirlingshire.

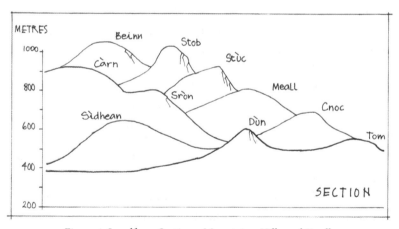

Figure 4: Landform Section - Mountains, Hills and Knolls

Popular enthusiasm for place-names has been driven by the growing interest amongst urban dwellers, once their leisure time had increased after the Second World War, in hillwalking and climbing. As a result, the excellent and comprehensive series of guides produced by the SMC tend to focus on hills and mountains rather than the full spectrum of Gaelic place vocabulary. Nevertheless, these pioneering if rather selective early books still manage to illustrate the diversity and richness of the named landscape of the Highlands. From the very beginning, the SMC has sought to pronounce and understand the language attached to the mountains it reveres.

Margaret Gelling has argued that in contrast to Gaelic, much of the variability and subtlety of Old English terms, which described hill names has been lost from the contemporary language. So without a comparable specific vocabulary in English, it is difficult to translate the diversity of Gaelic topographical names (figure 4) neatly when describing qualities of form, character, texture and height. Nevertheless, such an eclectic vocabulary can tell us a great deal about the differing landscape characters prevailing in the Gàidhealtachd. Aspects of place which have shaped the language.

In an attempt to explore such observations, a study area was chosen extending from Rannoch in the north to the Trossachs in the south and from Breadalbane in the west to Strathbraan in the east. This area, which is broadly the Highland part of the former pre-1974 County of Perthshire, was selected because its toponymy is not only almost wholly Gaelic, but also includes a representative diversity of toponymic terms. It must be noted, however, that in the study area, the words *meall* (lump, mass of any matter, heap, hill, eminence, great shapeless hill, mound) and *tom* (round hillock or knoll, rising ground, swell, green eminence - any round heap) account for over 50% of the names mapped at 1:25,000 scale on OS Explorer sheets. It is reasonable to assume that such a preponderance of two name types reflects the relatively rounded, rolling and smooth nature of upland Perthshire when compared with more rugged areas of the Scottish Highlands. In Kintail and the Cuillins of Skye *sgùrr* or *sgòrr* (high, sharp pointed hill) seems to be the default generic. In the study area the word is much less frequent, whilst in the Cairngorms, *càrn* (heap or pile of stones loosely thrown together, cairn), perhaps reflecting the dominance of stony plateaux in the range, is more frequent.

The choice of study area has a disadvantage. As living Gaelic is almost wholly absent, native speakers cannot inform field investigations. Some of the last attempts to do so were made in the late nineteenth century and the 1920s in Balquidder by Mrs Carnegie of

Stronvar, in Breadalbane by W. J. Watson and in Blair Atholl by Ó Murchú in the 1960s.

The 650 names studied and their occurence are shown in **Table 5.** These are *Beinn (76), Bioran (8), Caisteal (11), Càrn (23), Cnap (5), Cnoc (34), Cruach (6), Dùn (33), Maol (10), Meall (193), Sgiath (22), Sgòr / Sgòrr (8), Sìthean (13), Sliabh (4), Sròn (54), Stob (38), Stùc (16), Tom (89),* and *Tòrr (7).* This large sample size may perhaps compensate for cartographic inaccuracies, omissions and inconsistencies. *Creag* (rock) was omitted from the study because of the large numbers (422) involved and the likelihood that a translation is straightforward.

A map search of the terms was carried out at 1:25,000 scale on OS Explorer sheets and distributions were mapped at 1:250,000 scale. For each entry the following data was recorded: National Grid Reference, elevation, relative relief or ruggedness, categories of qualifying nouns or adjectives, whether named features were summits or outliers, and the presence of corries and outcrops. The information for each name type was then collated, tabulated and analysed.

Consideration of geology was omitted from the study, as it appears that there is little relationship between the distribution of name and

Table 5: Frequency of Perthshire Mountain Names

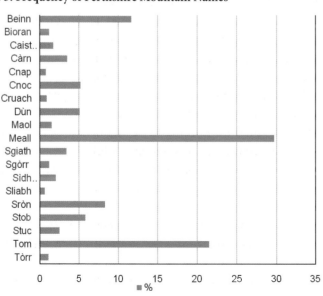

Table 6: Mountain Name, Elevation (metres) and Relative Relief (metres)

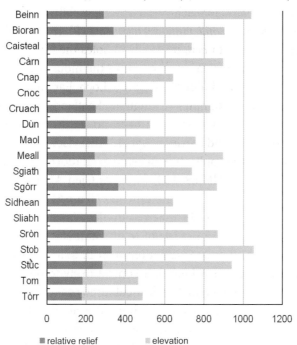

rock type as shown on the 1:250,000 geological sheets 56N 04W and 56N 06W.

There appears, for example, to be no broad toponymic change in name type or distribution reflecting the major outcropping of granite to the north-west of Comrie in Glen Lednock. Although there are three, and the only references to *bioran - stick, staff or any pointed thing*, in nearby Dalchonzie, which is also located on hard rock, in this case metamorphic schist. In contrast, different name types appear to be more directly related to geomorphology, in particular degrees of ruggedness. The concept of ruggedness has been adapted from Whittow (1992). When applied to a point in the landscape, it is measured as the maximum difference in elevation within the kilometre square in which the point is situated. Very rugged has been defined as a height difference of over 300 metres, moderately rugged as lying between 200 and 300 metres and rolling as being below 200 metres (**Tables 6** & **7**). Definitions of hill form should be read in conjunction with **Table 9**, where gender, genitive and plural forms and a grid referenced example are also given. Results for each name type are as follows.

Beinn - *mountain, hill, pinnacle, high place* (**Plates 3, 4, 15 and 19**)

Often anglicised to *ben*, it usually denotes the highest elevation in an area. The name is most frequent in the mountainous areas of Mamlorn, west Balquhidder and south Loch Earnside. There are nearly a thousand examples throughout Scotland. Although only moderately rugged, they are very likely to be dominant summits possessing outcrops and corries. It appears that visual dominance is a factor that drives the application of *beinn* to landform. Its diminutive form, *Am Beannan* (NN 693135) in upper Glen Artney is the only subsidiary peak recorded in the study area (**Plate 6**). 'S Àirde Bheinn at NM479539, although 292 metres in elevation, is certainly not the highest mountain in the Isle of Mull, but it is the highest in the district of Mishnish and visually dominant in that locality. *Beinn* is always qualified and if coloured, it is most likely to be grey *(liath)*, red *(dearg)*, grey-green *(glas)* or dun-coloured *(odhar)*.

In Irish, *ben* originally meant a horned peak, but this connotation has been lost from Scottish Gaelic, though it survives as *beannachar* in horn-shaped Loch Venachar in the Trossachs. Another diminuitive form, *binnean,* has now adopted the older meaning, which is supported by the visual evidence. *Beinn* can be qualified according to its intrinsic qualities, such as form, colour and pattern. Or qualification may reflect a feature of the landscape context. Ben Lawers - *Beinn Labhair* (NN634415) takes its name from the noisy

Plate 6: Glen Artney - Am Beannan and Coire na Fionnarachd (in the background)

burn, which descends loudly from its corrie to Loch Tay below. This phenomenon is known by toponymists as back formation.

Bioran - *stick, staff, any sharp pointed thing* (Plate 7)

These are rare, of medium height, but very rugged. They are very likely to be lesser summits with both corries and outcrops. They are seldom qualified, which implies a specific and distinct form. *Am Bioran* (NN694222) to the South of St Fillans is a dramatic example. There is another *Am Bioran* far away in the Gàidhealtachd, on *Stac an Àrmainn* off St Kilda, which is a very pointed landscape. The name is shown on Mathieson's 1928, 6 inch to the mile map as *Am Biran* (NA153063), but not on OS Explorer sheet 460.

Plate 7: St Fillans - *Dùn Dùirn (in the foreground) and Am Bioran (in the background) (also in colour section)*

Caisteal - *Castle, fort, tower, garrison* (Plate 8)

These are rare, of medium height and moderately rugged. They are likely to be lesser summits with outcrops, but are less likely to possess corries. Some are unqualified, several are steep *(corrach)*. Almost half of them are slopes. Only one in eleven is associated with any archaeological artefact, such as a fortification. Such a low figure suggests that the name, like *dùn* is used to suggest a steep, castle-like form in the landscape rather than an actual fortress.. The summit ridge of *Caisteal Abhail* in Arran (NR965445), whose full meaning is unclear, is distinguished by turret-like granite torrs. There are about fifty examples, mostly in the central and south west Highlands.

*Plate 8: Arran - Cìr Mhòr, Ceum na Caillich and
Caisteal Abhail, (to the right of the picture)*

Càrn - heap of stones loosely thrown together

These are infrequent, yet widespread, high and moderately rugged. They are reasonably likely to be a lesser summit or slope with outcrops and corries. They are always qualified, usually by colour. *Càrn Gorm* (NN635502) in Glen Lyon shows such qualities. Of course the famous Cairngorm range has been named after a mountain with the same name further north.

Cnap - *knob, button, lump, boss stud, little hill*

These are very rare, low, but very rugged and concentrated to the east of Loch Lomond. They are likely to be an outlying summit with outcrops, but no corries. They are always qualified, usually according to size. *Cnap Mòr* - Big Button (NN324164) at the head of Loch Lomond is an example. The word has given its identity to the entire lumpy district of Knapdale in Argyll.

Cnoc - *hill, knoll, hillock, eminence* (Plate 9)

These are frequent and sometimes paired, in the low, rolling country to the south of the study area. They are likely to be lesser and lower summits without any outcrops or corries. They are always qualified, just under a quarter by colour - especially *dubh* or *odhar* - and just over a quarter biotically, with references to flora being twice as common as those to fauna. There are nearly 3000 mapped examples throughout Scotland, with a concentration in Kintyre, the Inner Hebrides and the Northern Highlands. Like *beinn, cnoc* can be qualified according to intrinsic qualities, but it is more likely to be

Plate 9: Glen Artney - Cnoc Brannan and Cnoc nan Oighreag to the left

named after another aspect of the landscape and to be grammatically complex as a result.

Cruach - *rounded hill standing apart, mountain pinnacle*
These are rare, of medium height and ruggedness, and concentrated on Loch Lomondside. They are likely to be lesser summits with outcrops, but less likely to have corries. Half are unqualified, which indicates a form so specific it needs no qualification. *Cruach Ardrain* (NN 409213), south of Crianlarich, resembles the kind of peat stack, *cruach-mhòna,* which can still be seen next to croft-houses in the Outer Hebrides.

Dùn - *heap, hill, hillock, mound. Fortified house or hill* (Plate 10)
These are frequent, and sometimes paired, in the low, rolling country found in the valley floors of upper Glen Dochart and Strathearn. They are likely to be rocky and outlying summits without corries. None, in contrast to the similar likening to a fortress, *caisteal,* is a slope. They are usually qualified by size or biotically. Only 12% are related to the existence of any archaeological artefacts, usually a fort. OS maps are unlikely, however, to show all archaeological remains. Nevertheless, it seems reasonable to conclude, in the study area, that *dùn,* like *caisteal,* applies to landform which suggests a fort-like appearance or occupies a fort-like position, relating to an outlook for example. *Dùn 'n Aon Duine* (NN675233), the Fort of the Lone (literally one) Man (Plate 10), in its prominent position above

Plate 10: St Fillans - Dùn 'n Aon Duine (right) and Creagan na Mòint(e)ich (left)

south Loch Earnside is a good example of such a position in the landscape, possessing a good outlook in both directions along the loch. Its constrained summit perhaps suggesting that it could only accommodate one man. **Plate 21** also shows duns, one large and one small. Only the latter possesses a fort, however.

Maol - *brow of rock, great bare rounded hill (literally: a bald head)*
These are rare in the study area, of medium height, but very rugged and concentrated between Lochs Katrine and Lomond. Their different physical qualities suggest that they are not a dialectic substitution for the rounded *meall* type - even though these are absent from the same area. They are likely to be rocky outliers with corries. They are always qualified, most often with an association with flora or fauna. *Maol* names are more common in Mull. In Berneray, Harris, the word is also applied to the top of a large sand dune, *Maol Bhàn* - Fair or White Bald Head (NF909831) - which is clearly a feature without landcover and therefore perceived as bald, due to continual accumulation and movement of wind-borne sand. It is fairly common on north-western coastal promontories, such as *Rubha na Maoile* on the South side of Eddrachillis Bay (NC145345) in Sutherland.

Meall - *lump, mass of any matter, heap (as of earth), hill, eminence, great shapeless hill, mound*
These are very common and widespread, moderately rugged and high summits, although 5% are slopes. They are unlikely to be rocky or have corries. They are always qualified. If by colour, *odhar* and

*Plate 11: Suilven - Ùidh Fheàrna, Caisteal Liath, Meall
Meadhonach and Meall Beag (Ùidh Fheàrna is to the left of
centre below the dome of Suilven) (also in colour section)*

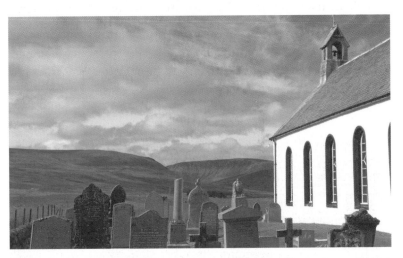

Plate 12: Amulree - Meall Mòr, Coire a' Chearca(i)l and Meall nam Fuaran (centre)

dubh are the most common - suggesting an association with blanket
peat. If by form, fat (*reamhar*) accounts for 10% of instances, but
contrarily, rough (*garbh*) also accounts for another 5%. Indeed, *Meall
Garbh* (NN644437), near Ben Lawers, drops precipitously to the pass

below *An Stùc* (NN638432). At the eastern end of the very rugged ridge of Suilven in Assynt (**Plate 11**), we also find *Meall Meadhonach* (NC164177) and *Meall Beag* (NC166177). A wide range of qualifiers indicates a very general type of landform, providing a vehicle for a diversity of differentiating specifiers.

Sgiath - *wing, portion of land jutting into sea, shield* (Plate 13)

These are infrequent, of moderate height and ruggedness and, like *maol*, concentrated between Loch Katrine and Loch Lomond. Their physical similarity to *sròn* types, and the latter's absence from the same area, suggest a dialectic substitution. However, Peter Drummond, citing *Sgiath Mhic Griogair* - one of Rob Roy's hiding-places in the Trossachs (NN527074) - suggests a developed meaning of a refuge or shelter. Indeed, several hills of the name lie athwart the prevailing wind, providing shelter in the crook of the wing, so to speak. God is sometimes described as a *sgiath* in the Bible. They are more likely to be outliers than summits. Nearly half are slopes, but with both corries and outcrops. They are always qualified, usually by colour: blue (*gorm*) is the most frequent; or with a biological association.

*Plate 13: Glen Dochart - Sgiath Chrom and Sgiath Chùil
lying across the prevailing westerly wind direction*

Sgòrr / sgòr / sgùrr - sharp steep hill, rising by itself, or a little steep precipitous height on another hill or mountain, peak, pinnacle **(Plate 14)**

These are rare, moderately high, but very rugged. They are likely to be rocky, outliers with corries. Over half are slopes which suggests a different usage to that prevailing in the Cuillins of Skye and Kintail, where the spelling is *sgùrr* and the name identifies a peak in its own right rather than an outlier. In the study area all are qualified, usually biotically. In his long poem *An Cuilithionn - The Cuillin,* Somhairle MacGill-Eain / Sorley MacLean captures the physical nature of a *sgùrr.*

> *An Sgùrra Biorach sgùrr as àirde,*
> *Ach Sgùrra nan Gillean sgùrr as fheàrr dhuibh,*
> *An sgùrra gorm-dhubh craosach làidir,*
> *An sgùrra gallanach caol cràcach,*
> *An sgùrr iargalta mòr gàbhaidh,*
> *An sgùrra Sgitheanach thar chàich dhuibh.*

> *The Sgurr Biorach is the highest sgurr*
> *But Sgurr nan Gillean the best sgurr,*
> *The blue-black gape-mouthed strong sgurr,*
> *The tree-like slender horned sgurr,*
> *The forbidding great dangerous sgurr,*
> *The sgurr of Skye above the rest.*

(MacLean 1989, 65)

Plate 14: Trotternish, Skye - Baca Ruadh, Coire an t-Seasgaich and Sgùrr a' Mhadaidh Ruaidh to the right of the picture (also in colour section)

Biorach means sharp-pointed or piercing and can be applied to the points of antlers. In northern Argyll, it can also apply to a 2 year-old heifer. It shares the same root as *Am Bioran* cited above.

Sìthean / Sìdhean - *little hill or knoll. Fairy hill. Big rounded hill.* Sìthean is now the recommended form. (Plate 15)

In Perthshire these are infrequent, moderately rugged and low – in contrast to the last phrase in the definition. They are mostly outliers, with nearly a quarter being slopes. They are often paired, without outcrops or corries. 33% are unaccompanied by adjectives. If qualified, they are usually black (*dubh*). *Sìtheanan* are associated with *na sìthean,* the fairies who reputedly inhabited such hillocks. References to the other world abound in Strathyre, where *Beinn an t-Sìdhein* (NN547178), Mountain of the Fairy Hill, dominates the western skyline above the village.

Plate 15: Glen Conghlas - Ais an t-Sìdhein. (Sìthean Mòr is to the left Sìthean Beag to the right, below Beinn a' Chùirn and Beinn Mhanach to the right) (also in colour section)

Sliabh - *mountain of the first magnitude, extended heath, alpine plain, moor ground* (Plate 16)

These are very rare in the study area, of medium height and moderately rugged. They are usually rocky. Half of them are outlying summits with corries. All are qualified. Given the generality of the dictionary meaning, which is broadly similar to the physical nature of the study area, it is surprising that they are not more common. This supports the view that, although *sliabh* is still used in Scottish Gaelic, it had, at least in Perthshire, ceased to be active in the naming process long ago, in contrast to Ireland and the Isle of Man, where it seems to have become the default term for mountain. In Scotland, the name is concentrated in Galloway and the southern Inner Hebrides. It also appears in literature. *Sliabh Fuar – Cold Moor* (NN709379) south of Ardtalnaig is a rare Perthshire example, which does not reflect the first part of the definition above. Other examples in the study area are equally non-compliant with this description. It is still common in Tiree, where it refers to moorland or muir beyond the arable land.

Plate 16: Ardtalnaig - Sròn na Ceàrdaich and Sliabh Fuar (Sròn na Ceàrdaich centre background, Sliabh Fuar - the slope below, and Tom Fluir centre middle ground (note stone pickings below Tom Fluir indicating former arable land)

Sròn - *nose, promontory, headland rising from a mountain to a strath. Ridge of a hill*

It has the equivalent usage in naming as shoulder in English. As a result it seldom forms a summit. These are frequent and widespread, yet with a significant concentration in Glen Artney along the Highland Fault. *Sròn Àileach* (airy) at NN677153, *Sròn nam Broighleag* (of the blaeberries) at NN684185, *Sròn na Maoile* (of the bald hill) at NN693173, *Sròn nan Cabar* (of the logs) at NN697173, *Sròn na Leacainn* (of the slabby place) at NN708183 and *Sròn a' Mhill* (of the

Plate 17: Glen Artney - Sròn Àileach (on the left of the picture), Càrn Labhruinn, Cnocan Dubha, Cachaileith Liath and Sròn na Maoile (on the right)

rounded hill) at NN727202 are examples. They are of medium height and moderately rugged. Half are outlying summits, though only 5% are slopes, in contrast to *sgiath*, which they otherwise resemble. They are likely to have corries and rocky outcrops and seem formally equivalent to the geomorphological concept of the truncated spur. All are qualified, with references to fauna being the most frequent (37%).

Stob - *stake, any pointed stick, prickle, thorn. Remaining stump of anything broken or cut. Any sharp pointed stick* (Plate 18)

These are infrequent, high and very rugged and rocky. They are concentrated in the more glaciated, western part of the study area, in Mamlorn, west Balquhidder and north Loch Lomondside. The great majority have corries. The presence of the less rugged, yet dominant *beinn* type throughout these areas argues that *stob* is not a dialectic substitution for the former, more common name, but a name attached to a form which is distinct to *beinn*.

Plate 18: Glen Artney - Stob Chaluim MhicGriogair and Stùc an Fhorsair (to the right of the picture)

Stùc - *little hill jutting out from a greater, steep on one side and rounded on the other. Cliff, rock, conical steep rock, precipice* (Plate 18 & 19)

These are infrequent, high and moderately rugged, concentrated along Loch Lubnaig and Loch Earn. They are likely to be outlying summits with outcrops and corries. 25% are unqualified, but 20% are, by colour. Typical examples, which illustrate its meaning of an asymmetric form, are *Stùc Garbh – Rough Asymmetric Hill* (NN668174) at the head of Glen Artney and *An Stùc* (NN639431) to the north of Loch Tay, in the Lawers range.

*Plate 19: Loch Tay - Beinn Ghlas, Beinn Labhair and
An Stùc (to the right of the picture)*

Tom - *round hillock or knoll, rising ground, swell, green eminence. Any round heap*

These are frequent in low, rolling country. Half are outlying summits, without rocks or corries. 20% are slopes. All are qualified. Cultural references (40%) are commonest. There are four references to hanging or hangmen, for example. **Plate 3** includes reference to a herdsman in *Tom a' Bhuachaille* and **Plate 20** to a place of worship, *Tom Cràbhachd*. Biotic qualifiers (31%) come next. Like *cnoc* and *meall*, if colour is specified, *Tom* is likely to be *dubh* or odhar, suggesting a link with peaty ground. Indeed, there are four occurrences of *Tom na Mòine*, hillock of peat, and, many more all over the Highlands. The word came from Irish and can mean a copse. In Arran it meant thicket. In the clearance of flatlands for farming, many barren and unploughable hillocks may have retained their woodland cover, and so the older meaning of *tom* became associated more with a certain type of landcover than with a landform.

Plate 20: Glen Lednock - from left to right, Cnoc na Sìthe, Tom na Cràbhachd and Sgòrr Racaineach (in the background)

Tòrr - *hill, mountain of an abrupt or conical form, lofty hill. Eminence. Mound. Large heap. Rock*

These are very rare and in Perthshire found in low, rolling country. Their occurrence tends to contradict the dictionary meaning of lofty hill. It may be, however, that local ruggedness is too fine-grained to be detected at the search scale of 1:25,000. They are all outliers rather than summits and more common in the Southern Hebrides. None have corries, but half have rocky outcrops. The majority is qualified, usually by size and then by colour, which is often grey (*liath*). *Tòrr* can also refer to a great amount of anything in Gaelic, as in the English 'piles of....'

Table 7: Frequency, Elevation (metres) and Ruggedness (metres) of Hill Names

Name	Quantity	%	Elevation (m)	Ruggedness (m)
Beinn	76	11.7	749	290
Bioran	8	1.2	562	339
Caisteal	11	1.7	500	235
Càrn	23	3.5	656	239
Cnap	5	0.8	283	358
Cnoc	34	5.2	354	183
Cruach	6	0.9	580	250
Dùn	33	5.1	328	197
Maol	10	1.5	448	308
Meall	193	29.7	652	244
Sgiath	22	3.4	462	276
Sgòrr / Sgòr / Sgùrr	8	1.2	501	363
Sìdhean	13	2.0	389	253
Sliabh	4	0.6	464	253
Sròn	54	8.3	577	291
Stob	38	5.8	721	332
Stùc	16	2.5	655	285
Tom	89	21.5	284	182
Tòrr	7	1.1	312	177

In his study of Scottish place-names, Nicolaisen asks whether differences in name distribution are a reflection of different dialects or are determined by differences in the landscapes the words describe, or are attributable to different phases in the expansion of the Gaelic settlement of Scotland.

Some name types studied above do indeed possess distinguishing and identifiable physical attributes. For example, *sgòrr, cnap* or *bioran* can be expected to be very rugged, but relatively low in elevation, when compared to *beinn*. The name *stob,* in contrast, is not only both high and very rugged, but also rocky. In complete contrast, the names *cnoc, dùn* or *tom* are more likely to be found in low, rolling country and to be without any rocky outcrops.

Table 8: Frequency (%) of Qualifying Adjectives

name	colour	texture	form	biotic	culture	none
Beinn	22.0	8.0	6.5	13.0	4.0	
Bioran			12.5	25.0		50.0
Caisteal	9.0		27.0		18.0	18.0
Càrn	26.0		7.5	17.0	17.0	
Cnap			40.0			
Cnoc	23.0	3.0	12.0			
Cruach			16.5			50.0
Dùn	9.0		27.0	15.0	3.0	3.0
Maol	10.0	10.0	20.0	30.0	10.0	
Meall	18.0	5.0	22.0	23.0	5.0	
Sgiath	32.0		18.0	36.0		
Sgòrr / Sgòr / Sgùrr		12.5		37.5	12.5	
Sìthean	23		23.0			31.0
Sliabh			25.0		25.0	
Sròn	5.5	7.5	7.5	37.0	5.5	
Stob	13.0	13.0	5.0	18.5	8.0	
Stùc	19.0	6.0	6.0		25.0	25.0
Tom	12.0	2.0	2.0	31.5	40.5	
Tòrr	43.0		57.0			14.0

Qualification by adjectives can further distinguish between the different names describing distinct landforms. Contrasting patterns of association between noun and adjective can be found. For example, *cnoc, dùn* or *sìthean* are often black or light brown-coloured, suggesting a link with peaty ground. Observation in the field also indicates an association with valley floor morraines. *Meall,* on the other hand, when, in 18% of instances, a colour is identified, is also linked with peaty hues, but at the much higher level of the rounded and dissected plateau. *Cnoc, dùn* and *sìthean* are sometimes also found in pairs, denoted by opposing adjectives such as big or small, black or white. *Beinn,* as the idea of a pre-eminent peak would imply, is never paired and more likely to be grey or red, whilst *sgiath* is more likely to be blue, *gorm.* In the study area, however, only 15.5% of hill names are qualified by colour, and of these, over 50% are either black or dun-coloured. Such a preponderance of those colours may reflect the wide extent of blanket peat in the dissected plateau of Highland Perthshire.

Some names, such as *bioran, caisteal, cruach* or *stùc,* seem to possess such a specific formal meaning that they often require no qualification by any adjective or dependent genitive noun. Others such as *meall* are always qualified, implying a form so general that it can be pointed, round, rough, notched, forked but most often fat, *reamhar* – thus emphasising the dictionary definition. Cultural associations qualify *tom* in about 40% of cases, which may reflect greater human activity at lower elevations. In contrast, over a quarter of the much higher *sròn* types are associated with animal descriptors. This may relate to their position as outlook points overlooking valleys, like Glen Artney, which define the edge of a mountain complex and are positions which experience a relatively lower level of human activity. Their general position suggests an equivalence with the geomorphological concept of the truncated spur.

Comparison of the distribution of different name types reflects contrasts, at the larger scale, between landscapes of differing character. The common occurrence of *stob* in Balquidder, for example, reflects the greater ruggedness prevailing there than in the rest of the study area. The parallel occurrence of *beinn* in the same locality implies that this is not a case of dialectic substitution, but a name attached to a distinct form. A similar situation exists with the parallel distribution of *maol* and *meall* in the area between Loch Lomond and Loch Katrine. However, in the same area *sgiath* does seem partly to substitute for *sròn,* which is similar in form and absent from the locality.

Understanding landscape through its common toponymic themes and associations can in this way inform the study of language and vice versa. Generally the findings support the argument that irregular distributions of landscape terms present in place-names are more due to differences in landscape character rather than any regional variation in naming trends.

Consideration of the study area data shows that there is not a clear relationship between the density of names and the complexity of the landscape. This may be due to cartographic error or omission, or the quality and nature of informants, and is discussed more fully in the earlier chapter on mapping.

Ian Fraser has written about the phenomenon of pairing in place-names shown in particular amongst the hill name generics: *cnoc, dùn* and *sìthean*. Examples of the same noun can often occur quite close together, distinguished by east or west, great or small, upper and lower. Such distinctions are sometimes more symbolic than representational and have evolved within a dual classification system of naming. *Tom an Rìgh* (NN488127) and *Tom na Banrighinn* (NN492128) in Glen Finglas are less than 300 metres apart and do not materially differ from each-other. Fraser argues that there is a natural tendency amongst namers to find opposites in the landscape serving as triggers in the naming process. Such pairing can relate to patterns of living and working, which sees places paired through naming as particular to specific functional activities. Such distinctions may not always be embodied in the actual names. In **Plate 21,** however, there is a real difference in size between the two duns.

Plate 21: Trotternish - Dùn Mòr and Dùn Beag; Lòn Garbh
is at the foot of the hill and An Corran in the background to
the right of Staffin Island (also in colour section)

Table 9: Landform - Mountains, Peaks, Crags, Hills and Knolls

Name	Gender	Sound	Meaning	Example
Àird / ard, àird, àirdean	f	*ahrsht*	height, point	Garbh-Àrd, Benderloch, NM877375, Rough Point
Aonach, aonaich, aonaichean	m	*oenuch*	steep height, plateau, ridge	Aonach Eagach, Glen Coe, NN155583, Notched Ridge
Bàrr, barra, barran	m	*bahr*	top, summit	Bàrr Mòr, Lismore, NM817388, Big Top
Beannan, beannain	m	*BYOWnan*	little hill	Am Beannan, Glen Artney, NN693136, Little Hill (Plate 6)
Beinn, beinne, beanntan	f	*byn*	mountain, hill, pinnacle, peak	A' Bheinn Mhòr, South Uist, NF808312, Big Mountain
Bidean, bidein, bideanan	m	*BEETchan*	pinnacle, peak, sharp pointed hill	Bidean nam Bian, Glen Coe, NN143542, Peak of the Hides
Binnean, binnein, binnein	m	*BEENyan*	pinnacle, high conical hill, apex of a hill	Binnean Mòr, Glen Nevis, Lochaber. NN212673, Big Pinnacle
Biod / bioda, biodan	m	*beet*	pointed top	Bioda Buidhe, Staffin, NG439664, Yellow Pointed Top (Front Cover)
Bioran, biorain	m	*BEERan*	little pointed stick	Am Bioran, St Fillans, NN695222, Little Pointed Stick (Plate 7)
Bràigh, bràighe / bràghad,bràigheachan	m	*bry*	the upper part or place	Am Bràigh Riabhach, Cairngorms, NO953999, Brindled High Place
Bruach, bruaich, bruaichean	f	*BROOuch*	bank, brink, brim	Bruach na Frìthe, Cuillins, Skye, NG461252, The Bank of the Deer Forest
Bruthach, bruthaich, bruthaichean	m/f	*BROOuch*	ascent, hillside, brae	Loch na Bruthaich, Assynt, NC071315, the Loch of the Hillside

64

Caisteal, caisteil, caistealan	m	*CASHtyal*	castle, tower, fort, castle-like hill	Caisteal Abhail, Arran, NR965445, Castle Abhail (Plate 8)
Càrn, càirn, cùirn, càrnaichean	m	*caahrrn*	heap or pile of stones, rocky hill or mountain	Càrn Bad an Fhraoich, Glen Almond, NN799373, Cairn of the Heathery Spot
Cleit / cleite, cleite, cleitean / cleiteachan	f	*clehtch*	rock, cliff, rocky eminence	Cleit an Rùisg, Harris, NB1777048, Rock of the Fleece or Hide
Cnap, cnaip, cnapan	m	*crahp*	knob, button, lump, boss, stud, little hill	Cnap Mòr, Ardlui, Loch Lomond, NN323164, Big Lump
Cnoc, cnoic / cnuic, cnocan	m	*crawchk*	knoll, hillock, eminence	Cnoc nan Càrn, Tobermory, NM498557, Knoll of the Cairns (also Plate 9)
Creag, creige, creagan	f	*craik*	rock, crag, cliff, precipice	Creag Ìochdair, Glen Lednock, NN733287, Lower Rock
Creachann, creachainn, creachannan	m	*CRAYchun*	rock, summit of a rock, hard rocky surface, shell-like	Beinn a' Chreachain(n), Water of Tulla, NN374442, Mountain of the Rocky Surface
Cruach, cruaiche, cruachan	f	*CROOuch*	pile, heap, stack of hay or peats	Cruach Tairbeirt, Arrochar, NN313058, The Heap of Tarbert
Cùl, cùile, cùiltean	m	*cool*	the back of anything	Cùl Mòr, Assynt, Sutherland, NG162119, The Big Back
Dùn, dùin, dùin, dùintean	m	*doon*	heap, hill, hillock mound, fortress, castle	Dùn 'n Aon Duine, St Fillans, NN675233, The Fort of the One or Lone Man (Plate 10)
Fireach, fìrich, fireachean	m	*FEEruch*	hill, moor, top of a hill	Fireach Beag, Strath Avon, NJ154238, Little Hill Top
Maol, maoil, maoil	m/f	*moeul*	brow of a rock, bare / bald top, promontory, bare round hill	Maol Buidhe, Ardnamurchan, NM464626, Yellow Bald Hill

Table 9 (cont.)

Name	Gender	Sound	Meaning	Example
Meall, mill, mill	m	*meeowl*	lump, mass, great shapeless hill	Meall nam Fuaran, Glen Quaich, NN826362, Rounded Hill of the Springs (Plate 12, also Plate 11)
Monadh, monaidh, monaidhean	m	*MAWnugh*	moor, range, heath	Meall Fuar-mhonaidh, Loch Ness, NH457223, Rounded Hill of the Cold Moor
Mullach, mullaich, mullaichean	m	*MOOluch*	top, summit	Mullach Mòr, Holy Island, Arran, NS063297, Big Summit
Òrd, ùird, òrdan, ùird	m	*awrsht*	hammer	Uchd an Ùird, Duirinish, NG793315, Breast-Shaped Hill of the Hammer
Sgàirneach, sgàirnaich	m	*SKARNyuch*	continuous heap of loose stones covering a hillside like a deserted quarry	Sgàirneach nam Broc, Glen Lochay,Perthshire, NN494377, Loose Scree of the Badgers (Plate 24)
Sgiath, sgèith / sgèithe, sgiathan	f	*SKEEuh*	wing, shield	Sgiath Chrom, Glen Dochart, NN465313, Crooked Wing (Plate 13)
Sgòr / sgòrr / sgurr, sgòir / sgòirr / sgùrra, sgòran / sgòrran / sgurran	m	*skawr*	sharp, steep hill rising alone, a conical sharp rock, a little precipitous height on another hill	Sgùrr nan Gobhar, Cuillìns, NG426225, Steep Hill of the Goats
Sithean, sithein, sithein	m	*SHEEahn*	knoll, fairy hill,	Sithean Glac an Ime, Scalpay, Skye, NG608307, Fairy Hill of Butter Hollow (also Plate 15)
Sliabh, slèibh, slèibhtean	m	*SLEEuv*	high moorland, heath, the face of a hill	Sliabh Fuar, Ardtalnaig, NN708379, Cold Moor (Plate 16)

66

Slios, sliosa, sliosan	m	*SLEEuhs*	side, extending and sloping declivity	Slios Meall na Saobhaidhe, Torridon, NG880480, Rounded Hill Slope of the Den
Spàrdan / spàrdain, spàrdain, spàrdanan	m	*SPARStan*	little eminence, or hill - flat at top, short and steep acclivity, level shelf on a hillside where one would naturally rest (literally: a hen-roost)	Creag an Spàrdain, Assynt, NC222327, Rock of the Little Eminence
Spidean, spidein, spideanan	m	*SPEETyan*	pinnacle, sharp pointed hill	Spidean Choinnich, Assynt, Sutherland. NG205278, Kenneth's Pinnacle
Sròn, sròine, srònan	f	*srawn*	nose	Sròn Àileach, Glen Artney, NN677153, Breezy Nose (**Plate 17**)
Stac, staca / staic, stacan	m	*stachk*	high cliff, precipice, projecting rock.	An Stac, Loch Ailort, NM763793, The High Cliff
Stob, stuib, stoban	m	*stawp*	point, stake	Stob Chaluim MhicGriogair, Glen Artney, NN660190, Calum MacGregor's Stump (Plate 18)
Stùc, stùic, stùcan / stùcannan	m	*stoochk*	little hill jutting out from another, steep on one side and rounded on the other	An Stùc, North Loch Tayside, NN639432, The Jutting Hill (Plate 19)
Suidhe, suidhean, suid-heachan	m	*SOOHyuh*	seat, level shelf on a hillside	Suidhe Bhlàin, Kilchattan, Bute, NS096527, Saint Blane's Seat
Tom, tuim, tomannan	m	*towm*	knoll, round hillock, green eminence	Tom Cadalach, Glen Beich, North Loch Earnside, NN, Sleepy Hillock (Plate 4)
Tòrr, torra, torran	m	*tawr*	heap, hill, mound, tower.	Tòrr nan Con, Morvern, NM582583, Tower of the Dogs

6.2: Landform - Hollows, Valleys, Ridges, Plains and Passes

Like *beinn, gleann* is so common and applied at many scales across the Highlands, it has entered the English language and Scots as 'glen' and is the default word for valley. Highlanders were deeply attached to their glen, and that attachment survived clearance, the pressgang and exile. In 1928, William Watson collected a story from a farmer at Auchlyne in Glen Dochart, about two soldiers from that Glen meeting in Canada, and one asking the other for proof of his provenance. The reply is a recitation of place-names, all lying within a short distance of one another, which showed that he knew his home turf intimately.

> '*Tha Fas a' Ghràig an Leathad a' Charraigh[1]*
> *Is Coille Chasaidh an Ardchoille[2],*
> *Caibeal na Fairc(e) an Achadh-loinne[3],*
> *Tom an Taghain[4] 's Meall na Samhna[5],*
> *Lochan nan Arm anns an t-Suidhe,*
> *Is Tom Ruigh an Innis Eòghain[6],*
> *Dail Clachaig am Both Uachdair[7],*
> *Is daimh air cruachan Beinne Mòire[8].*'

(in Watson 1928, 264)

The last line refers to stags on the shoulder of Ben More. In order of appearance in the text, the following can still be found, mostly in anglicised form on OS explorer sheet 365 as: Ledcharrie[1] - Slope of the Stone Pillar (NN506282), Ardchyle[2] - Wood Height (NN526294), Auchlyne[3] - Pleasant or Productive Field (NN512296), Tom an Taghain[4] (Plate 22) - Hillock of the Pine Marten (NN505512) , Meall na Samhna[5] - The Rounded Hill of Hallowtide or All Hallows (NN493325), Innisewan - Ewan's Meadow[6] (NN483283), Bowachter[7] - the Upper Hut and Ben More[8] - Big Mountain. *An Suidhe* - the Seat, refers to *Stob an t-Suidhe* - the Stump-shaped Hill of the Seat (NN474268) or in its vicinity to the south-west, at *An Suie*. Other place-names in the rhyme do not appear on OS sheets. The storyteller's companion responds with an observation on the swiftness of the Burn of the Turner near Upper Lix, which is now Wester Lix. This list shows the detail and depth of the psychogeography possessed by Highlanders in the eighteenth century. It also shows how the anglicisation of Gaelic names began and spread along the glens, through the influence of trade and commerce with the Low-

Plate 22: Glen Dochart - Tom an Taghain (in the foreground), Meall Sgallachd, Creag Mac Rànaich, Creag Loisgte & Dùn Meadhonach

lands. Names in the uplands, which were important to transhumance culture, were for the most part left intact in their original form.

Glen Nevis below Scotland's highest mountain is described in *An Duanaire – A Collection of Gaelic songs and poems* made by Donald MacPherson in 1868.

> *Gleann Nibheis, gleann na gcloch,*
> **Glen Nevis, glen of stones,**
> *Gleann am bi an gart anmoch;*
> **Glen where the corn ripens late;**
> *Gleann fada, fiadhaich, fàs,*
> **A long, wild, waste glen,**
> *Sluagh bradach an mhìoghnàis.*
> **With thievish folk of evil habit.**

(in MacPherson 1868, 45)

It is a wonder any corn ever ripened in such a wet place. In quoting the poem, Watson translates *gart*, which means an enclosed plot of arable land, or garden, as corn.

The pairing phenomenon discussed in the previous section occurs amongst valleys as well. Fraser describes *Gleann Dubh - Black Glen* (NM725535) and *Gleann Geal - White Glen* (NN725505) in Morvern. The first is deep and dark with a river meandering through peat bogs, where hills to its east cast a long shadow in winter. To the north lies *Beinn nam Beathrach* NN753573, Mountain of the Thunderbolts. *Gleann Geal* is wide and shallow by comparison with good grazing on grassy haughs flanking the river. Here pairing is directly representative of landscape by using a colour or shade contrast indicating different agricultural land capabilities.

Srath, which has also come into Scots and English as Strath, can be larger in scale than *gleann.* Its real distinguishing feature is the flatness of its valley floor, as it mostly occurs lower downstream along river systems in broad valley bottoms, in haughs or floodplains. *Bealach* is the second most common word in the category of concavity and is found throughout the Gàidhealtachd. It signifies a pass for travellers. Indeed, its original meaning was way or route. Many of the drove roads in the Highlands typically pass through *bealaichean.* Passes of the cows and of the cow exist in the Trossachs, *Bealach nam Bò* (NN480075), and Applecross, *Bealach na Bà* (NG782414). The former is mentioned in Scott's poem, *The Lady of the Lake. Above the Goblin Cave* (Coire na Uiruisgean) *they go, Through the wild pass of Beal nam Bo.* Scott's rendering of *bealach* no doubt reflects Gaelic pronunciation with its stress on the first syllable, but the contraction to *Beal* could be confused with the word for mouth: *beul or bial.* In some dialects, final syllables in a word like bealach can be elided in speech.

Though both of these *bealaichean* are very steep, cattle would have had many more problems negotiating *Bealach nam Fàradh* - the Pass of the Ladders, also in Applecross (NG787447), and incorrectly shown as Bealach nan Arr on OS Explorer sheet 428. *Bealach a' Mhorghain - Pass of Shingle* (NG455623) in Skye also climbs steeply across the peninsula of Trotternish to the South of *Beinn Eadarra - Mountain Between.* It is spelled incorrectly on the OS explorer map as Bealach a' Mhòramhain. Watson quotes the melancholy chant of a headless corpse who dwelled in this eerie place after the ghost was exiled to Morar.

> '*Is fada bhuam féin bonn Beinn Eadarra,*
> *is fada bhuam féin Bealach a' Mhorghain.*'

> '*Far from me is Beinn Eadarra's foot,*
> *far from me is the Shingle Pass.*'

> (in Watson 1926, 483)

Like other place-name elements associated with the land, *bealach* can also apply to sea passages, as discussed in the hydronymy section, below.

Làirig has a much patchier distribution than *bealach*. Perhaps the most well-known example is the high level route of the Lairg Ghru (*Làirig Dhrù*) at NH964027, whose meaning in Gaelic may refer to a dripping river, and which cuts through the Cairngorms. The word is also very common in Highland Perthshire. In most cases *làirig* seems to involve a longer and more gradual ascent across a watershed than *bealach*. *Làirig nan Lunn* (NN450387), running between Glen Lyon and Glen Lochay, and *Làirig an Lochain* (NN594414), also running from Glen Lyon to Loch Tay, are good examples of more relaxed crossings of the watershed. The former is part of an old coffin route to Killin (*Cill Fhinn*), the sacred burial place of Fionn (Fingal or Finn Mac Cumhail) in Celtic mythology, and where *lunn* can, among other things, mean a pole for carrying a bier. Further upstream *Làirig Mhic Bhàtaidh* (NN 382345) - wrongly shown on the OS map as *Làirig Mhic Bhaidein* also runs between these two glens. This pass features in *Òran Coire a' Cheathaich - Song to the Misty Corrie*, composed by Duncan Ban MacIntyre in the second half of the eighteenth century. The poem also uses the rare generic hill name of *sliabh*.

> '*Tha sliabh na làirig an robh Mac Bhàididh,*
> '*na mhòthar fàsaich 's 'na stràca trom...*'

> ' *The moor of the pass where MacWattie was*
> *is a tufted forest and flush with heavy growth.*'

(in MacLeod 1978, 166)

Cumhang, which also has an adjectival form, means a narrow place or defile. The Passes of Leny and Brander were originally known as *An Cumhang Lànaigh* and *Cumhang a' Bhrannraidh*, where Brander means a trap or snare. In a maritime context, it gives *An Caolas Cumhang - the Narrow Strait*, which has been anglicised to Kylesku. It can also qualify other words for valley like Glen or stand on its own. *Cumhang a' Ghlinne - the Narrow of the Glen* (NG873407), between Lochcarron and Kishorn, shows such refinement of meaning. Also in Wester Ross, and at the summit of *Bealach na Bà* in Applecross, is *Allt a' Chumhaing - the Burn of the Defile* (NG782415). Close at

Plate 5: Loch Katrine - Bealach nam Bò and Coire na(n) Ùruisgean (Bealach nam Bò is the break of slope in the left background below the rock face, Coire na(n) Ùruisgean is above the steamboat and Eilean Molach is at the bottom right.)

hand can be found *Creag a' Chadha - the Rock of the Steep Pass* (NG 863407) and *Cadha nam Fèidh (Fiadh) - the Steep Pass of the Deer* (NG877844). Whilst a *bealach* can vary in dimension, *cadha* is always narrower and steeper and sometimes cuts across a hillside, as shown in both these cases. Unlike *bealach* and *làirig*, it usually does not encompass both sides of a watershed. *Clais,* literally a furrow, is steeper than either *bealach* or *cadha*, and signifies a gorge or cleft. Its primary meaning, of ploughable land, is the origin of several settlement names in Sutherland.

In his poem '*Coin is Madaidhean Allaidh - Dogs and Wolves,*' Sorley MacLean imagines his poetic motivation chasing its inspiration, love and beauty, through an archetypal Highland landscape of hill and valley.

> *gadhair chaola's madaidhean-allaidh*
> *a' leum thar mullaichean nan gàradh,*
> *a' ruith fo sgàil nan craobhan fàsail,*
> *ag gabhal cumhang nan caol-ghleann;*
> *a' sireadh caisead nan gaoth-bheann.*

lean greyhounds and wolves
leaping over the tops of dykes,
running under the shade of the trees in the wilderness
taking the defile of narrow glens,
making for the steepness of windy mountains;

(MacLean 1989, 134)

In the text *caol* and *gaoth* meaning narrow and windy are in the emphatic position, which causes the nouns following, *gleann* and *bean,* to be lenited to *ghleann* and *bheann.*

Leitir, which has been derived from *leth tìr,* and literally means half land, and *leathad* both mean slope or hillside, though *leathad* does not share this derivation. They are commonly anglicised in the names *letter* and *led,* such as Letterfinlay by Loch Lochy and Ledmore in Assynt. *Leitir* usually slopes towards a watercourse or body, that is, with land on one side only, in other words *leth thioram* (half dry) and *leth fhliuch* (half wet). *Leitir Mhòr - the Big Slope* (NN032594), to the West of Ballachulish, was where Colin Campbell of Glenure (the Red Fox) was assassinated, reputedly by an Appin Stewart. The murder provided much of the plot for Stevenson's novel 'Kidnapped.' In the story, David Balfour and Alan Breck evade capture, after the event, by climbing, circling above and then descending *Stac an Eich - Steep Cliff of the Horse* (NN030593), though this is not identified in the book. Later, the pair camp and fish in a hidden cleft called Heugh of Corrynakiegh, which is *Coire na Cìche* in the novel, at the back of the Pap of Glencoe or *Sgòrr na Cìche - Steep Peak of the Breast* (NN124594). From there, and late at night, Alan Breck descends to the clachan of Kaolisnacoan in the book, which is *Caolas nan Con* (NN136613) - the Narrows of the Dogs, on Loch Leven, where he leaves a miniature fiery cross on the window sill of his kinsman, John Breck MacColl.

'Whole land' is *tìr* in Gaelic. It is the origin of *Cinn Tìre* or Kintyre, literally, Heads of Land, though originaly it may have been *Ceann Tìre*. If the plural is correct, it may signify the several promontories terminating the peninsula and separating the Firth of Clyde from the Irish Sea. In modern Gaelic the mainland is *tìr-mòr* or sometimes *tìr-mhòr*. *Tìr* is used to distinguish dry land from the sea and indeed applies to the act of coming ashore, *a dol air tìr,* literally, going on land, from a vessel.

Table 9: Landform - Hollows, Valleys, Ridges, Plains and Passes

Name	Gender	Sound	Meaning	Example
Amar, amair, amaran / amraichean	m	*AMur*	trough, channel, ditch	Amar Stob a' Choin, Balquidder, NN415167, Trough of the Stump of the Dog
Bac, baca / baic, bacan	m	*bachk*	pit, hollow, bog, bank, peatbank	Bac Mòr, Treshnish Isles, NM244388, Big Bank
Bealach, bealaich, bealaich	m	*BYALuch*	pass, mountain gorge, glen, gap	Bealach na Seann Làirige, Glen Finglas, NN550128, Pass of the Old Gorge
Beàrn, bèirn / beàirn, beàrnan	m/f	*byaarn*	gap, crevice	Tobar Bun na Bèirn, NR163537, Mull of Oa, Islay, The Well at the Foot of the Gap
Blàr, blàir, blàran	m	*blaar*	cleared space	Còinneach-bhlàr, Braeleny, NN644107, Moss Plain
Cadha, cadhan, cadhachan	m	*CAHuh*	narrow place, ravine	An Cadha, Rhiconich, NC234506, The Ravine
Caigeann, caiginn, caigeannan	m	*KEHkown*	rough mountain pass	Rubha a' Chaiginn, Kingairloch, NM855510, Point of the Rough Mountain Pass
Càthar, càthair	m	*CAAhur*	mossy, soft boggy ground	Càthar an Fhèidh, Lochaber, NN404763, Boggy Ground of the Stag. Càthar can be confused with *cathair* meaning seat e.g. A' Chathair Bheag, Gairloch
Coire, coireachan	m	*CAWruh*	corrie, hollow on the side of a hill (literally: kettle)	Coire Gabhail, Glen Coe, NN163550, Taking Corrie
Crasg, craisg, crasgan	f	*crask*	crossing	Beinn a' Chraisg, Kinlochbervie, NC237597, Mountain of the Crossing
Cuithe, cuitheachean	f	*COOyuh*	pit, narrow glen, deep moist place, patch of snow. The very similar *cuidhe* can mean a cattlefold in the Western Isles.	Cuithe Mheadhonach, Arran, NR969452, Middle Pit
Cumhang, cumhaing	m	*COOung*	narrow place, defile	Creag a' Chumhaing, Kishorn, NG794405, Rock of the Narrow Place

74

Gaelic forms	Gender	Pronunciation	Meaning	Example
Cunglach, cunglaich, cunglachan	m	COONgluch	narrow defile, cleft	An Cunglach, Trossachs, NN553096, The Cleft
Dìg, dige, dìgean	f	jeek	ditch, wall of loose stones	Meall na Dige, Balquidder, N452226, Rounded Hill of the Ditch
Diollaid, diollaide, diollaidean	f	JEEOlitch	saddle	Diollaid a' Chàirn, Lochaber, NG488758, The Saddle of the Cairn
Eag, eige, eagan	f	ek	notch, gap	Eag a' Chait, Abernethy Forest, NJ039124, Notch of the Cat
Easg, easga, easgan	m/f	esk	marsh, swamp, ditch formed by nature	An t-Easg Leathain(n), Atholl, NN805697, The Broad Marsh
Glac, glaic(e), glacan	f	glachk	hollow, small valley	Glac an Amair, Mull, NM728338, Hollow of the Channel
Gleann, glinne, gleanntean	m	glown	narrow valley, glen	Cumhang a' Ghlinne, Lochcarron, NG872407, The Defile of the Glen
Lag, laig / luig, lagan	m/f	lak	hollow, pit, cave	Lag an Fhiodha, Ardnamurchan, NC548648, Hollow of the Timber
Làirig, làirige, làirigean	f	laarik	moor, hill, sloping hill, pass	Làirig nan Lunn, Glen Lyon, Perthshire, NN450387, Pass of the Poles
Lèana, lèanan, lèanachan	f	LEEUHnuh	swampy plain, meadow, field of green	Lèana Mhòr, Barra, NF663007, Big Swampy Plain
Lèanag / lianag, lèanaig, lèanagan	f	LEEUHnak	wet plain or lea	Lianag Mhòr, Assynt, NC220064, Big Wet Plain.
Leathad, leathaid / leothaid, leathaidean / leòidean	m	LEHut	declivity, slope, side of hill, half ridge	Leathad Fear Asain, Assynt, NC219070, Slope of the Assynt Man.
Leitir, leitire / leitireach, leitirean / leitirichean	f	LEHtchir	slope, side of a hill	Leitir Mhòr, Ballachulish, NN024887, Big Slope
Lòn, lòin, lòintean	m	lawn	marsh, morass, pool, meadow, small brook with marshy banks	Lòn Garbh, Staffin, Syke, NG490687, Rough Marshy Stream (Plate 21)

Table 9 (cont.)

Name	Gender	Sound	Meaning	Example
Machair, machrach, ma-chraichean	m/f	*MAchehr*	extensive, low lying fertile ground, long ranges of sandy plains fringing the Atlantic side of the Outer Hebrides	A' Mhachair, Iona, NM267237, The Machair
Magh, magha, magaidh	m/f	*mugh*	plain, field	Magh-cùl, Kinloch Laggan, Badenoch, NN558904, Back Plain
Rèidh, rèidhean	m	*ray*	smooth and level ground, plain, meadow	Druim Rèidh, Mull NM432574, Level Ground Ridge
Riasg, rèisg	m	*REEusk*	moor, fen, marsh, place where sedge grows, land that cannot be ploughed owing to the amount of dirk-grass it grows.	Tom an Rèisg, Strath Avon, NJ156154, Hillock of the Fen
Sloc(hd), sluic, slocan	m	*slochk*	pit, den, hollow, cavity, dell, hold, hole	Sloc na Beinne, Applecross, NG725388, Pit of the Mountain
Slugaid, slugaide	f	*SLOOgetch*	slough, deep and miry place, quicksand	Allt na Slugaide, Am Boc, Isle of Lewis, NB484398, Burn of the Slough
Srath, sratha, srathan	m	*srah*	valley, riverside land	Srath a' Bhàthaich, Torridon, NG890480, Valley of the Byre.
Talamh, talaimh / talmhainn, talamhan	m/f	*TAluv*	earth, land, soil, T glas – unploughed land, T dearg – ploughed land	Seann Talamh, Strathyre, NN556174 , Old Land
Tìr, tìre, tìrean	m/f	*cheer*	the land (sometimes as distinct from water)	Tìr Èilde, Glen Quaich, NN831420, Hind Land
Toll, tuill, tuill	m	*towl*	hole, hollow	A' Chlach Thuill, Assynt, NC037267, The Stone Hollow
Uamh / uaimh, uaimhe / uamha, uaimhean, uamhan	f	*OOah*	cave	Uamh Fhliuch, Kerrera, NM801292, Wet Cave

6.3: The Gaelic Seascape

Admiralty charts and Ordnance Survey maps differ in their coverage of both land and sea. The Admiralty is only really interested in land where it provides navigational reference points, especially when these become critical for setting sail or dropping anchor. Depths and hazards at sea as well as tidal effects are covered as fully as possible on these charts. Land is shown in an amorphous shade of milk chocolate brown, which does not invite inquiry. Ordnance Survey measures the depth of still <u>freshwater</u> bodies but this only applies to larger, natural lochs. OS sheets only cover marine skerries and reefs, when these are visible from land or form land above the high water mark. Strong tidal streams, such as *Caolas Ùpraid - Narrows of Uproar* (NR155538), between Frenchman's Rocks and the mainland of Islay, are not always mapped. Troublesome rocks, which 'dry,' or are only visible at low water and are often called *bogha* or *bodha* in Gaelic, are also not always on OS maps. It is worrying therefore to see many sea kayakers using land-based maps as navigational tools. *Port Duine na h-Èiginn - Port of the Man in Difficulty* NR160539 on the Rhinns of Islay would provide a refuge for a small boat whilst waiting for favourable conditions, but it is unmapped by the OS.

The best known place-name element in the category of freshwater or marine hydronymy must be the word *loch*, which has retained its Gaelic spelling without alteration. It has entered Scots, and to a lesser extent English, or it is at least known, if often mispronounced, in English. Unlike the word 'lake,' *loch* applies both to fresh and salt water. Many long and fjord-like sea lochs serrate the Highland west coast from Kintyre to Cape Wrath. The name encompasses an enormous difference in application, from the grand inland waterways of the Great Glen to the merest moorland puddle, though *lochan* is its diminutive form. Words like *poll* and *glumag* also meaning pool, or puddle are used much less frequently. The word *linne,* also meaning pool gives its name tautologically to Loch Linnhe, one of the largest sea lochs in Scotland. The situation in Gaelic is more complex and more interesting. North-east of Corran the loch is called *An Linne Dhubh*, which may reflect its increasingly dark character as the water becomes progressively enclosed by the high mountains of Lochaber. South-west of Corran it is called *An Linne Sheileach - the Brackish*

Pool. Neither of these old Gaelic names is mapped. *Linne* has come into Scots as Linn, whose spelling retains the double N, even though this is redundant in its Scots pronunciation. Linn can be the pool below a waterfall or the waterfall itself, as in the Reekie Linn on the River Isla in Angus or Stichill Linn, north of Kelso.

Many other name elements of the coast can also be applied to large freshwater bodies like Loch Shiel and Loch Awe, such as *camus, cladach, inbhir, geodha, òb, port, ros* and *rubha.* The last is sometimes shown as *rudha,* and is anglicised in the settlement of *Rhu* near Helensburgh. Natives of Point district in Lewis are known as *Rudhaich,* whilst those of Ness are *Nisich.* People defined by peninsulas. *Geodha* can also apply to inland cliffs, like *Geodha Fir Chata,* near Inchnadamph at NC298193. Its meaning is obscure, but could be the Ravine of the Men of Sutherland.

Sgeir also occurs inland in adjectival form as *sgeireach* and as a plural at *Sgeirean an Amadain - Skerries of the Fool* on Loch Maree at NG946705. This name perhaps speaks of reckless helmsmanship in shallow waters. *Camas* or *camus,* which often refers to a curving, horseshoe-shaped bay, has in the past described land within the curve of a river, at Cambuskenneth by the Forth at Stirling and Cambuslang on the Clyde near Glasgow, where *cambus* is the old Scots form. *Camas* is similar in physical form to the Norse-derived *ùig.* Where the curve becomes tighter and smaller, *camus* is replaced by *sàilean.* This word, as its closeness to Latin indicates, only applies to salt water, however. It is most common in mainland Argyll and the islands of Mull and Jura.

Terms for what on land would be concavities are also used at sea for deep holes. There are several examples of *sloc* along the west coasts of Lismore and Seil. *Poll* is also widespread in the same area. Yachts would be well advised to anchor in *Poll Creadha - Clay Pool* (NG710410), where a good hold might be had, rather than *Poll Bhrochain - Pool of Porridge,* where the anchor might drag unpredictably in a loose slurry of mud. *Port Lobh - Rotting Port* (NR350928) on the West side of Colonsay, no doubt so named because of the mass of seaweed cast upon its shore by Atlantic swells, would provide a less than fragrant berth. *Acarsaid Fhalaich - Hidden Anchorage* (NF906570) on the east coast of North Uist

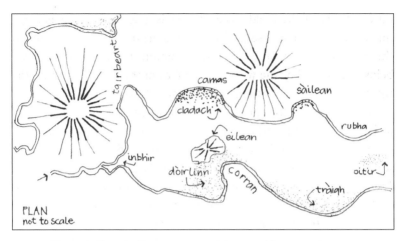

Figure 5: Generic diagram summarising coastal toponymic terms

implies a sheltered or concealed spot, if its entrance from the sea can be found. *Acarsaid* or *acarseid* is yet another Gaelic word of Norse origin and literally means anchor seat - *akkar-sæti*. Caladh, also meaning harbour or haven, though common in house names and often shortened to *cala*, is rare in place-names. *Port,* which is cognate with Latin *portum*, implies a smaller anchorage than the same word in English.

Given the complexity and diversity of how water meets in the land along the West Coast, there is a great degree of specificity in several other words such as *dòirlinn* and *fadhail* or *faodhal*. The first, which is common in coastal place-names, means a small island to which one can wade in low water, or conversely a narrow sound separating an island from the mainland, which is likely to dry out at low tide. The *dòirlinn* across to the island on which *Caisteal Tioram* (dry castle) stands near Acharacle at NM663724 is perhaps the best known example. *An Fadhail* meaning the ford or space between islands made passable on foot by the ebbing tide is less common and applies to large tidal expanses of sandy beach. This seascape is typical of Benbecula, whose name in Gaelic is *Beinn nam Fadhla*.

The best known word in this distinctive set is probably *tairbeart*, which is anglicised to tarbert and sometimes gives rise to settlements of that name. It has a compounded meaning of an isthmus over which it is possible to draw or pull (*tàirn* or *tarraing*) a boat (*bàta*) on wooden rollers. There are examples throughout Scotland in Easter Ross, Gigha, Harris, Kintyre, Jura, Loch Lomond, near Handa Island in Sutherland and even on the Garbh-Eileach, which shows how widespread the practice of taking shortcuts overland must have been. The longest, and one which escapes the colliding tidal races below the cliffs of its Mull, crosses Kintyre at Tarbert, Loch Fyne. There, in 1097AD, Magnus Barelegs claimed the peninsula as an island and his right under the terms of a treaty with Edgar, King of Scots. An engaging and smaller instance, only 200m long, lies at the mouth of Loch Moidart (NM660736) and separates Eilean Shona from Shona Beag. *Tairbeartan* are widely variable in scale.

In the mid 19th century, George Rainy, the owner of Raasay, made use of another Tairbeart at one of the narrowest parts of the island (NG592476) to build a two metre high stone wall to separate deer in the fertile south of the island from crofters, whom he had displaced to the rough and infertile north.

As Norse invasions of the isles and the West Coast were seaborne, and permanent settlement under their rule lasted nearly 500 years, many words for coastal features have Scandinavian origins. Some have later been gaelicised. These include: *bodha / bogha, geodha, nis, sgeir* and *ùig*, which in Old Norse are: *boði, gjá, nes, sker* and *vik. Vik* also exists as the suffix *aig* in many Gaelic place-names. Hence the many *Sandaigs, Sanndaigs* and *Sanndabhaigs*, or sand bays. Another suffix, *øy* meaning island, has been gaelicised to -*aigh* and is anglicised to *a* and *ay* in *Barraigh*, Barra and Soay. These words and suffixes are also common in the Northern Isles of Orkney and Shetland, where they remain closer to their original form. *Sker* has also come into Scottish English as skerry. *Na Sgeirean Fiaclach* - the Toothed Skerries, (NR398447) just off the South coast of Islay, would, no doubt, make a meal of any timber-hulled galley. *Cleiteadh*, meaning a ridge of rocks, appears to displace *sgeir* around the Isle of Arran.

Eilean is the modern gaelic word for island. It is thought to be Norse in orign. The older word was *innis*. This is the source of the Scotticised *inch*. There are many examples in Loch Lomond, Inchmurrin (*Innis Mearan – St Mirren's Isle*) and the Firth of Forth, Inchcolm (*Innis Colm – St Columba's Isle*). *Innis* came to refer to a riverside meadow (see section on land use), which can be understood visually as an island of cultivation amidst unploughable land.

Navigational hazards in the form of rocks have often been individually, even mischievously named. In the name *A' Bhratag* or *A' Bhradag* (NM888353), the Impudent Girl, which is inconveniently situated at the mouth of Loch Etive, one can almost sense the irritation of the Gaelic mariners felt at being caught out. The same word also occurs by the anchorage at Castle Sween, Knapdale (NR712787). *Am Buachaille* (the Herdsman) lies off Staffa at NM326352 and is a herdsman one should not heed. Hazardous rocks may also be named after animals. Wariness may have motivated the naming of *Eich Donna* - Brown Horses (NM792098), a line of drying rocks just off Arduaine – Green Point (ard OOanyuh, not the ardoonee of yachting usage). *Làir Bhàn - White Mare* (NM766065) is another equine example to the south of Shuna. There is a rare example of a boar skerry off the south west coast of St Kilda, at *An Torc* (NF086990). Famously, three dogs, using the older word for that animal, *Am Madadh Beag, Am Madadh Mòr* and *Am Madadh Gruamach* (grim) are rocks standing guard, like the three headed Cerberus of Greek myth, at the entrance to Loch nam Madadh, the ferry port of North Uist. Whilst between Lunga and Scarba, the modern word for dog, *cù*, in its genitive singular is used in *Bealach a' Choin Ghlais - the Pass of the Grey Dog* (NM713071), known as the Grey Dogs in yachting guides.

This last name is interesting for two reasons. The place is also called Little Corryvreckan on account of its tide race, which can reach eight knots. At the height of the Spring tides, a breaking standing wave occurs in mid-channel, or in the *bealach*. So the name seems to describe the flowing tidal process on the move, rather than a fixed physical entity. Secondly, *bealach* is a name more usually associated with mountain passess than the sea. A parallel lies in the use of the word *coire* in the whirlpool of Corryvreckan between Jura and Scarba. The origin of the second part of its name is unclear, but it is thought to refer to the cauldron of St Breccan. Corries are more usually found as scooped out hollows on mountainsides.

The tide also runs fiercely over another *An Coire* (NR162511), just off Portnahaven in Islay. *Sruth a' Chòmhraig - Stream of the Battle* (NF856459), North Uist could refer to the current (*sruth*) and how the helmsman has to fight to remain on course, rather than any historical reference to a real battle (*còmhrag*). Between Lewis and the Shiant Islands runs *Sruth nam Fear Gorm* - The Current of the Blue Green Men, another fierce tidal stream running over a submerged reef which connects the islands, beneath the sea, to Lewis.

According to Adam Nicholson, whose family owns the Shiants, *gorm* 'describes that dark half colour which is the colour of deep sea water at the foot of a black cliff.' The blue green men

'are strange, dripping semi-human creatures who come aboard and sit alongside you in the sternsheets, sing a verse or two of a complex song and, if you are unable to continue in the same metre and with the same rhyme, sink your boat and drown your crew.'

(Nicolson 2002, 38)

With hazards like that, little wonder Lewis is renowned for the quality of its singers and songs. Tides are not always so fierce as they move in response to the moon. *Loch an Dàil* (NR260580) in Islay, anglicised to Loch Indaal, means the Loch of Delay, because, owing to its gradual profile, it takes almost an hour longer to dry at low tide, compared to the narrower Loch Gruinart on the north side of the island.

Some rocks at sea also make a noise. According to Ian Fraser, *An Tudan* (NM694087) off Lunga in the Firth of Lorn, means The Farter, whilst two examples of *Sgeir Phlocach*, off the coast of Jura at NR524642 and NR522634, are plopping skerries. Other names describe the voyage into wider horizons. Perhaps the most well known is *An Dorus Mòr* - *The Big Door* (NM757986), which separates Loch Craignish from the more open water of the Sound of Jura. *Sgeir Leth a' Chuain* - *Half Skerry of the Sea* is similar: lying between the Garvellachs islands, it separates inshore waters from the wider Firth of Lorne. A most evocative name of this kind is *Camus Cùil an t-Sàimh*, which may mean -*The Bay at the back of the Breaking Waves* (NM265237), in Iona. Another possible translation is '*The Bay of the Nook of Peace,*' but the name could also be a gaelicisation of the norse *háfn*.

Donald MacIver from the western machair of Uig in Lewis celebrates the Atlantic swell in a famous song of exile called *An Ataireachd Àrd* - *The High Surge of the Sea,* sung by Capercaillie, Ishbel MacAskill and Runrig.

An ataireachd bhuan,
The ceaseless surge

Cluinn fuaim na h-ataireachd àird
Listen to the surge of the sea;

Tha torann a' chuain
The thunder of the ocean is

Mar chualas leams' e nam phàist
As I heard it when I was a child,

Gun mhùthadh, gun truas,
Without change, without pity,

A' sluaisreadh gainneamh na tràigh'd:
Breaking on the sand of the beach:

An ataireachd bhuan,
The ceaseless surge,

Cluinn fuaim na h-ataireachd àird.
Listen to the high surge of the seas.

'S na coilltean a siar
In the woods of the West

Chan iarrain fuireach gu brath:
I would not want to remain forever:

Bha m' inntinn 's mo mhiann
My mind and my desire were always

A-riamh air lagan a' bhàigh;
On the little hollow by the bay;

Ach iadsan bha fial,
But those folk who were generous in affection

An gniomh an caidreabh, 's an àgh
In their happiness and in their acts

Air sgapadh gun dion,
Have been scattered defenceless,

Mar thriallas ealtainn ro nàmh.
As a flock of birds flees in front of their enemy.

(in Lorne Gillies 2005, 74)

Foragers may find places which are *sligeanach / sligeach / sligeachach* or *na slige* or refer to *faochag,* good for collecting shellfish and buckies or whilks. Curiously, and despite being as common as the humble buckie, mussels *(feusgain* - literally beardies) and cockles *(coilleagan)* do not receive as frequent a mention in place-names as *faochagan.* Not even on Barra's famous Cockle Strand, which is called merely *An Tràigh Mhòr* – *The Big Beach,* do they receive a mention. Curiously, the inhabitants of Mackinnon country in Strath, Skye are nicknamed *Na Faochagan.*

Good sea fishing points are more often named after potential catches, *nan sgadan* (herring) or *cudaigean* (cuddies or coal fish) than those who catch them *(iasgairean). Rudh' an Tacair* on Loch Sween (NR735891) in Argyll may indicate a bountiful catch. Fish traps, *cairidhean,* often generate a place-name. They usually consist of a low wall or weir between high and low water marks, low enough to admit the high tide but high enough to leave fish stranded behind their stones upon the ebb. *Eileach,* literally meaning a mill dam, can also represent a bank of stones built to guide fish into a bag net.

6.4: Still Freshwater

In some places in the Highlands such as Benbecula or the Reay Forest (*or MacKay's Country - Dùthaich MhicAoidh*), terra seems more aqua than firma. The Lochs there tend to retain their pure Gaelic names more than many other surrounding generic names, especially those attached to rivers. They can be classified according to colour, size, shape, surrounding vegetation, animals, function, or they can be named after people. For the trout fisher, the ability to understand Gaelic place-names may well increase their catch, or at least their expectations.

Any *Loch Dubh* will probably be dark, peaty, infertile and acidic and yield many small and hungry, but very old, trout. *Dubh* might also indicate enclosure by landform, which hides the sun for most of the day. Such waters will be slow to warm up in Spring and not be worth fishing until high summer. *Am Feur-loch* or a *Loch an Fheòir* (genitive of grass) will be fertile, grow many water plants, which provide a safe habitat for trout and abound in food. Casting may well be a problem, as well as playing a hooked fish, which will instinctively head for cover in the vegetation and so entangle and even break the line. It is best to fish such lochs early in the season, before summer's growth chokes the open water. *Loch Gaineamhaich* or *na gaineimh* (genitive of sand) will be sandy and clear, but not necessarily fertile, unless it lies over limestone or calcareous shelly sand. In the latter instance it is sometimes known as a *machair* loch. Lochs of this nature can be found in the Uists and Assynt. As such waters are famously 'gin clear,' their residents are easily 'gliffed,' so stealth and a minimum of wading are required.

Loch Sgeireach (skerried) or *Garbh* (rough) may be difficult to wade and present hazards to those using a boat. *Loch Leacach* (slabby) or *na Lice* (genitive of *leac*) may have solid and flat wading inshore but could also have abrupt fall-off points into deeper water. Lochs which are qualified by *cam* or *crom* (crooked), *cròcach* (antlered or branched), *eileanach* (islanded) or *na h-Achlaise* (of the oxter or armpit) are likely to have a complex form and a greater length of shoreline than mere area would imply. This gives a diversity of nooks and crannies for trout to inhabit and a greater exposure of the water to windblown insects. Such waters may hold a great number of fish, but not necessarily of any great size. When fishing lochs that are *fraochach* or *an Fhraoich* (genitive of *fraoch*) or *sgitheach*, it may, depending on season, be worth putting on a heather or hawthorn fly. Sometimes lochs are fertilised by the droppings of geese or seagulls, so those which are *ealach* (abounding in swans), *nan eun* (of the birds), *nan gèadh* (of the geese), *a' Gheòidh* (genitive of goose), *nam faoileag / faoileann* (of the seagulls) may be more productive than their neighbours. Trees, supposing they still remain, are a good sign, as they provide shelter and invertebrate food. Peat, however, *mòine* or *mona* in genitive form, is what makes *Loch Dubh* acidic and infertile. *Lochan Tiormachd* (NC762648) in North Sutherland might dry out in summer. So too might *Lochan an Tairt* (NH446338) – The Loch of Thirst, in the same County. *Loch nam Breac-adhair* (sky), which is now mapped as *Loch nam Breac-odhar* near Port Henderson in Gairloch at NG767721, where trout once fell from the sky, must be an answer to the angler's prayer.

More directly, *Loch nam Breac Reamhar* (of the fat trout), *Loch nam Breac Mora* (of the big trout), *Loch nam Breac Ruadh* (of red trout) or *nam Breac Buidhe* (of the yellow trout), or *Loch a' Bhradain* (of the salmon), should be worthy of exploration, as should *Loch an Iasgair* (of the fisherman). But it should be noted that Osgood Mackenzie in Wester Ross translates a *Loch an Iasgair* (NG922845), near *Fionn Loch,* as the Osprey's Loch. In Gaelic the osprey is known as *Ailean Iasgair,* or Alan the Fisherman. On the other hand *Lochan nan Geadas* (NM601297), high in the hills to the East of Glen Ogle, may only contain a few specimens, large enough to escape the appetites of pike. Though in Staffin, North Skye *geadas* is also used for the Artic charr, which inhabit Loch Mealt.

6.5: Running Freshwater

In contrast to the near universal application of *loch* and *lochan* as naming elements, running water is identified in several different ways, which can be distinguished by scale, position and size. The geographical concept of stream order is helpful, to some extent, in their differentiation (Figure 6). *Abhainn* (river) is closest to the sea, has many tributaries and in Gaelic hydronymy can be ranked as 3rd order. *Allt* (burn or stream), which is often corrupted to alt or ault, tends to feed into *abhainn,* and is, therefore, usually 2nd order and has a few tributaries.

Dwelly in a poetic mood describes *caochan* as a streamlet or purling rill. Sometimes, particularly in Strathdearn, it seems to be of a lesser order than *allt.* Generally, it can be seen as primary when it flows into *allt* or secondary in the absence of, or in place of the latter. Interestingly, Dwelly also cites *caochan* as applying to the first distillation of whisky or the sound made by fermenting wort, which supports such a classification. Watson, citing the Old Irish word *caeich* meaning one eyed or blind, defines the morphology of *caochan* as *'a river so overgrown with herbage it cannot see out of its bed.'* To which Jake King adds 'that it is not blind in itself but rather people are blind to it.' The majority of these occur in the Spey catchment and the Central Highlands.

Stream order and the scale of a watercourse have to be seen in context. There is an *Abhainn Mhòr* on St Kilda, NF097994, which is barely one kilometre in length, has no tributaries, but does flow directly to the sea. In Highland Perthshire a watercourse of that size would be more likely to be called *Allt Mòr.* St Kilda's river might not even be perceived as big in the southern Highlands.

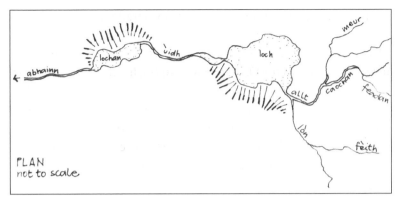

Figure 6: Gaelic Stream Order.
Caochan, feadan, fèith and meur are shown as primary order, allt as
secondary and ùidh and abhainn as third order.

Feadan, which variously means a chanter, spout or water-pipe, is commonly applied to small streams and seems to be equivalent or perhaps slightly diminutive, as its name would suggest, to *caochan.* Dwelly is expansive: the word can also apply to a crevice through which the wind whistles or an opening in the wall of a barn to admit the wind for winnowing grain. Both applications support the small-scale connotations of *feadan.*

Things are not always quite so simple. Non-aqeous terms can also apply to watercourses. Sometimes these are local variants. Lòn, which elsewhere means a meadow, is a small stream in Skye, particularly in Trotternish where there seems to be no other word in use. It appears to be of primary order (Plate 21).

In upper Strathavon, near Tomintoul, the word for a finger, *meur,* is used for a small stream. There is even a *Meur an Lòn.* Moreover, in upper Glen Lyon, we find *Allt Meurain,* a diminutive form. Presumably these examples were not tautologies for those who coined them. The word *meur* also means a branch of stream, and locations suggest it is primary in order. The great majority occur at a high altitude in the Spey catchment. *Ùidh* is another word, which is peculiar to a locality-in this case Assynt or *Asainte.* It applies to a stream with a slow, yet strong current running between two freshwater lochs. *Ùidh Fheàrna* (NC150158) below Suilven in Assynt, connecting Fionn-loch and Loch Veyatie, is an ample and powerfully flowing example (Plate 11).

More generally, *uisge,* simply meaning water, is the origin of many Scottish 'Waters of … ' which preserve Gaelic word order in translation and are found throughout the Highlands. It appears to be either primary or secondary in order and is often described as rough, *garbh.* Though *Garbh-uisge* (NN614080) on the River Teith, west of Callander, running as broken water across the Highland Fault, is more like *abhainn* in order.

What is surprising and lost to contemporary knowledge is that the commonplace *allt* applied originally, not to watercourses, but cliffs, which ran adjacent to the burn in question. Significantly, *Allt* is not used in Ireland for a watercourse. When early Irish colonists encountered the landscape of parallel rocks, glens and streams, which typifies much of mainland Argyll, particularly Knapdale, *allt* quickly became a dominant word linked to watercourses. Its original meaning and association were subsequently lost.

Fèith, vein or sinew, has also been applied to watercourses in a secondary sense. Here it applies to torn strips or rents in a moor or bog, which, at a distance, resemble their primary meaning. *Lùban Fèith a' Mhadaidh - Bends of the Dog's Bog Stream* (Plate 23), Rannoch (NN517532), is a good example, where the *'veins'* of the stream appear almost varicose in their contortions. *Lùb* is a common word attached to the meanders of streams.

One early Celtic word - *dobhar*, though it is no longer used in modern Gaelic, has nevertheless, been influential in naming in the distant past. This accounts for the absence of its original and correct Gaelic spelling from the mapped record. Dobhar gives, Edradour near Pitlochry (*Eadar Dà Dhobhar* - between two streams). *Inbhir Dhòbhran*, near Glen Orchy, shows the dimunitive form *dòbhran*, which elides with *inbhir* to lose the DH sound, and is thus mapped as *Òrain* in the burn of the same name. *Allt Òrain* flows from *Coir' Òrain* and joins Loch Tulla (*Toilbhe*) at NN278417. It would have been satisfying to find places named after the Gaelic word for song, *òran*, on the home turf of Duncan Ban MacIntyre, but the truth is more prosaic. *Dobhar* in the plural can also be confused with the word for otter, also *dòbhran*. So, and again on MacIntyre's home turf, *Beinn Dòbhrain*, which is mapped incorrectly as Beinn Dòrain (NN326377), is the mountain of streamlets instead of the more

Plate 23: Rannoch - Lùban Fèith a' Mhadaidh in the foreground

alluring mountain of otters. There are a great many streamlets grooving the western flanks of this mountain from which to choose. Several of them have their source in *Fuaran Mòr – Big Spring* (NN325371). Just to the south is *Feadan Mhart Donna – Streamlet of Brown Cows* (NN326366).

Allt Kinglas to the south of *Beinn Dòbhran* conceals another Old Celtic word for stream, *glais*. Conghlais, which is quoted in Duncan Ban's '*Òran do'n Inbhir - Song to the Inver*,' means dog stream, or rivulet. It is easy to be critical about how the anglicisation of the Gaelic spelling of place-names has obscured their meaning. The tautological examples of *Allt Dhòbhrain* and *Allt Conghlais* shows that Gaelic was also well capable of doing the same, once the meanings of root elements had been lost in earlier words and languages. The quality of *Allt Conghlais* was so highly prized that the burn was one of the three waters of Scotland in a Gaelic saying.

> '*Caor is Cadan is Conghlais,*
> *Trì uisgeachan na h-Alba.*'

> '*Caor and Cadan and Conghlais,*
> *Three waters of Scotland.*'

(in Watson 1926, 452)

Caor and Cadan are mapped as *Allt Chobhair* (NN626445) in Glen Lyon and Innerhaden (*Inbhir Chadain*) Burn in Rannoch (NN667554). They seem very small streams to have attracted such iconic status, but at one time this area formed the frontier between advancing Scotland and retreating Pictland. *Glais* is another older name for a watercourse no longer used in modern Gaelic. It gives Strath Glass, *Strath Ghlais* in Invernesshire and Glen Finglas, *Gleann Fionn-ghlais,* in the Trossachs. The district of Douglas in Lanarkshire is *Dubh Ghlais*, which is also the origin of *Inbhir Dhubhghlais* or Inveruglas, on the west bank of Loch Lomond.

Some mention must given to the Gaelic word for well - *tobar,* which has generated settlement names such as Tobermory on the Isle of Mull and Tibbermore in Lowland Perthshire. These should not be confused. The first is the well of Mary, *Tobar Mhoire*, and the second is merely a large well, *Tobar Mòr*. The old Scots version of Tibbermore retains the typical Gaelic softening of B to P in Tipper-muir. Several wells, *Tobar an Fhìon,* by Castle Lachlan, Loch Fyne-side (NS006948 as shown on the OS 6 inch to the mile map), and indeed streams, such as *Allt an Fhìon* (NN683260), near St Fillans are associated with the word for wine, *fìon* (feeuhn). This does not mean that wine actually flowed in them, but rather that their water was especially pure or perhaps holy. Knowing where clean water supplies were relative to an anchorage would be of service to MacLachlan's Galleys and other seafarers on Loch Fyne *(Loch Fìn)*. According to Watson, the very name of the Loch comes from the eponymous *Gleann Fìn,* where *Fìn* means vine, citing tradition and the songs of Duncan Bàn Macintyre, in whose 'Praise of Ben Dobhrain' deer slake their thirst.

> '*Cha Bhiodh ìot' air an teangaidh*
> *Taobh shìos a' Mhill Teanail*
> *Le fìon Uillt na h-Annaid,*
> *Blas meala r' a òl air.*'

> 'Down below Meall Teanail
> Their tongue would not be parched
> When there is wine of Annat Burn
> Honey-flavoured to drink:'

(in MacLeod 1978, 214 and 215)

He argues that such waters deserved their reputation through proximity to the holy places past which they flowed. *Allt na h-Annait* (NN34385) tumbles briskly past an ancient burial ground. *Beinn Mhana(i)ch – Mountain of Monks* lies 4 kilometres to the north-east in Glen Lyon.

Tobar Loch Shianta - The Well of the Holy Loch (Loch Sheanta NG472698), near Staffin in Skye, was one of the most renowned healing wells on the island. Martin Martin's account of his visit at the turn of the seventeenth and eighteenth centuries is in his *Description of the Western Islands of Scotland.*

> *... it is much frequented by strangers, as well as by the inhabitants of the Isle, who generally believe it to be a specifick for several diseases; such as stitches, head-aches, stone, consumption, megrim* [migraine]. *Several of the common people oblige themeselves by a vow to come to this well, and make the ordinary tour about it, called dessil* [deiseil in modern Gaelic] *which is performed thus: they move thrice round the well, proceeding sunwise from East to West ... This is done after drinking the water; and when one goes away from the well, it's a never failing custom, to leave some small offering on the stone which covers the well. There is a little fresh-water lake within ten yards of the said well; it abounds with trouts, but neither the natives not strangers will ever presume to destroy any of them, such is the esteem they have for the water.*
>
> (Martin 1716, 93)

A full description of this site and other places and names of great interest in Staffin can be found at http://www.skyecomuseum.co.uk.

Table 10: The Gaelic Water-scape (Hydronymy)

Name	Gender	Sound	Meaning	Example
Abhainn, aibhne, aibhnichean	f	*AHvin*	river	Abhainn Bà, Rannoch Moor, NN350513, River of Cattle
Acarsaid / acairseid, acairsaide, acarsaidean	f	*ACHkur-setch*	anchorage, harbour	Acairseid Mhòr, Eriskay, NF794097, Big Anchorage
Aiseag, aiseig, aiseagan	m/f	*ASHek*	ferry	Rubha na h-Aiseig, Trotternish, Skye, NG441768, Point of the Ferry
Allt, uillt, uillt	m	*owlt*	burn, stream	Allt Port an Eòrna, Morvern, NM586574, Stream of the Barley Port
Alltan, alltain,alltain	m	*OWLtan*	small burn, rivulet	Alltan nam Breac, Loch Venachar, NN534056, Rivulet of the Trout
Àth, àtha, àthan	m	*aah*	ford	Àth a' Choire, Strathyre, NN585105, Ford of the Corrie
Bàgh, bàigh, bàghan, bàghannan	m	*baagh*	bay	Bàgh Mòr, South Uist, NF793144, The Big Bay
Bàta, bàta, bàtaichean	m	*BAAtuh*	boat	Port Bàta na Luinge, Ulva, NM414414, Port of the Boat Ship
Beum, beuma, beu-man / beumannan	m	*baym*	stream, torrent, gap	Beum a' Chlaidheimh, Carrbridge, NH937304, Torrent of the Sword
Bodha / bogha, bodhachan	m	*BOWuh*	sunken rock in sea, rock over which waves break	Bogha Caol Àrd, Ardnamurchan, NM473627, Sunken Rock of the Narrow Point
Bota, botaichean	m	*BOHtuh*	river bank, mound	Botan Ruairidh, Barvas, Lewis, NB373455, Rory's Little Bank
Bùrn, bùirn	m	*boorn*	freshwater	Creag Àird a'Bhùirn, Loch Morie, Easter Ross NH528755, Rock of the Water Point

Cairidh, cairidhean	f	*KEHhree*	weir, fish-pound	Allt an (na) Cairidh, Kylesku, NC228328, Stream of the Fish Trap
Caise	f	*KESHuh*	stream of water, steepness	Coire na Caise, Loch Spelve, Isle of Mull NM702250, Corrie of the Steepness
Camas / camus, camais	m	*CAmus*	bay, creek harbour, crooked rivulet	Camas Beag, Uig, Skye, NG379615, The Small Bay
Caochan, caochain, caochanan	m	*COEHchan*	streamlet, purling rill (see description in main text)	Caochan a' Bhric, Abernethy Forest, NJ018116, Streamlet of the Trout
Caolas, caolais, caolais	m	*COEHlus*	narrow, strait, firth	Rubha Beul a' Chaolais, Ross of Mull, NM297209, Point of the Narrow's Mouth
Carraig, carraige, carraigean	f	*CAHRrick*	rock, fishing rock, rock jutting into the sea, promontory, cliff, headland	Carraig nan Liùthaichean, Islay, NR432668, possibly Fishing Rock of the Coalfish
Ceann, cinn, cinn	m	*cyown*	head, headland, point, top	Beinn Ceann a' Mhara, Tiree, NM936405, Mountain of the Sea Headland
Cladach, cladaich, cladaichean	m	*CLaduch*	shore, beach, coast, stony beach	Port a' Chladaich, Ross of Mull, NM375224, Port of the Rocky Shore
Cleiteadh, cleitidh, cleitidhean	m	*CLAYtchugh*	ridge of rocks in the sea	Cleiteadh nan Sgarbh, Arran NR884298, Rock Ridge of the Cormorants
Comar, comair, comaran	m	*COHmur*	meeting or confluence of streams	Abhainn a' Chomair, Achnasheen, NH159578, River of the Confluence
Corran, corrain, corrain	m	*COran*	point of land running far into sea, island which comes into sight at low tide at the mouth of a river (west coast), sickle	An Corran, Staffin, Trotternish, NG490687, The Sickle-shaped Point, (Plate 21)

Table 10 (cont.)

Name	Gender	Sound	Meaning	Example
Crannag, crannaig, crannagan	m	CRAnak	fortified island in a loch, part artificial / part natural	Lochan na Crannaig, Ardnamurchan, NM464657, Loch of the Crannog
Cuan, cuain, cuantan / cuanta	m	COOHun	sea, ocean, large loch, the deep	Sgeir Lèith a' Chuain, Garvellachs, NM648108, Grey Skerry of the Ocean
Cuing, cuinge, cuingean	f	COOink	narrow strait or channel	Creag na Cuinge, Ord of Caithness, ND082194, Rock of the Channel
Dòirlinn, dòirlinne, dòirlinnean	f	DAH-WRleen	isthmus, peninsula, stream, islet to which one can wade at low tide (mainland), pebbly or stony part of shore (isles), narrow sound separating an islet from the mainland and liable to ebb dry	An Dòirlinn, Lismore, NM802397, The Isthmus
Eas, easa, easan	m	ess	waterfall, cataract, cascade	Eas Urchaidh, Glen Orchy, NN243322, Orchy Waterfall
Eilean, eilein, eileanan	m	EHlan	island	Eilean na Comhairle, Islay, NR387680, Council Island
Fadhail, fadhail / fadhlach, fadhlaichean	f	FOEUHuhl	extensive beach, tidal ford	See next entry in table.
Faodhal, faodhalach, faodhalaichean	f	FOEUHuhl	alternative form of fadhail	Faodhal Dhubh, Loch Moidart, NM645715, Black Tidal Ford

94

Word	Gender	Pronunciation	Meaning	Example
Feadan, feadain, feadanan	m	FEHtan	pipe, canal opening, streamlet (see description in main text)	Bràigh an Fheadain, Jura, NR548754, Brae of the Little Stream
Fèith, fèithe, fèithean / fèithichean	f	fay	bog, underground stream, bog channel (see description in main text)	Lùban Fèith a' Mhadaidh, Rannoch, NN517532, Bends of the Dog's Bog Stream (Plate 23)
Fuaran, fuarain, fuarain / fuaranan	m	FOOerahn	well, spring	Meall nam Fuaran, Glen Quaich NN827362, Rounded Hill of the Springs (Plate 12)
Gaineamh / gainmheach, gaineimh, gainmhich	f	GANyuv	sand, gravel, sea-shore	Rubha na Gainmhich, Loch Shiel, NM699684, Point of the Sand
Geodha, geodhachan, geodhaichean	m	GYAWuh	chasm, ravine, creek or cove formed by surrounding rocks	Geodha nam Faochag, Skye, NG293358, Chasm of the Buckies
Gil, gile, gilean	f	geel	ravine, water course	Allt na Gile, Jura, NR484777, Stream of the Ravine
Glumag, glumaig, glumagan	f	GLOOmak	puddle, deep hole or pool, deep pit full of water, usually applied to a pool in running water	Cairidh Ghlumaig, Trotternish, NG409740, Fish Trap of the Pool
Inbhir, inbhirean	m	EEnvur	place of meeting of rivers, confluence, cove or creek at the mouth of a river, angular piece of ground at the mouth of two rivers.	Eilean an Inbhire, Raasay, NG548242, Island of the River Mouth

Table 10 (cont.)

Name	Gender	Sound	Meaning	Example
Iola, iolaich, iolachan	f	*EEyula*	fishing rock, fishing bank, fishing station	Bàgh an Iolaich, Mull, NM433354, Bay of the Fishing Rock
Laimrig / làimhrig, laimhrige, laimrige, laimreagan	f	*LEHmrrick / LYVrick*	natural landing place, quay, harbour	Rubha Laimhrige, Jura, NR532667, Harbour Point
Linn / linne, linne, linneachan, linntean	f	*leenyuh*	pool, pond, lake, mill dam, channel	Loch Linne, Knapdale, NR798910, Pool Loch
Loch, locha, lochan	m	*lawch*	lake, arm of sea	Loch na h-Innis Fraoich, Assynt, NC163263 Loch of the Heather Meadow (Plate 26)
Lochan, lochain, lochain	m	*LAWchan*	small loch or lake,	Lochan Coire na Poite, Kishorn NG817453, Little Loch of the Corrie of the Pot
Lùb / lùib, lùib / lùibe, lùban / lùibean	f	*loob*	meander, bend, bending of the shore	Lùb an Fhigheadair, Rannoch, NN437582, Bend of the Weaver
Mol, moil / mola, molan	m	*mol*	shingly beach	Mol nan Eun, Torridon, NG894554, Shingle Beach of the Birds
Morbhach, morbhaich	f	*MORuvuch*	grassy plain so near the sea that it is often flooded by the tide	Morbhach a' Choire, Torridon, NG868568, Grassy Plain of the Corrie
Morghan, morghain	m	*MAWRuhghan*	gravel, shingle, pebbly beach	Loch a' Mhorghain, North Harris, NB153049, Loch of the Gravel

Word	m/f	Pronunciation	Meaning	Example
Muir, mara, maran-nan	m/f	*MOOeer*	sea, ocean, large loch, the deep	Sloc a' Mhuilinn, Lismore, NM849432, Pit of the Mill
Òb, òib, òbain	m	*awp*	small bay, creek, harbour	Òb Gorm Beag, Torridon, NG859548, Small Blue Bay
Oitir, oitire oitirean	f	*AWtcheer*	sandbank or ridge in the sea, shoal, shallow, low promontory jutting into the sea, rock projecting into the sea	Oitir Mhòr, Kerrera, NM824300, Big Sandbank
Òs, òsa, òsan	m	*aws*	mouth or outlet of a river, bar or sandbank in a harbour	Òs A-muigh, Uig, Isle of Lewis, NB039333, Outer Outlet
Poll, pull, pull	m	*powl*	pool, pit, deep stagnant water, dark and deep part of any stream	Poll na h-Ealaidh, Uig, Skye, NG375593, Pool of the Swan Place
Port, puirt, puirt	m	*pawrsht*	port, harbour, ferry (from Latin *portum*)	Port nam Marbh, Ardnamurchan, NM496629, Port of the Dead
Rinn, rinne, rinnean	m	*ryne*	point, promontory	Rinn nan Gruban (possibly Crùban?), Bragar, Lewis, NB307498, Point of the Crabs?
Rodh, rodha	m	*roe*	water edge, water mark	Rubha Rodha, Lochinver, Assynt NC054233, Water Edge Point
Ros, rois, rosan	m	*ross*	promontory, isthmus, peninsula	Ros a' Mheallain, Bracadale, Isle of Skye, NG375404, Peninsula of the Little Rounded Hill
Rubha / rudha, rubhaichean / rudhaichean	m	*ROOuh*	promontory, headland, point of land	Rubha nam Brà(i)th(ai)rean, Trotternish, Skye NG528629, Point of the Brothers

Table 10 (cont.)

Name	Gender	Sound	Meaning	Example
Sàilean, sàilein, sàileanan	m	*SAHlen*	little inlet, arm of the sea, deep bay	Bàgh an t-Sàilein, Loch Sunart, NM690640, Bay of the Little Inlet
Sgeir, sgeire, sgeirean	f	*skerr*	skerry, rock in the sea nearly covered by neap tides and covered by Spring tides	Sgeir an Duilisg, Islay, NR432673, Dulse Skerry
Sruth, srutha / sruith, sruthan	m	*stroo*	stream, current, tide	Creag an t-Sruith, Strathyre, NN578139, Rock of the Current
Stalla, stallachan	m	*STAluh*	sea rock, overhanging rock, lofty precipice, ledge on the face of a rock	Stallachan Dubha, Ardnamurchan, NC537622, Black Ledges
Steall, stèill / still, steallan	f	*shtchowl*	torrent, cataract	Lòn na Steill, Skye, NG444397, Marshy Stream of the Torrent
Tairbeart, tairbeirt, tarbeartan	f	*TEHrupersht*	isthmus, peninsula, crossing, portage	Ceann an Tairbeirt, South Uist, NF814403, Head of the Isthmus
Tobar, tobair / tobrach, tobraichean	m/f	*TOHpurr*	well, fountain, spring	Tobar na Slàinte, Trotternish, Skye NG455689, Well of Healing
Tolm, tuilm, tolman	m	*TOHlum*	island in a river or near shore	Eilean Thuilm, Stornoway, Lewis, NB449304, Holm Island

Gaelic	Gender	Pronunciation	Meaning	Example
Tràigh, tràighe / tràghad, tràighean / tràghannan	f	*try*	seashore, beach exposed at low water, shore of lake or river	Tràigh Bad a' Bhàigh, Scourie, NC223469, Beach of the Bay Place
Ùidh, ùidhe, ùidhean	f	*OOee*	isthmus, ford, part of a stream which leaves a lake before breaking onto a current, slow running water between two lochs	Loch na Garbh-Ùidhe, Assynt, NC161248, Loch of the Rough Stream running between two Lochs (Plate 11)
Ùig, ùige, ùigean	f	*OOik*	bay, nook, hollow, cave, den	Bealach Ùige, Trotternish, NG443643, Pass of Uig (Front cover)
Uisge, uisgean, uis-geachan	m	*OOSHkuh*	water, rain, river	Garbh-Uisge, Callander, NN614080, Rough Water

7: LANDCOVER AND ECOLOGY

7.1: Habitats, Woods and Forests

At the time of the first Ordnance Survey mapping, what kind of woodland cover had been recognised and described by Gaelic place-naming? After the Second World War, Fraser Darling applied the phrase 'wet desert' – and not in any charitable sense - to much of the Highlands. Today though we value some wet deserts like the Flow Country in Caithness, his opinion has lent contemporary credence to the well-established myth of the Great Wood of Caledon, which had circulated since Roman times and which preceded modern 'desertification.' According to Fraser Darling, some woodland had been destroyed by invading Romans and Vikings and more was cleared in the aftermath of medieval conflicts. He maintains that the great bulk of the trees were cleared by the iron smelting industry in the late eighteenth century and the widespread establishment of large scale sheep farming in the nineteenth century. Before that, it was, according to Fraser Darling, his idea of heaven. This idea of a paradise lost has been perpetuated by the Scottish Green Party and contemporary conservation bodies such as Re-afforesting Scotland.

It is impossible to be certain about the position and extent of the great wood. The Roman writers Pliny and Tacitus do not give any reason to believe that woodland covered Scotland from coast to coast. Ptolemy's map, which showed a *'Caledonia Silva'* in various locations, was reprinted up until the early eighteenth century, when the wood was centred approximately around Glen Orchy. From the early sixteenth century to Blaeu's Atlas of 1654 the mapped area of the wood seems actually to have increased, which is unlikely. Even at its greatest extent in 3000 BC and before the arrival of significant numbers of humans, the wood would have been a mosaic reflecting stages of primary and secondary succession and responses of the treeline to long-term climate change and short-term weather phenomena. After humans began to modify treecover, this patchwork developed a looser structure in response to burning and the grazing of domestic animals. It is perhaps significant that the Romans built the Antonine Wall from turf, which must have been plentiful and would have been difficult to cut in thickly wooded country.

Humans first started to alter Scotland's landscape in Mesolithic times, from about 10,000 BC. This became significant in its effects during the Neolithic period, from about 3500 BC, and accelerated with the development of metal tools. As the climate became increasingly wet and windy up to the Roman period, blanket bog began to replace woodland cover. Carbon dating of bog pine shows that very few individuals are younger than 4000 years old, which indicates a much earlier retreat of 'Caledonia Silva' than suggested by Fraser Darling. Perhaps as much as half of the forest had gone by the time of the birth of Christ. At the end of the medieval period, as little as 4% of the original area may have remained, well before the influences of wider economic and industrial forces. Modern claims by conservationists that the extent of native pine forest is only 1% of its original area relate to its coverage at its maximum around 3000 BC, well before the mass arrival of humans.

There are several sorts of evidence which support this assessment. Comparisons can be made between maps drafted at different periods. Secondly, Government documents commented quite frequently on the state of the nation's woods. Finally, accounts of travellers in the Highlands can be examined.

Shortage of timber is mentioned in several Acts of the Scottish Parliament throughout the sixteenth century. As early as 1503, the Nation's woods are referred to as being utterly destroyed. In the late sixteenth and early seventeenth century, legislation attempted to limit damage caused, perhaps by, amongst other activities the practice of transhumance. Specific reference to the use of shielings suggests that the Highlands were included in this destruction. In 1564, the Privy

Council deplored the mismanagement of woodland in the North. As a result, imports of Scandinavian timber increased dramatically between 1580 and 1640.

The earliest maps drafted from a Scottish viewpoint were those made by Timothy Pont at the end of the sixteenth century. Woodland coverage can be compared with later maps by Blaeu, which were based on Pont's work, with additional material supplied by Robert Gordon of Straloch, and those made over 100 years later by William Roy in the mid-eighteenth century. But the maps of these pioneering cartographers are hard to interpret where trees and woods are concerned. Often their first priority was to record built form and watercourses, or, in the case of Roy, elements of strategic military importance. They also had difficulty in deciding how to represent woods, especially if they were unenclosed - that is, if they had no defined boundary - which would have been the case in the Highlands of that time, and how to distinguish between trees in open country and continuous canopy. Cartographic symbols for woodland were also unrefined and often inconsistent. Sometimes mapmakers such as Blaeu, when copying Pont's work, favoured appealing graphic symbolism in their reworking, over evidence derived from primary sources. Sometimes woods were omitted because they were irrelevant to the map's purpose. Roy left out half of today's ancient woodlands, because they would have been of little use to troops on the march.

Despite these difficulties of interpretation, none of these maps suggests continuous woodland cover. Instead, they represent surviving and disconnected patches, which map reasonably well onto today's pattern of ancient and semi-natural woods. In a comment on his sketch map of the Gruinard district in Wester Ross, Pont observes: 'excellent hunting place wher are deir to be found all year long as in a mechtie parck of nature' (in Smout 2006, 87). What he describes is an open landscape with clumps of trees. These maps suggest that woodland represented about 4% of the landcover, though this figure could have been 7% in parts of the Highlands. There are exceptions. The pine woods that Pont maps at the head of Glen Coe and the ancient woodland in Glen Esk had disappeared by the time of the first Ordnance Survey mapping in the late nineteenth century.

Between 1767 and 1771, prior to the establishment of shooting estates and the rapid growth of large scale sheep farming, Professor John Hope of the University of Edinburgh commissioned James Robertson to carry out a botanical survey of the Highlands. Between Braemar and Ben Avon in the Cairngorms he found copses of birch and scrub species on the hillsides. On the steep slopes above Loch Ness, he described more continuous cover which included woodland trees. Matters were more variable between Tyndrum and Kinlochleven, where there was either forsaken waste, bare mountains or woods of birch, pine, hazel and ash. Similarly in Glen Dochart, hills were either covered in good grass or woodland. In the eastern Highlands, between Deeside and the Spittal of Glenshee, between Inverness and Carrbridge and amongst the hills above Blairgowrie, the terrain was barren and produced only heather and bearberry. Robertson's reports do not suggest continuous woodland cover spread all over the Highlands.

It would be interesting to record the distribution of Gaelic tree and wood names in comparison to what we know to be the potential extent of different species. Without such a comprehensive document, how do place-names support the mapped evidence? In general, those referring to trees and woods, just like what they describe, seem to have a fragmented distribution. The extensive vocabulary for open moors, marshes, plains and wet meadows, as well as the frequency of these words, seems much more prolific than words for specific woodland types or specifically named woods. Individual tree types are more usually associated with features like rocks, cliffs and islands - in another words, places which are less accessible to grazing animals - rather than attached to Gaelic words for woods, such as *bad, coille* and *doire* (thicket, wood and grove). *Bad* and *doire* have acquired secondary meanings of spot or place and hollow, perhaps in the absence or the erosion of their primary association with trees. Place-name evidence does not support the case for continuous woodland cover at the time of progressive Gaelic colonisation and settlement.

In a specific area like Trotternish in Skye, where tree cover seems to have been reduced to nothing between 2200 and 600BC, there are only two place-names mapped on the OS Explorer sheet which refer to woodland. One is *Loch Droighinn* - Blackthorn Loch (NG456713). The dense and suckering habit of this thorny bush means that it would not be favoured by grazing animals. The other is *Druim na Coille - Ridge of the Wood* (NG435643), which is seven kilometres to the south and lies upon high stony ground which would provide little forage. More widely, the frequency of words for view, *sealladh*, and *faire* and *freiceadan,* meaning watching and watch, even at the low elevations of *tom* and *cnoc,* suggests the existence of wide-ranging visual interconnections. Similarly, the way that the colour, texture, pattern and form of the landscape have been a constant preoccupation of Gaelic toponymy suggests a landscape whose flesh and bones were not concealed, at the time of naming, beneath an obscuring mantle of trees.

Table 12 shows many words for wet, marshy and boggy habitats, plains and meadows. Michelle Cotter and Jake King collected an un-mapped name on Islay which describes uncertain ground underfoot in a graphic manner. It is *Sùil-Chrith - The Trembling Eye,* NR392746, to the north-west of Bunnabhainn. On the OS Explorer sheet, the place has a note saying 'shake holes.' *Crith* also gives us *critheann,* the aspen, which also shows its nerves in its Latin name of *Populus tremula,* the unworthy tree, so called because it is said to have provided the wood, which was used to make the cross of Christ. In Gairloch the term is *sùil-chruthaich.*

Plate 1: 'A Little Place' - Creagan nam Plaoisg –
Little Rock of the Husks, Brig o' Turk, Trossachs

Plate 5: Loch Katrine: Bealach nam Bò, Coire na(n) Ùruisgean and Eilean Molach.
(Bealach nam Bò is the break of slope in the left background below the rock face, Coire
na(n) Ùruisgean is above the steamboat and Eilean Molach is at the bottom right).

Plate 7: St Fillans - Dùn Dùirn (in the foreground) and
Am Bioran (in the background)

Plate 14: Trotternish, Skye - Baca Ruadh, Coire an t-Seasgaich and
Sgùrr a' Mhadaidh Ruaidh to the right of the picture

*Plate 11: Suilven - Ùidh Fheàrna, Caisteal Liath, Meall
Meadhonach and Meall Beag (Ùidh Fheàrna is to the
left of centre below the dome of Suilven)*

Plate 15: Glen Conghlas - Ais an t-Sìdhein. (Sìthean Mòr is to the left Sìthean Beag to the right, below Beinn a' Chùirn and Beinn Mhanach to the right)

Plate 21: Trotternish - Dùn Mòr and Dùn Beag; Lòn Garbh is at the foot of the hill and An Corran in the background to the right of Staffin Island

Plate 26: Assynt - Loch na h-Innse Fraoich and A' Chuinneag

Plate 27: Loch Tay - Ruined Shieling Huts in Ardeonaig Glen. Meall Greigh, Rounded Hill of the Stud, is the highest peak to the left of the Loch

Plate 28: Balquidder - Meall an Fhiodhain to the right of the picture

*Plate 30: Balquidder - Leum an Èirionna(i)ch
is on the right of the picture*

Plate 33: Trotternish, Skye - Leac na(n) Fionn, just to the right of centre

Plate 36: A Gaelic colour chart

Table 12: Landcover and Ecology - Habitats, Woods and Forests

Name	Gender	Sound	Meaning	Example
Bogach, bogaich, bogaichean	m/f	*BOKEuch*	marsh, bog	Bogach nan Sgadan, North Uist, NF810687, Marsh of the Herring
Boglach, boglaich, boglaichean	f	*BAWkluch*	marsh, bog	Boglach nan Tarbh, Islay, NR410735, Marsh of the Bulls
Borrach, borraich	m	*BAWruch*	mountain grass	Meall Ùr a' Bhorraich, Applecross, NG720377, Fresh Rounded Hill of the Mountain Grass
Càrnach, càrnaich	m/f	*CAARnuch*	stony place, rocky ground	Cadha Càrnach, Raasay, NG583394, Stony Defile
Càthar, càthair	m	*CAAhur*	mossy ground	Càthar nan Tarbh, Jura, NR548743, Moss of the Bulls
Coille, coilltean	f	*CAWLyuh*	wood, forest, grove	Druim na Coille, Trotternish, Skye, NG437644, Ridge of the Wood
Dithreabh, dithreibh, dithreabhan	f	*JEEruv*	waste, wilderness, higher ground	Loch Dithreabh na Cuileige, Applecross, NG773415, Wilderness Loch of the Fly
Doire, doirean, doireachan	m/f	*DAWryuh*	grove, thicket, clump of oak trees	Doire Domhain(n), Raasay, NG555438, Deep Wood
Easg, easga, easgan	m/f	*esk*	marsh, swamp, ditch formed by nature	An t-Easg Leathain(n), Atholl, NN805697, The Broad Marsh.
Fàsach, fàsaich, fàsaichean	m/f	*FAAHsuch*	wilderness, desert, stubble, grassy headland of a ploughed field	Fàsach, Glendale, Isle of Skye NG190492, (The latter two meanings are more likely given the fertile location of Glendale).
Frith, frithe, frithean	f	*free*	deer forest, heath, moor	Bealach na Frithe, Balquidder, NN455230, Pass of the Deer Forest

Table 12 (cont.)

Name	Gender	Sound	Meaning	Example
Lèana, lèana, lèanachan	f	*LEEuhnuh*	swampy plain	Lèana Mhòr, Barra, NF664006, Big Swamp
Lèanag, lianag, lèan-aig, lèanagan	f	*LEEuhnuk*	wet plain or lea	Lianag Mhòr, Assynt, NC220064, Big Wet Plain
Lèig, lèige, lèigean	f	*layk*	marshy or miry pool	Druim na Lèige, Isle of Lewis, NB215266, Ridge of the Marshy Pool
Lòn, lòin, lòintean	m	*lawn*	marsh, morass, pool, small stream with marshy banks (Skye)	Lòn Garbh, Staffin, Syke, NG490687, Rough Marshy Stream, (**Plate 21**)
Luachair, luachair, luachrach	f	*LOOuchihr*	place where rushes grow	Lochan na Claise Luachrach, Loch Laxford, NC223498, Small Loch of the Rushy Ditch
Machair, machrach, machraichean	m/f	*MACHehr*	large, low-lying fertile plain, often on the coast e.g. long ranges of sandy plains fringing the Atlantic coast of the Outer Hebrides	A' Mhachair, Iona, NM267237, The Machair
mòinteach, mòintich, mòintichean	f	*MAWN-tyuch*	mossy, moor ground, peat moss	Creagan na Mòint(e)ich, St Fillans, Loch Earn, NN677229, Rocks of the Peat Moss (**Plate 10**)
Riasg, rèisg	m	*REEusk*	moor, fen, marsh, place where sedge grows, land that cannot be ploughed owing to the amount of dirk-grass it grows	Tom an Rèisg, Strath Avon, NJ156154, Hillock of the Fen

7.2: Flora

Letters in the Gaelic or Old Irish alphabet used to be symbolised by types of tree, and some other species of shrubs, as listed below. Only birch, alder and elder share the same ancient and modern forms, whilst old and new versions of oak, yew, willow and, at a stretch, ash bear some resemblance to each other. Only birch and willow show any similarity with their Latin species name. The Irish origins of the alphabet perhaps account for the omission of pine as a letter representative, since that species is infrequent there, in comparison to the Scottish Highlands.

Table 13: the Gaelic Alphabet in Tree names

Letter	Old Gaelic	Modern Gaelic	Latin Name	English Name
a	ailm	leamhan	*Ulmus spp.*	elm
b	beithe	beithe	*Betula pendula*	silver birch
c	coll	calltainn	*Corylus avellana*	hazel
d	dair	darach	*Quercus petraea*	oak
e	eadha	critheann	*Populus tremula*	aspen
f	fearn	feàrn	*Alnus glutinosa*	alder
g	gort	eidheann	*Hedera helix*	ivy
h	uath	sgitheach	*Crataegus monogyna*	hawthorn
i	iogh	iubhar	*Taxus baccata*	yew
l	luis	caorann	*Sorbus aucuparia*	rowan
m	muin	fionan	*Vitis vinifera*	vine
n	nuis	uinnseann	*Fraxinus excelsior*	ash
o	onn	conasg	*Ulex europaeus*	gorse or whin
p	peith bhog	beithe bhog	*Betula pubescens*	downy birch
r	ruis	ruis	*Sambucus nigra*	elder
s	suil	seileach	*Salix spp.*	willow
t	teine	cuileann	*Ilex aquifolium*	holly
u	ur	fraoch	*Calluna vulgaris*	heather

Tree species which appear most often in place names are birch, rowan, oak and pine. Ash is less frequent, perhaps because its name has been retained in its Old Norse form of *askr* in place-names like

Ascog and *Askaig*, both meaning Ash Bay. Certainly its hard timber would have been very useful to Vikings in boatbuilding. Alexander Carmichael in his collection of Gaelic traditions and folklore, *Carmina Gadelica*, quotes an anonymous mnemonic for some tree qualities and habitats (and incidentally for the genitive singular of feminine nouns and the genitive plural).

Tagh seileach nan allt.
Choose willow of the streams.

Tagh calltainn nan creag.
Choose hazel of the rocks.

Tagh feàrna nan lón,
Choose alder of the marshes,

Tagh beithe nan eas.
Choose birch of the waterfalls.

Tagh uinnseann na dubhair.
Choose ash of the shade.

Tagh iubhar na leuma,
Choose yew of resilence,

Tagh leamhan na bruthaich,.
Choose elm of the brae,

Tagh duire na gréine.
Choose oak of the sun.

(adapted from Milliken 2007, 135)

Note here how oak is synonymous with the old sacred word for grove, *doire*, in the last line. The association of this species with the sun may reflect its preference for south facing slopes, where it meets Scots pine at the northern limit of its range in the Highlands.

The great twentieth century Gaelic poet Sorley MacLean also uses trees in a spiritual manner. In his poem 'Hallaig', he imagines a lover and people who had been cleared from the Island of Raasay, moving through the landscape embodied as trees - not as the sacred oaks but as birch, hazel and rowan.

...'s tha mo ghaol aig Allt Hallaig,
and my love is at the Burn of Hallaig,

'na croaibh bheithe, 's bha i riamh
a birch tree, and she has always been

eadar an t-inbhir 's Poll a' Bhainne,
between Inver and Milk Hollow

thall's a bhos mu Bhaile-Chùirn:
here and there about Baile-chuirn:

tha i 'na beithe, 'na calltuinn,
she is a birch, a hazel,

'na caorunn dhìreach sheang ùir
a straight, slender young rowan.

Ann an Screapadal mo chinnidh
In Screapadal of my people

far robh Tarmad 's Eachunn Mór,
where Norman and Big Hector were,

tha 'n nigheanan 's am mic nan coille
their daughters and sons are a wood

ag gabhail suas ri taobh an lòin
going up beside the stream.

Uaibhreach a nochd na coilich ghiuthais
Proud tonight the pine cocks

ag gairm air mullach Cnoc an Rà
crowing on top of Cnoc an Ra,

dìreach an druim ris a' gheallaich
straight their backs in the moonlight

chan iadsan coille mo ghràidh
- they are not the wood I love.

Fuirichidh mi ris a bheithe
I will wait for the birch wood

gus an tig i mach an Càrn,
until it comes up by the cairn,

gus am bi am bearradh uile
until the whole ridge from Beinn na Lice

o Bheinn na Lice f' a sgàil.
will be under its shade.

(Maclean 1989, 227)

Several points are worthy of comment. In Gaelic grammar, people are literally in their birchness, hazelness, rowanness or wood-
ness. So the idea of transubstantiation is embedded in grammatical
construction. The poet echoes this idea by referring to a bird whose
name associates it with a tree - the pine cock though what species *coileach giuthais* denotes is unclear. In the poem Maclean also
employs the Skye usage of *lòn* (*lòin* is the genitive) for a stream,
which elsewhere means a meadow. We can also see the genitive
of *càrn* in *Bhaile Chùirn*, Township of a Cairn. Although the poet
portrays surreal happenings, these occur in a real landscape. *Baile
Chùirn* (NG554406) is on the west coast of Raasay (*Ratharsair*).
Poll a' Bhainne is not mapped but lies to the north of *Baile Chùirn*.
An t-Inbhir is also on the west at NG553422. The sonorous *Cnoc
an Rà - Hillock of the Fort* (NG549372) is three miles to the south,
whilst *Beinn na Lice - Mountain of the Slab*, rises on the south-east
coast of the island just to the south of Hallaig itself. It is wrongly
shown with its adjective in the nominative case, *leac,* at NG593370.
It is almost as if MacLean is swooping and soaring in his imagina-
tion like a bird, as he flies repeatedly across a collaged landscape of
Ratharsair.

In his visionary dreamscape, the poet sees his love as a birch.
First at *Allt Hallaig,* NG593380, then as a hazel and after that as a
rowan on the other side of the island, at the mouth of a burn, in
the fertile milk hollow of *Poll a' Bhainne* and near the township of
Baile Chùirn. From there he moves three miles to the north-east and
sees his ancestors as a wood regenerating in the short, steep bowl of
Screapadal. At night he hears birds crying in the trees on *Cnoc an Rà,*
and there decides to wait until all of the mountain of *Beinn na Lice*
to the south of Hallaig, is covered in birch trees, as if his people have
returned from the dead to repossess their landscape.

It is worth reading the entire work to understand MacLean's
psychogeographic itinerary. The sequence of his dream journey
suggests a reweaving of the past with the present. The cleared
townships of Screapadal and Hallaig in the east are reconnected with
later habitations in the south and west. *Ratharsair* is made whole
again, as she once was, and is finally surveyed in her entirety from
the height of *Dùn Cana.*

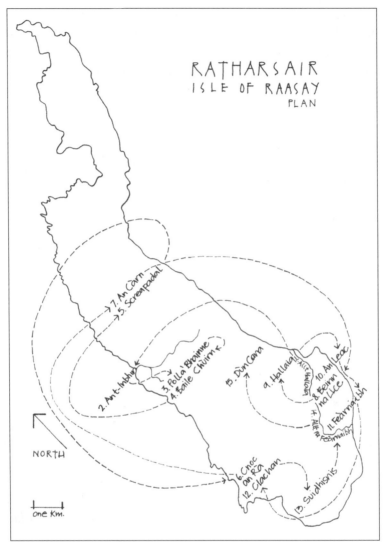

Figure 7: Place-names in Sorley MacLean's 'Hallaig' – the broken line shows the sequence of the poet's psychogeographic journey through the landscape.

In contrast to most other tree species, blackthorn, elm and aspen are very localised in their distribution, perhaps because these species tend to reproduce vegetatively through suckering, and so form dense isolated thickets. Holly is more common in place-names than one might expect, perhaps because its berries are spread far and wide by birds. Whatever the species, woods or other places associated with trees are more likely to be named after a dominant constituent than any other attribute. This suggests that woodland ecosystems were not highly structured or floristically diverse during the period when names were coined. The predominance of birch, a pioneer species, suggests a history of partial woodland clearance and recolonisation by this fast-growing species in a cyclically disturbed habitat. Many references to the bramble also indicate a scrubby, secondary succession of vegetation. There is a curious mention of apples at *Creag nan Ubhal*, Drumochter, NN637753, Rock of the Apples. To quote the band Runrig, the tree must be *An Ubhal as Àirde - the Highest Apple* growing at over 1500 feet, if, indeed, it still lives. Perhaps the specimen is, or was, a crab apple, *Malus sylvestris;* or the name may be fanciful or even false.

Dry, open country is frequently covered by heather (*Calluna vulgaris* or *fraoch)*, blaeberry (*Vaccinium myrtillus* or *broighleag*) and cloudberry (*Rubus chaemorus* or *oighreag).* The first two often occur below the tree line. Heath (*Calluna vulgaris*) is not distinguished from ling (*Erica cinerea*) and there is also little mention of bearberry (*Arctostaphylos uva-ursi* or *cnaimhseag*), which is now quite common on the hilltops. Wetter areas commonly support moss, rushes and reeds. Bog myrtle (*Myrica gale* or *roid*), which is common on the ground in these areas, is rare in place-names, as is bog cotton (*Eriophorum angustifolium* or *canach*). Perhaps the land was better drained in the past. Similarly, bracken (*raineach*) seems more widespread today, than it was when names were recorded. The cresses, herbs and flowers so beloved by eighteenth century Gaelic poets are very infrequently remembered in names.

All this evidence supports the existence of an open landscape, which has been shaped by long term grazing, rather than woodland clearance, at the time names were coined. The likely consequence of nineteenth century sheep farming was an impoverishment in the diversity of the herb layer by selective grazing rather than the destruction of primary woodland. Rare references in place-names to the primrose are interesting. This plant favours the woodland floor, but can also survive in the open. Its presence in the latter situation can indicate the former existence of woodland. It seems that trees clung on, growing on cliffs, rocks and islands, in gullies and along stream courses, which are harder for grazing animals to reach. Only in the Cairngorms and parts of the North can be found large and extensive tracts of woodland growing on relatively flat land. These are typified by Scots pine (*Pinus sylvestris* or *giuthas*). The broad, rounded canopies of 200 - 300 year old individuals can only have developed in open situations. Such specimens are now popularly known as 'Granny Pines.'

Without deliberate and intensive grazing, the pine woodland of the Cairngorms would have been a mix of tree generations all competing for light. Mature trees would not have had the opportunity to develop the wide and beautiful crowns seen today. The rapid increase in sheep grazing in the surviving pine forests after the Highland Clearances put an end to woodland succession. Individual trees, large enough to be immune to grazing, would no longer have had the competition growing up from below to restrict their crowns. Without the intensive grazing, after the Clearances, there would have been lower numbers of the large pines we see today. So the 'Granny' pine is really a rather unnatural and relatively modern phenomenon. Whilst considered to be an icon of our enduring Highland landscape, the much-loved Granny should really be considered as our only living link with, and memorial to, the Clearances.

Flag Iris (*Iris pseudoacorus* or *seileastair*) is mentioned surprisingly often in place-names throughout the Highlands. This may be because it is a plant whose various parts, when treated with different mordants, can yield several dye colours. These include blue-grey when treated with copperas mordant, dark green when treated with alum and black if iron sulphate is used. When thatching, iris leaves provide an initial flat bed for the second layer of marram grass. Conveniently for this purpose, iris in the Western Isles grows along burns which thread their way through dunes, bound together with marram. Calum MacDonald, the writer of Runrig's lyrics celebrates his native North Uist in the song 'Tìr a' Mhurain.'

Trobhad is coisich rium
Come and walk with me

Ri taobh a' chuain
By the side of the ocean
Is seallaidh mi dhuit
Let me show you
Tìr a' Mhurain
The land of the marram grass.
(http://www.jimwillsher.co.uk/Site/Runrig/Lyrics/)

Marram is also celebrated in another song from the island, *O Mo Dhuthaich - O My Land* which is a song of longing, composed either by Allan MacPhee or Alan MacInnes of South Uist who were both exiled to Manitoba.

O mo dhùthaich 's tu th' air m' aire
Uibhist chùbhraidh ùr nan gallan,
Far am faighte na daoin' uaisle,
Far am bu daoin' uaisle Mhac ic Ailein.

Tìr a› mhurain, tìr an eòrna
Tìr sam pailt' a h-uile seòrsa
Far am bi na gillean òga
Gabhail òran 's 'g òl an leanna.

Oh, my land, you're always in my thoughts
Fresh, fragrant Uist , home of heroes,
Where the noble people live,
Hereditary territory of Clan Ranald.

Land of bent-grass, land of barley,
Land fertile in every way,
Where the young lads
Sing songs and drink ale.

(extract from Lorne Gillies 2005, 284)

Here marram is translated as 'bent-grass.' The species is vital in binding the sand of the dunes of the Uists and Benbecula against blow-outs which would threaten the fertile machairs in their lee. Marram is such an important plant that it has been chosen to define the land's identity in these two songs.

Table 14: Flora

Name	Gender	Sound	Meaning	Example
Aitean, aitinn	m	*EHtchun*	juniper (Juniperus communis)	Caochan Aitinn, Glen Avon, NJ139102, Juniper Rill
Bealaidh	m	*BYAHlee*	broom (Cytisus scorparius)	Creag a' Bhealaidh, Atholl, NN903572, Rock of the Broom
Beith(e), beithe	f	*BAYhuh*	birch (Betula pendula or pubescens)	Eilean na Beithe, Tobermory, NM517550, Island of the Birch
Biolair, biolaire, biolairean	f	*BEEolihr*	watercress	Fuaran nam Biolaire, Glen Lyon NN514400, Spring of the Cresses
Broighleag, broighleig, broighleagan	f	*BROYlak*	Blaeberry (Vaccinium myrtillus)	Cnoc nam Broighleag, Loch Fyneside, NM937936, Knowe of the Blaeberries
Calltainn / cailltuinn, calltainn(e) / calltuinnn(e)	m	*COWLteen*	hazel (Corylus avellana)	Lag a' Challtuinn, Braeleny, Callander, NN646135, Hollow of the Hazel
Canach, canaich	m/f	*CAnuch*	cotton grass, bog cotton (Eriophorum angustifolium)	Lochan na Canaich, Morvern, NM683558, Little Loch of the Bog Cotton
Caorann, caorainn	m/f	*COEUrun*	rowan (Sorbus aucuparia)	Sròn a' Chaorainn, Glen Almond NN84308, Nose of the Rowan
Cnaimhseag, cnaimhseig, cnaimhseagan	f	*CREH-Vshak*	Bearberry (Arctostaphylos uva-ursi)	Beinn nan Cnaimhseag, Inchnadamph, Assynt NC274177, Mountain of the Bearberries
Còinneach, còinnich	f	*CAWNyuch*	moss	Coire na Còinnich, Glen Almond NN850305, Corrie of the Moss

Table 14 (cont.)

Name	Gender	Sound	Meaning	Example
Conasg, conaisg	m	CAWnusk	whin, gorse (Ulex europaeus)	Cnoc a' Chonaisg, Strathconon, NH390564, Hillock of the Gorse
Conasgach	adj	CAW-nuskuch	whinney, gorsey (Ulex europaeus)	Tom Conasgach, Loch Venachar, NN578064, Whinney Hillock
Craobh, craoibhe, craobhan	f	croeuv	tree	Eilean na Craoibhe, Loch Sunart, NM638606, Island of the Tree
Creamh, creamha	m	crehv	wild garlic, gentian, leek (Allium spp.)	Bad a' Chreamha, Strome, Lochcarron, NG857366, Spot, Hillock or Clump of Wild Garlic
Critheann, crithinn	m	CREEuhn	aspen (Populus tremula)	Torr a' Chrithinn, Loch Shiel, NM672692, Hillock of the Aspen
Cuilc, cuilce, cuilcean	f	COOeelk	reed (Juncus spp.)	Cnoc nan Lochan Cuilce, Loch Laxford, NC194480, Knowe of the Small Reed Lochs
Cuileann, cuilinn	m	COOlun	holly (Ilex aquifolium)	Rubh' Àird a' Chuilinn, Reay Forest, NC298421, Point of the Height of the Holly
Cuiseag, cuiseig(e), cuiseagan	f	COOshak	stalky grass, possibly Rye Grass (Lolium Perenne)	Coire na Cuiseig, Arran, NR960392, Corrie of the Stalky Grass
Darach, daraich	m	DAHruch	oak (Quercus petraea)	Meall an Doire Dharach, Kinlochleven, NN207627, Rounded Hill of the Oak Grove
Dearcag, dearcaig, dearcagan	f	JARkak	little berry	Meall nan Dearcag, Rannoch, NN657559, Rounded Hill of the Berries

Gaelic	Gender	Pronunciation	Meaning	Example
Dris, drise, drisean	f	*dreesh*	bramble, briar (Rubus spp., Rosa spp.)	Beinn na Drise, Mull, NM475427, Mountain of the Bramble.
Droigheann, droighinn	m	*DROYuhn*	blackthorn (Prunus spinosa)	Loch Droighinn, Trotternish, Skye, NG455713, Blackthorn Loch
Duileasg, duilisg	m	*DOOlushk*	dulse	Camas Geodhaichean an Duilisg, Uig, Lewis, NB043384, Bay of the Dulse Ravines
Eidheann, eidhne	f	*EHunn*	ivy (Hedera helix)	Creag na h-Eidhne, Gruline, Isle of Mull, NM554397, Rock of the Ivy
Fathan, fathain, fathanan	m	*FAHhan*	coltsfoot	Allt Fathan Glinne, Balquidder, NN495178, Burn of Colts-foot Glen
Fearna	f	*FYAARnuh*	alder (Alnus glutinosa)	Loch na Claise Feàrna, Scourie, NC200468, Loch of the Alder Furrow
Feur, feòir	m	*FEEar*	grass, hay	Lochan Feòir, Assynt, NC228253, Loch of Grass
Fiantag, fiantaige, fiantagan	f	*FEEuntak*	black heath berry or crow berry (possibly Empetrum nigrum)	Allt Fhiantagan, St Fillans, NN693233, Black Heath Berry Stream
Fiodhag, fiodhaige, fiodhagan	f	*FEEdak*	gean, bird cherry (Prunus avium)	Gleann Fhiodhaig, Glencarron and Glenuig Forest, NH150485, Cherry Glen
Fraoch, fraoich	m	*FROEUuch*	ling, common heather (Calluna vulgaris)	Loch na h-Innis Fraoich, Assynt, NC163263 Loch of the Heather Meadow (**Plate 26**)
Freumh, freumha, freumhan	m	*FREHuv*	root, stem	Tòrr nam Freumh, Arran, NR955374 Tower of the Roots
Giuthas, giuthais	m	*GYOOuss*	Scots pine (Pinus sylvestris)	Eilean na Creige Giuthais, Loch Maree, NG927714, Island of the Pine Rock

Table 14 (cont.)

Name	Gender	Sound	Meaning	Example
Gòinean	m	GAWNyan	couch grass	Gleann Ghòinean, St Fillans, NN703224, Glen of Couch Grass
Iubhar, iubhair, iubharan	m	YOOur	yew (Taxus baccata)	Loch Iubhair, Glen Dochart, NN424268, Yew Loch
Leamhan, leamhain, leamhan	m	LEHvan	elm (Ulmus spp.)	Beinn Leamhain(n), Ardgour, NM957624, Elm Mountain
Lus, luis, lusan	m	loos	herb, plant, weed, flower	Beinn nan Lus, Mull, NM593405, Mountain of the Herbs
Meacan, meacain, meacanan	m	MEHCH-kan	root, bulb	Creag Meacan, St. Fillans, Loch Earn, NN680256, Rock of Bulbs
Muran, murain	m	MOOran	marram grass	Eilean a' Mhurain, North Uist, NF704727, Island of Marram Grass
Oighreag, oigh-reig, oighreagan	f	OYrak	cloudberry, mountain strawberry (Rubus chaemorus)	Cnoc nan Oighreag, Glen Artney, NN742153, Knowe of the Cloudberries (**Plate 9**)
Preas, pris, preasan / pris	m	prehs	bush, shrub, thicket	Cnoc a' Phreasan Challtuinne, Scourie, NC187467, Knowe of the Little Hazel Bush
Raineach, rainich	f	RAHNyuch	fern, bracken	Meall Raineach, Flodigarry, Skye, NG456736, Fern Hill
Roid, roide, roidean	f	rotch	bog myrtle (Myrica gale)	Tòrr Roid, Sleat, Skye, NG672094, Myrtle Tower
Seamrag, seam-raig, seamragan	f	SHEMrak	clover, wood sorrel	Leathad na Seamraig, Loch Laxford, NC226492, Slope of the Clover

Gaelic	Gender	Pronunciation	English (scientific)	Example
Seasg, seasga, seisg / seisge	m/f	*shesk*	sedge (Carex spp.)	Coire an t-Seasgaich, Trotternish, Skye, NG476581, Corrie of the Sedge Place
Seileach, seilich, seileachan	m	*SHEHLuch*	willow (Salix spp.)	Druim Àirigh nan Seileach, Trotternish, Skye, NG475608, Ridge of the Shieling of Willows
Seileastair, seileastairean	m	*SHEHlus-tehr*	yellow flag iris (Iris pseudoacorus)	Creag an t-Seilisdeir, Loch Earnside, NN658252, Rock of the Iris
Sgitheach, sgithich	m	*SKEEuch*	hawthorn (Crataegus monogyna)	Cnoc nan Sgitheach, Arran, NR882461, Knowe of the Hawthorns
Sùbh, sùibh, sùbhan	m	*soo*	raspberry (Rubus idaeus)	Meall nan Sùbh, Glen Lyon, NN459398, Rounded Hill of the Raspberries
Ubhal, ubhail, ùbhlan	m/f	*OOuhl*	apple (Malus sylvestris)	Creag nan Ubhal, Drumochter, NN637753, Rock of the Apples
Uinnseann, uinnseinn	m	*OOEENs-hun*	ash (Fraxinus excelsior)	Cnoc an Uinnseinn, Strathyre, NN557174, Knowe of the Ash

7.3: Fauna

Questions arise when comparing the full complement of fauna known to have existed before natural extinctions and migrations caused by post-glacial climate change, with the range of animals, which have been active in Gaelic place-naming. Amongst large mammals, badgers, cat, red and roe deer, foxes, otters, pine marten and hare are commonly referred to in names, though the last species is the least mentioned. There is also no distinction made between the brown and mountain species, which is the white hare in Gaelic, *a' mhaigheach gheal,* owing to its winter coat.

We know that at the time of the Gaelic colonisation of Scotland from about 500AD, bear, beaver, elk, wild boar and wolves were all still present in the Highlands. Lynx and reindeer may have been present as well. Elk may have survived until the ninth century, bear until the tenth and wild boar until the thirteenth. Beaver populations lasted longer, until the sixteenth century, perhaps because they could exist in scrubby wet woodland, which persisted along watercourses in spite of grazing by domestic animals. Yet none, except perhaps the boar, is active in place-naming. Indeed, the only extinct mammal which has been employed reasonably widely in place naming is the wolf (*madadh-allaidh* – literally, wild dog), and then only infrequently. Though the widespread mapping of lairs or dens *(saobhaidh)* is perhaps a secondary reference to them, it may also apply to fox dens. Only one reference to bear can be found at *Allt Mhathain – Bear Stream* two kilometres to the east of *An Nead – Nedd* at NC163315, in Assynt.

With the exception of the wolf, can we assume that these large species, which are now extinct in the Highlands, had little significance in the act of naming and remembering places? Or, if names citing them did once exist, were they superseded or lost after species extinction? This last explanation would not account for the survival of wolf names. Perhaps the animal could persist throughout the period of active naming in Gaelic because woodland cover is not an essential component of its habitat. For other conspicuous species, it seems likely that names referring to them may have been altered at some time after their various extinctions.

The last *madadh-allaidh* is thought to have been killed in Inverness-shire in 1743. The problems that the wolf caused for man, apart from the obvious ones, were such that there was a tradition of siting burial grounds on small offshore islands. Examples are well distributed throughout the Highlands, which indicates a widespread problem. These can be found on Handa, Sutherland (NC145475), *Tannara Mòr*, Wester Ross (NB993699), Inishail, Loch Awe (NM102245) and on Eilean Munde *or Eilean Mhunna*, Loch Leven, Argyll (NN084591).

There may be more references to wolves than is apparent, as the qualifying adjective wild (*allaidh*) may have been dropped since there are also numerous mentions of *madadh*; another word for dog, which is not common in contemporary usage. To distinguish it from the wolf, the older name for fox is *madadh-ruadh* – literally the red or ruddy dog. However, in his *Òran nam Balgairean* – *Song to the Foxes,* Duncan Ban MacIntyre refers to the animal *balgair,* which can also mean a thief. In some dialects of contemporary Gaelic *sionnach* is used for fox, which also occurs in some areas in place-names. Similarly, reference to wild boar, *torc allaidh*, may have been compounded with ones to the domestic animal. An older and rare name for the otter is *madadh-uisge* (literally, water dog), but it is more commonly represented throughout the *Gàidhealtachd* as *dòbhran*, which may, as has been discussed, be confused with *dobhair*, water, in its plural form. Other large mustelids, the badger (Plate 24), *broc* (cognate with Old English brock) and the pine marten, *taghan* are well represented in names, but absent in the Outer and some of the Inner Hebrides. Just as the wolf and the fox are linked with the word for den, *saobhaidh,* badgers and wild cats are sometimes associated with the word *sgàirneach* at *Sgàirneach a' Chait* (NN5761222), to the west of Loch Lubnaig and *Sgàirneach nam Broc* (NN494377) in Glen Lochay. *Sgàirneach* means a continuous heap of loose stones covering a hillside, a great number of stones like a deserted quarry on a hill – a perfect hiding-place for such species.

A surprising omission in place-names, at least in the Central Highlands, given the frequency of sightings and its current iconic status in that area, is the red squirrel, *feòrag*. An explanation may be that the species could have been exterminated during the progressive deforestation of the Highlands, which would have fragmented its vulnerable aerial habitat of continuous tree canopy. Today's healthy populations have bred from reintroductions sourced in Dalkeith and

Scandinavia in the late eighteenth and early nineteenth century, well after active Gaelic naming of the landscape may have ceased. There is an older name for the species, *easag,* which is present in Kintessack *(Ceann na h-Easaig),* near Forres (NJ300860).

Pride of place in the Gaelic toponymic bestiary, and one which anticipates the Victorian predilections painted by Landseer, must go to the deer. *Fiadh* covers both roe and red. Stags and hinds / does of these species are *boc* and *damh, eilid* and *earb* respectively. The forest which they inhabit is *frìth,* and may well abound in hinds, and so might be termed *èildeach.* At one time, in contrast to how they appear today, deer forests would have abounded in trees as well as deer. An *eilleag* or *ailleag* was a funnel-shaped walled trap, open at its wider end, where deer were slain en masse up until the sixteenth century. There is an example in Glen Bruar, where landform may have also contributed to this purpose, and where the valley of the *Fèith Ghorm Ailleag - Bog Channel of the Blue Deer Trap* (NN814805) narrows to a defile. In 1564 the fourth Earl of Atholl organised such a deer hunt for Mary Queen of Scots. The Queen camped to the east of nearby Beinn a' Ghlò at a spot since known as *Tom na Bànrigh - Queen's Hillock,* though this cannot be traced on OS maps. Once inside the trap, deer were brought down in huge numbers by wolfhounds and archers.

In the eighteenth century, *Donnchadh Bàn Mac an t-Saoir* (Duncan Ban Macintyre), who for a time was one of the Earl of Beadalbane's gamekeepers, or foresters, was still using deerhounds, but in combination with stalking and a gun – the modern technique. In the

Plate 24: Glen Lochay - Sgairneach nam Broc

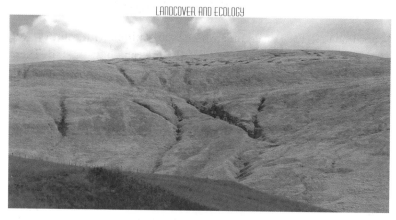

Plate 25: Glen Artney - Allt Eas nan Earb

following extract from his most famous poem, which was intended to be sung, *Moladh Beinn Dòbhrain* (Praise of Ben Dobhrain), and which is more about praising deer and their habitat than the mountain itself, he follows the movement of a party of hinds through the landscape around the peak.

Siubhal (a movement in classical pipe music or piobaireachd)

Bu ghrinn leam am pannal
Methought the troop graceful

A' tarraing an òrdugh,
deploying in order,

A' dìreadh le faram
ascending with bustle

Ri Carraig na Sròine:
the Cliff of the Nose;

Eadar sliabh Craobh na h-Ainnis
between the moor of the Pauper's Tree

Is beul Choire Dhaingein,
and the mouth of the Corrie of Fastness,

Bu bhiadhchar greigh cheannard
lusty was the haughty herd

Nach ceannaich am pòrsan;
that pays not for its portion;

Dà thaobh Choire Rainich,
on both sides of Ferny Corrie,

Mu sgèith sin a' Bhealaich,
around the flank of the Pass,

Coire Rèidh Beinn Ach-Chaladair,
in the Smooth Corrie of Ben Achallader,

'S thairis mu'n Chònnlon,
then over by the Dog Meadow;

Air Lurgainn na Laoidhre
on the Shank of the Cleft,

Bu ghreadhnach a' chòisridh;
gay was the party;

Mu Làrach na Fèinne,
about the Field of the Fianna,

'Sa' Chraig Sheilich 'na dheidh sin,
on Willow Rock thereafter,

Far an cruinnich na h-èildean
where gather the hinds

Bu neo-spèiseil mu 'n fhòlach.
that disdained the rank field grass.

… Cha bhiodh ìot' air an teangaidh
… Down below the Hill of Gathering

Taobh shìos a' Mhill Teanail,
their tongue would not be parched,

Le fìon Uillt na h-Annaid …
when there is wine of the Annat Burn,

Blas meala r' a òl air …
Honey-flavoured to drink …

(in Macleod 1978, 215)

Donnchadh lived for a time at *Àis an t-Sìdhein*, around which the place-names quoted in the poem are spread. Most of these underlined in the text can still be traced on OS Explorer sheet 378 (Figure 9). Others appear not to have been recorded, whilst *bealach* and *sròn* are too general and frequent to locate with any accuracy. By tracing the route of the deer observed in the poem from *Coire Daingean(n)* to *Coire Rèidh* and then to *Creag Sheileach* on *Meall Tionail (Teanail* in the song)* to drink from the pure waters of *Allt na h-Annait*, it is possible to hypothesise a position for *Coire Raineach* (Figure 9).

Cònnlon may lie near *Allt an Lòin*. Whilst *Lurgann na Laoidhre*-shank of the fork, promontory or land converging between two rivers, may be *Lurg Luibheach*. This is mapped on the OS 1:25,000 sheet at NN353398. Here *Allt an Lòin* and *Allt Coire a' Ghabhalach* meet below a sloping shank of land. The poem is the work of a man who intimately observed and understood the behaviour of deer, where and what they liked to eat, what springs quenched their thirst and what shelter they sought. Donnchadh was an acute interpreter of ecology and ethology long before these words were invented.

Birds most commonly used in place-names are raptors: the eagle (*iolair[e]*), hawk (*seabhag*) and the sparrow hawk (*speireag*). The golden and the sea eagle are not distinguished. The latter has 10 names. Most are qualifications of iolair. *Bhàn, bhuidhe, chladaich, fhionn, mhara* and *riabhach*- all attributes of the bird, but breaccan apply to both species. To further confuse, ospreys are known as *iolair-uisge, -iasgaich* or *iasgair*, so it is difficult to know which species place-names remember, but their context may help. The buzzard (*clamhan*) is rarely mentioned and harriers and merlin not at all, which is surprising given many references to sparrow hawks. Scavengers are recorded, but ravens (*fitheach*) are more common than crows (*feannag*). Gulls are not distinguished by species and are either *faoileag* or *faoileann*. Other water birds mentioned in place-names are the heron, *corra-ghritheach*, sometimes abbreviated to *corra*, and the cormorant, *sgarbh*. The latter comes from the Old Norse *scarfrand* gives Scarfsferry, near Thurso. Geese (*gèadh*) and swan (*eala*) are also common.

Another surprising omission, given the extent of muir burn, is the red grouse. There is no collective noun for the species in Gaelic. Females are appropriately called heather hens (*cearc-fhraoich*), whilst *coileach-ruadh* (red cock) is the male, mentioned by Duncan Ban MacIntyre in his '*Cead Deireannach nam Beann – Final Farewell to the Bens*.' *Cearc*, is common in the landscape and in places unlikely to be frequented by poultry. Again, records may be abbreviated. Or ridges and summits may have a hen or cockerel-like appearance. Its relative, the ptarmigan, *tàrmachan*, is reasonably frequent in place-names, perhaps because its niche habitat, at a higher altitude than the grouse, has been less altered by human agency. Another contributory factor may be that the existence of large scale grouse moors only dates from the nineteenth century, well after active Gaelic naming ceased.

Besides the plover, ptarmigan and the grouse, the only other small bird mentioned in place-names is the swallow, *gòbhlan-gaoithe,* which literally means the wind forkie. The formal idea of forking is powerful in naming other birds of the same family. The sand martin is the sand forkie, *gòbhlan-gainmhich*; the house martin is the house forkie, *gòbhlan-taighe;* whilst their larger cousin the swift is *gòbhlan mòr* or *an gòbhlan dubh.* Amongst unrelated species, Leach's petrel is the sea forkie, *gòbhlan na mara.* Forking, or *gòbhlach,* is also an attribute commonly applied to landforms.

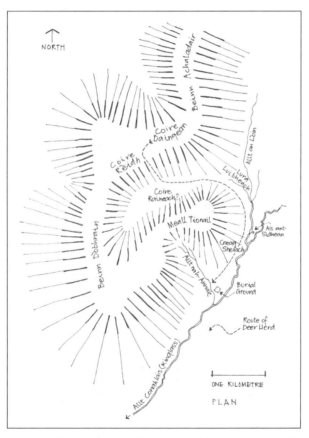

Figure 8: Sketch Map of some Place-names in 'Praise of Ben Dòbhrain.'

Table 15: Fauna

Name	Gender	Sound	Meaning	Example
Bàirneach, bàirnich	m/f	BAAH-RNyuch	limpet	Rubha nam Bàirneach, NB551308 Eye Peninsula (An Rubha), Lewis, Point of the Limpets
Boc, buic, buic	m	bochk	buck, billy goat	Creag Chath Bhoc, Glen Finglas NN548103, Roebuck Battle Rock
Bradan, bradain, bradain	m	BRAtan	salmon (Salmo salar)	Leac a' Bhradain, Loch Assynt, NC244218, Slab of the Salmon
Breac, bric, bric	m	BREHchk	trout	Loch nam Breac Mora, Assynt, NC322276, Loch of the Big Trout
Broc, bruic, bruic	m	BROCHk	badger (Meles meles)	Sgàirneach nam Broc, Glen Lochay,Perthshire, NN494377, Loose Scree of the Badgers (**Plate 24**)
Calman, calmain	m	CALaman	dove (Columba spp.)	Uamh nan Calman, Kerrera, NM803294, Cave of the Doves
Cat, cait, cait	m	caht	cat (Felix sylvestris)	Lochan nan Cat, Loch Tayside, NN644427, Little Loch of the Cats
Cearc-fhraoich, circe-fraoich	f	cyerk roeuch	female red grouse (Lagopus lagopus)	Meallan na(n) Circe Fraoich, Kinlochewe, NH008607, Small Rounded Hill of the Grouse Hen
Clamhan, clamhain, clamhain	m	CLAvan	buzzard (Buteo buteo)	Cnoc a' Chlamhain, Assynt, NC109249, Knowe of the Buzzard
Coinean, coinein, coineanan	m	CAWNyan	rabbit (Oryctolagus cuniculus)	Eilean nan Coinean, Crinan, NR777967, Island of the Rabbits
Corra, corran	f	CAWRra	grey heron (Arda cinerea)	Rubha nan Corra, Loch Shiel, NM745685, Point of the Herons
Cudaig, cudaige, cudaigean	m	COOtik	young coalfish, cuddy.	Rubha nan Cudaigean, Loch Snizort, Skye NG406410, Point of the Cuddies

Table 15 (cont.)

Name	Gender	Sound	Meaning	Example
Cuileag, cuileige, cuileagan	f	*COOlak*	fly	Àirigh nan Cuileag, Rannoch, NN596542, Shieling of the Flies
Cuthag / cubhag, cuthaige, cuthagan	f	*COOak*	cuckoo (Cuculus canorus)	Creag na Cuthaige, Braeleny, NN629107, Rock of the Cuckoo
Damh, daimh, daimh	m	*dahv*	stag (Cervus elaphus)	Dùn Damh, Strathyre, NN571133, Stag Fort
Dòbhran, dòbhrain, dòbhrain	m	*DAWran*	otter (Lutra lutra)	Sgiath an Dòbhrain, Braeleny, Callander NN629139, Wing of the Otter
Druid, druide, druidean	m/f	*DROOitch*	starling (Sturnus vulgaris)	Cnoc Druidean, Iona, NM273232, Starling Knowe
Eala, eala / ealaidh, ealachan	f	*YAluh*	swan (Cygnus spp.)	Rubha na h-Eala, Loch Shiel NM693683, Point of the Swan
Earb, earba, earban / earbaichean	f	EHrap	roe deer (Capreolus capreolus)	Allt Eas nan Earb, Glen Artney, NN684135 Stream of the Roe Deer Waterfall, (**Plate 25**)
Eilid, èilde, èildean	f	*EHYlitch*	red deer hind	Sàil Eilid a' Mhoraire, Reay Forest, NC358429, Heel-shaped Hill of the Lord's Hind
Eun, eòin, eòin	m	*AYun*	bird	Loch nan Eun, Lochnagar, NO230854, Loch of the Birds
Faochag, faochaige, faochagan	f	*FOEUchak*	little whelk, winkle, buckie, whirlpool	Poll nam Faochag, Lunga, NM708104, Pool of the Buckies
Faoileag, faoileige, faoileagan	f	*FOEUlak*	seagull	Eilean nam Faoileag, Loch Rannoch, NN530577, Island of the Seagulls

Gaelic	Gender	Pronunciation	English	Example
Faoileann, faoilinn, faoileannan	f	*FOEUluhn*	seagull	Biod na Faolinn, Ross of Mull, NM441182, Pointed Peak of the Seagull
Feadag, feadaige, feadagan	f	*FEHtak*	plover	Loch na Feadaige, Lochnagar, NO226857, Loch of the Plover
Feannag, feannaige, feannag	f	*FYOWnak*	crow (Corvus spp.)	Cnoc na Feannaige, Ross of Mull, NM434194, Knowe of the Crow
Fiadh, fèidh, fèidh	m	*FEEugh*	deer	Mainnir nam Fiadh, Mull NM673357, Fold of the Deer
Fitheach, fithich, fithich	m	*FEEuch*	raven (Corvus corax)	Cnoc an Fhithich, Rannoch, NN712567, Knowe of the Raven
Geàdh, geòidh, geòidh	m/f	*GYEUgh*	goose	Loch Geòidh, Loch Aweside, NS951035, Goose Loch
Gòbhlan-gaoithe	m	*GAWHlan GOEUyuh*	swallow	Creag Gòbhlan-gaoithe, Loch Lomond, NS344028, Swallow Rock
Guilbneach, guilb-nich	f	*GOO-lupnyuch*	curlew (Numenius arquata)	Meall nan Guilbneach, Trossachs, NN428063, Rounded Hill of the Curlews
Iolair(e), iolaire, iolairean	m/f	*YOOluruh*	eagle (Aquila chrysaetos)	Eilean na h-Iolaire, Rannoch Moor, NN326509, Island of the Eagle
Lach, lacha, lachan	f	*lach*	wild duck	Bealach nan Lachan, Braeleny, NN623102, Pass of the Little Wild Ducks
Losgann, losgainn, losgannan	m	*LOSgunn*	frog	Loch an Losgainn Mòr, Kilmelfort, NS865120, Big Loch of the Frog

Table 15 (cont.)

Name	Gender	Sound	Meaning	Example
Madadh-allaidh, madaidh- …, madaidhean- …	m	*MAHtugh ALLee*	wolf (lit: wild dog - Canis lupus)	Saobhaidh Madaidh Allaidh, Glen Dochart, NN440317, Wolf's Lair
Madadh-ruadh	m	*MAHtugh ROOugh*	fox (lit: red dog - Vulpes vulpes))	Sgùrr a' Mhadaidh Ruaidh, Trotternish, Skye, NG474584, Sharp Peak of the Fox (**Plate 14**)
Madadh-uisge	m	*MAHtugh OOSHkuh*	otter (lit: water dog - Lutra lutra))	Loch nam Madadh Uisge, Loch Ainort, Skye, NG568274, Loch of the Otters
Maigheach, maighiche, maigheachan	f	*MOYuch*	hare (Lepus capensis)	Meall nam Maigheach, Glen Lyon, NN586436, Rounded Hill of the Hares
Mang, maing, mangan	f	*mang*	yearling fawn	Coire nam Mang, Reay Forest, NC277421, Corrie of the Yearling Fauns
Nathair, nathrach, nathraichean	f	*NAHehr*	snake, adder	Cnapan Nathraichean, Braemar, NO223888, Little Lumpy Hills of Snakes. *Nathrach* – snake-like, can also apply to meandering streams
Partan, partain, partain / partanan	m	*PAHshrtan*	small crab	Port nam Partan, Calgary, Mull, NM350528, Port of Crabs
Ròn, ròin, ròin	m	*rawn*	seal	Clach nan Ròn, Loch Etive (Èite), NN103425. Stone of the Seals
Seabhag, seabhaig, seabhagan	m/f	*SHEHvak*	hawk	Càrn nan Seabhag, Atholl, NN740721. Cairn of the Hawks

130

Seangan, seangain, seanganan	m	SHEHNgan	ant	Creagan Sheangan, Glen Lochay, NN503363, Little Rock of Ants
Sgadan, sgadain, sgadain	m	SKAHtan	herring	Geodh' nan Sgadan, Badcall, NC144417, Ravine of the Herrings
Sgarbh, sgairbh, sgairbh	m	SKAHRrav	cormorant (Phalacrocorax carbo)	Creag nan Sgarbh, Ardnamurchan, NM630673, Rock of the Cormorants
Sionnach, sionnaich, sionnaich	m	SHOOnuch	fox (Vulpes vulpes)	Creag nan Sionnach, Atholl, NN714733, Rock of the Foxes
Speireag, speireig, speireagan	f	SPAYRrak	sparrow hawk (Accipiter nisus)	Creag na Speireig, Loch Ailort, NM707789, Rock of the Sparrow Hawk
Taghan, taghain	m	TOEUghan	pine marten (Martes martes)	Tom an Taghain, Glen Dochart, NN505303, Hillock of the Pine Marten (**Plate 22**)
Torc, tuirc, tuirc	m	tork	wild boar, boar (Sus scrofa)	An Torc, The Boar of Badenoch, Dalwhinnie, NN622764, The Boar
Trilleachan, trilleachain	m	TREELyuchan	plover; sandpiper	Àird Trilleachan. Loch Etive, NN102432, Plover Point

8: LAND USE

8.1: Agriculture and Crops

This section has been much informed by Ian Fraser's publications on Gaelic agricultural names and Albert Bil's work on the shieling in Highland Perthshire. As has been argued, Gaelic names are a late nineteenth century snapshot taken at the time of Ordnance Survey mapping. The landscape they documented predated crofting and depending on the history of an area, existed before or after the clearance of people from the land. It was also one of transhumance, even though that practice had largely ceased at the time of survey. The recording of the landscape took place at a watershed, after its naming and during the period when large scale sheep farming, grouse moors and deer forests were being introduced. The place-names mapped mostly describe an earlier landscape of pastoral transhumance agriculture. Agricultural names can be divided into four categories. Only the first three need concern us in any detail. These are: arable (potential tillage), grazing (limited tillage) and enclosures (untilled) and shelters for livestock.

Arable

The first word in the table below is *achadh*. Such names represent land with a potential for supporting arable crops, or in Scots, inby land, distributed around the home farm. Throughout Scotland, *achadh* names, except in the Western Isles and Berwickshire, have the widest and most even distribution, when compared with (town / township) or *cill* (church), which are concentrated in the east and west of the country respectively. *Baile* is primarily a settlement name, but many places with *achadh* names also became settlements and thus, this is a secondary expression of the name. *Achadh* is often anglicised as a prefix, to ach or auch.

In the Western Isles, the Norse *geàrraidh*, anglicised to garry, bears the same meaning. In Perthshire, where the climate is drier, *achadh* names are found in the most remote areas and close to the limits of cultivation. *Gàrradh* is similar to *geàrraidh* and means garden. *Lios* also means garden and applies to the fertile limestone island of *Lios Mòr*. It is almost completely absent in place-names however.

The most common crop names refer to barley *(eòrna)* and oats *(coirce)*, which are more suited to upland areas than corn. Despite the reliance on potatoes *(buntàta)* in the early nineteenth century, there seems to be only one name associated with that plant (Table 16). Perhaps its introduction came after active naming in Gaelic ceased.

Dail, which is anglicised to dal, is a level field by a river often prone to flooding and is equivalent in meaning to the Scots word haugh. It has also developed a secondary meaning as a settlement. *Dail* becomes more limited in usage as one proceeds upstream and inland, and as land adjacent to rivers becomes more constrained by steepening valley form.

Goirtean often appears as the prefix gort or gart, and refers to a small enclosure of arable land, especially frequent in Argyll. Fraser cites two interesting examples – both unmapped: *Goirtean gun Fhios* (without knowledge) in Ardnamurchan, where an old woman grew potatoes without the knowledge of the factor, and *Goirtean an Sgadain* on the south side of the Beauly Firth, where surplus herring catches were spread as fertiliser.

Grazing

Blàr is equivalent to field, and like the English word it has a wider meaning of field of battle or a battle itself. There can be fields of green, but also fields of peat and moss as well, and it is a very general term applying to any flat area devoid of treecover. *Cluain* meaning pasture, green field, meadow or lawn, is no longer in current use, but has in the past provided the scotticised clunie or cluny and appears in verse 2 of the ever popular 23rd Psalm:

'Ann an cluainibh glasa, bheir e orm laighe sìos
In pastures green he leadeth me down to lie.'

Innis can variously mean: island riverside meadow, pasture and resting place for cattle. In an extended sense the word can be understood as an island of cultivation in amongst the waste, even though now it is often found in areas of intense cultivation.. *Innis a' Chròtha* (NG970213) near Loch Duich, anglicised to Inchnacroe 300 metres to the west, and the *innis* of *Loch na h-Innis Fraoich - Loch of the Heather Meadow* (NC163263) near *Leitir Easaidh* in Assynt represent the pastoral meaning. In Plate 26, it is easy to see remnants of once green islands of cultivation amongst the surrounding heather. There are many well-built, ruined habitations nearby, which testify to former agricultural activity. *Innis* meaning island has been superseded by *eilean* in modern Gaelic (see section 6.3 on the Gaelic Seascape).

Plate 26: Assynt - Loch na h-Innse Fraoich and A' Chuinneag
(Quinag) (also in colour section)

Lèana and *lòn*, which are also listed in section 7.1 under habitats, can both mean a meadow. Meadows are often wet and thus can provide a source rushes for thatch. Indeed in Skye, *lòn* is also attached to small streams, particularly in Trotternish, *Lòn an Ime* - stream of the butter (NG433631), for example. *Lèana* is found in the anglicised Braeleny and Stroneslany in Callander and Balquidder respectively.

Dwelly's Dictionary defines *machair* as a large, low-lying fertile plain, often found on the coast along the sandy plains fringing the Atlantic coast of most of the Outer Hebrides. It is not so much an example as a defining occurrence. These areas are flat and wide raised beaches. In the past the word could apply to low-lying land in general and gave rise to the Machars district of Wigtonshire. Despite its physical ubiquity in the Western Isles, place-names including *machair* are rare.

Enclosures

Buaile meaning a fold for sheep or cattle is perhaps the most common type of enclosure for stock. Typically it is found closer to arable land or settlements, but does not usually generate settlement names – an exception being Buailnaluib, Aultbea (NG870900). *Crò* is usually circular in form and about the same scale as a sheep pen. It can be a wattled structure or temporary hut or stall. Dwelly quotes the well known saying:

'Cho fad 's bhitheas monadh an Ceann Tàil,
cha bhi MacCoinnich gun àl sa chrò.'

'As long as there are moors in Kintail,
MacKenzie will not be without cattle in the pen.'

(in Dwelly 1988, 274)

Kintail has given its name to the famous song *Crò Chinn t-Sàile*, (note the correct Gaelic spelling of Kintail), which means the head of the sea or salt water. The cattle pen gives its name to the River Cro. In Gairloch in Wester Ross, the meaning of *crò* has been extended to describe *Bad a' Chrò*, which is a circular inlet of the sea enclosed by land on three sides. This usage is yet another example of how generic Gaelic terrestrial names can apply equally well to seascape.

Mainnir is the kind of animal fold furthest from settlements and is sometimes formed by natural terrain making a place where beasts can be gathered. The name is mostly found in the mountainous parts of Skye and Mull. *Mainnir nam Fiadh - Fold of the Deer* (NM673357) in eastern Mull is so high that the animals involved here must have been wild deer. The Gaelic word for gathering, *cruinneach*, is often attached to landforms such as corries, where the terrain lends itself to the herding of grazing animals. The cup-shaped *Coire Cruinneachan* NN733392), near Ardtalnaig, lying above the now ruined township of *Tom Flùir* (flour hillock), may be a contraction of the word for gathering. At *Tom Flùir* evidence of the fertility of former arable land can be seen in the heap of stone pickings accumulated after many ploughings (Plate 16).

8.2: Transhumance and the Shieling

This subject will be dealt with in some detail since the landscape mapped by Ordnance Survey and its names was one where transhumance took place as a matter of course. The place-name most indicative of this practice is *àirigh*, sometimes spelled *àiridh* and often anglicised to *ari*. It must have been a very useful word, since Norsemen exported it to the Faroes, where it appears in place-names as ærgi. The visit in summer to the shieling in the uplands used to be a distinguishing feature of agriculture in the Highlands. Sandy Fenton paints a vivid picture in *Scottish Country Life*.

'The movement of people and stock to the shielings is spoken of as an occasion of great delight, the highlight of the year. People in Lewis who have experienced shieling life always speak of it with nostalgia. The day for the journey was a day of high excitement and community effort that made hard work a pleasure. In the Western Isles, the stock are said to have travelled in sequence, first the sheep, then the younger cattle, then the older cattle, followed by the goats ... and the horses, on whose wooden pack saddles all kinds of equipment was carried. The men carried spades, timber, heather ropes that had been previously twisted by hand, and other things required to repair the huts. In some places, such as mainland Argyll, the roofing timbers were brought home and taken back each year. It was the work of the men to repair the huts in which their women folk lived, either in advance, or on the day of flitting. The women carried bedding, dairy utensils, and oatmeal. Their long skirts were drawn up under a belt to let them walk more freely and they knitted stockings as they walked along. They also took with them spindles and distaffs for spinning wool, for ... this was where young girls would learn the art of spinning ... In Perthshire where there was the possibility of taking

light peat carts, spinning wheels were carried, and the bleaching of previously woven cloth was also a shieling occupation. The women and sometimes the herds also collected roots, herbs and lichens for making dye ...Once the huts had been prepared for occupation, and the souming or allocation of stock per familiy had been checked ... fires were lit ... and after a meal, often with cheese, and perhaps with a prayer and a hymn, the men returned to the village or wintertown (Baile Geamhraidh).'

(Fenton 1976, 137)

Fenton's portrait suggests a broader function of the shieling than Dwelly's definition of 'summer residence (*Baile Samhraidh*) for herdsmen and cattle'. Indeed, the transhumance system involved an infrastructure of halfway houses on the way to and from remoter shielings, which were progressively occupied as the growing season permitted. Some temporary halts, especially those in the islands, are called *Àirigh na h-Aon Oidhche - Shieling of the One Night* in Barvas, Lewis. Though *Loch Àirigh na h-Aon Oidhche* in Benbecula tells a different tale. Here a man who was spending his first night, and as it turned out his only night, in a newly completed sheiling hut awoke to a noise outside. He went out to investigate and saw his cattle being chased by a monster. The man never returned to *Loch Àirigh na h-Aon Oidhche*.

Also in Lewis, there is a *Taigh Earraich - House of Spring*, which was occupied after winter fodder had been exhausted and until the beginning of summer. Other kinds operated according to a haughland model in areas prone to winter flooding. In Perthshire, with its better climate and soils, shielings could be at altitudes of up to 2400ft and grow some arable crops, but most lay between 900 and 1500ft, whilst in Skye they rarely existed above 500ft and were unsuitable for crops. The journey to the shieling is remembered in the many references to flitting *(imrich)* (moving house in standard English), usually as *Bealach na h-Imriche - Pass of the Flitting*.

In modern day parlance, transhumance is sustainable practice. In upland areas or those at the margins of cultivation, it makes sense to use pastures as they progressively come into production. In unenclosed, mixed agricultural systems (those without fences or dykes separating fields), where arable crops have to be grown

*Plate 27: Loch Tay - Ruined Shieling Huts in Ardeonaig
Glen. Meall Greigh, Rounded Hill of the Stud, is the highest
peak to the left of the Loch (also in colour section)*

during the summer on better, low-lying land, it is more practical if animals, which could destroy crops without continual minding, are moved up the hill where they can range freely. Most shielings were within five miles of the home farm, but some could be as far away as twelve miles. Hence the need for staging-posts. Where transport was difficult and slow, it is also good sustainable practice to convert milk from pasturing goats, sheep and cows into something portable like cheese. Shielings were, therefore, usually sited near running water for the washing of cheeses. Sheltered and free-draining slopes were also chosen.

There are many references to milk *(bainne)*, butter *(ìm)* and cheese *(càise)* in place-names. In Balquidder the spectacular Hill of the Cheese Press or Vat - *Meall an Fhiodhain* (NN548248) commemorates the dairy process in its resemblance (plate 28). Whilst in Glen Lednock, there is *Càrn Luig Bainneiche - Cairn of the Pass abounding in Milk* (NN782267). On St Kilda at *Clach a' Bhainne*, every summer and autumn, milk was poured into a cleft in a rock as an offering to the spirit *Gruagach*, the long-haired maiden. If one looks at some of these places now, whose herbage has been impoverished by decades of unsustainable overgrazing by sheep and deer, it is difficult to imagine how productive they must once have been to deserve names so redolent of fecundity.

Popular reference is made to shielings in climbing books as small patches of green in the hills. These were probably just small areas or *todhairean*, where folds or pens stood and thus received a concentration of manure, whose effect persists today. In reality, most shielings were between 300 and 600 acres in extent, depending on the need of the home farm to maintain a balance between winter and summer feeding, and the density of stocking rates.

Plate 28: Balquidder - Meall an Fhiodhain to the right of the picture (also in colour section)

Many shielings are named after people and their occupations. Others indicate the kind of life lived among the hills. *Àirigh nan Cuileag - Shieling of the Flies* (NN597542) in Rannoch and *Coire na h-Àirighe Gruamaich - the Coire of the Gloomy Shieling* (NN888408) in Glen Quaich paint a less idyllic picture than Sandy Fenton's bucolic description quoted earlier. However, as family structures were loosened during the shieling time, opportunities for courtship arose. Elsewhere in Rannoch, in the anonymous song *Bothan Àirigh am Bràigh Raineach - a Shieling Hut on Rannoch's Brae (or Upper Rannoch)*, a young girl in the seventeenth century imagines rearing stolen cattle with her fine and noble lover in a shieling hut.

'S ann a bhios sinn gan àrach
We shall rear them

air àirigh am Bràigh Raineach,
on a shieling in Rannoch Moor,

ann am bothan an t-sùgraidh
in the little wooing hut

's gur e bu dùnadh dha barrach.
enclosed by brushwood.

Bidh a' chuthag 's a smùdan
The cuckoo and its singing

gabhail ciùil dhuinn air chrannaibh,
will play music to us from the trees,

bidh an damh donn 's a bhùireadh
the brown stag and its roaring

gar dùsgadh sa mhadainn.
will waken us in the morning.

(extract from Lorne Gillies 2005, 330)

In her book on Gaelic song, Anne Lorne Gillies likens the pair to medieval French lovers in a bower, where they bask in a perpetual summer. Referring to *Maighdeannan na h-Àirigh - Maidens of the Shieling*, she goes on:

'Gaelic song paints countless pictures of the shieling - the carefree girls, women and children tending the cattle on the sunny upland meadows of summer, far away from the grind of everyday life and the harsh uncertainties of the other three seasons. Of course they are usually the rose-tinted reminiscences of adults remembering the lost Arcadia of their youth.'

(Lorne Gillies 2005, 477)

In Perthshire and the eastern central Highlands, *àirigh* is replaced by *ruidhe* or *ruighe*, which can be confused with *righe* meaning a strip of sloping land, especially in corrupted forms of place-names. Glen Tilt has many examples of *ruighe*.

Not all shielings followed the general pattern. Some were associated with peat cutting or timber felling, whilst others like Arivurichardich (*Àirigh Mhuirich Cheàrdaich* – Moray's or Murdo's

Smithy Sheiling) in Braeleny (NN643138) were used for the smelting of bog iron. Shielings could also act as boundary markers between estates. *Clach Mhòr na h-Àirigh Lèithe - the Big Stone of the Grey Shieling* (NN658274), in Glen Tarken, Loch Earnside (Plate 29), is mentioned in property deeds as early as 1636 and as late as 1770.

Plate 29: Glen Tarken - Clach Mhòr na h-Àirigh Lèithe in the left foreground, *Sròn Mhòr Mhic La(u)rainn* is the centre of the picture

As the boundary between cultivatable and intractable land fluctuated with climate, population levels and market demand, shielings sometimes took over abandoned farms, or conversely shielings became permanently settled. What is named as a shieling may not have originated as one. In Perthshire, the shieling era came to an end as sheep farms progressively took over the upland pastures and broke the synergy between *Baile Geamhraidh* and *Baile Samhraidh*. Composing songs in the early nineteenth century, Duncan Ban MacIntyre from Glen Orchy in his *Cead Deireannach nam Beann - Final Farewell to the Bens* put it thus.

Bha mi 'n dè 'san aonach
Yesterday I was on the moor,
'S bha smaointean mòr air m' aire-sa,
and grave reflections haunted me:
Nach robh 'n luchd-gaoil a b' àbhaist
that absent were the well-loved friends

Bhith siubhal fàsaich mar rium ann;
who used to roam the waste with me;

'S bheinn as beag a shaoil mi
since the mountain, which I little thought

Gun dèanadh ise caochladh,
would suffer transformation,

On tha i nis fo chaoraibh
has now become a sheep-run,

'S ann thug an saoghal car asam.
the world, indeed, has cheated me.

'N uair sheall mi air gach taobh dhìom
As I gazed on every side of me

Chan fhaodainn gun bith smalanach,
I could not but be sorrowful,

On theirig coill is fraoch ann,
for wood and heather have run out,

'S na daoine bh' ann, cha mhaireann iad;
nor live the men who flourished there;

Chan 'eil fiadh r' a shealg ann,
there's not a deer to hunt there,

Chan 'eil eun no earb ann,
there's not a bird or roe there,

Am beagan nach 'eil marbh dhiubh,
and the few that have not died out

'S e rinn iad falbh gu baileach as.
have departed from it utterly.

(extract from Macleod 1978, 391)

Duncan Fraser describes a shieling tradition whose remnants prevailed until modern times in upper Glenlyon. Every year, when the people flitted up *Gleann Cailliche - Old Woman Glen* (NN375427) to the summer pastures, in order to encourage good weather and crops they moved the water-worn stones, which represent the Old Woman and her family, into the open air outside her hut, *T(a)igh nam Bodach - House of the Old Men* (NN381427), and then re-thatched its tiny roof. When the time came for them to return to the winter township, they replaced the family and removed the thatch. According to Fraser, writing in the late 1970s, the shepherd of the sheep farm was still keeping up this tradition, though the hut by then had a roof of stone and required no re-thatching.

8.3: Domestic and Farm Animals

In contrast to their ubiquity today, sheep were not the major livestock animal in the Highlands of the past. Those that were kept would also have been of smaller breeds, like the Soay or North Ronaldsay, rather than the Cheviot or Blackface, introduced in the nineteenth century. Place-name evidence shows that cattle names are both more numerous, and more diverse. This is not surprising, since before the development of large-scale sheep farming and deer forests, cattle were the major Highland export.

Calves, stirks, heifers and bulls are all commonly represented in place-names as well as by three collective nouns. Goat names appear to be at least as common, if not more so, than sheep names, though, like them, their presence in place-names is less diverse than those for cattle. Historically, goat's milk was an important dairy product. Thomas Pennant enjoyed their whey in Glen Tilt during his tour of Scotland in 1769. Loch Earnside and Dunkeld were also noted for the production of goat's whey well into the nineteenth century. Herds of feral goats, which can still be found in Colonsay, Jura, Rum and Kintyre, are the descendants of such domestic flocks. *Eireannach*, which is the modern spelling, and means a wedder or castrated goat, is a reasonably common place-name element. It can be confused with Èireannach meaning Irishman. It seems more likely that in a pastoral society a livestock word would be more active in naming rather than several wandering, often marooned and sometimes leaping Irishmen. There are also several 'islands of the wedder goat,' which would be good places to pasture an animal so destructive of crops and trees.

Less common are herds of feral ponies which, though once widespread, can still be found on Rum and Holy Island, off Arran. Horses were the only possible form of transport in the uplands and would have been used in the annual migration to the shielings and in the transport of peats and tools to and from the hill. In the

Table 16: Land Use - Agriculture and Crops

Name	Gender	Sound	Meaning	Example
Achadh, achaidh, achaidhean	m	*AHCHugh*	field, plain, meadow, agricultural holding	Achadh nam Bàrd, Trotternish, NG435501, Field of the Poets
Àilean, àilein, àilein	m	*AHLyan*	green, plain, meadow, enclosure	Glac an Àilean, Mull, NM396529, Hollow of the Green Meadow
Airbhe	f	*EHRuvuh*	dividing wall, fence	Tòrr an Airbhe, Kylesku (An Caolas Cumhang), NC194334, Tower of the Fence
Àirigh / àiridh, àirighe / àiridhe, àirighean / airidhean	f	*AHree*	shieling	Clach Mhòr na h-Àirighe Lèithe, Glen Tarken, NN658274, The Big Stone of the Grey Shieling (**Plate 29**)
Arbhar, arbhair	m	*AHRavur*	corn	Loch an Arbhair, Coigach, Wester Ross, NC079188, Loch of the Corn
Bainne	m	*BANyuh*	milk	Cnoc a' Bhainne, Assynt, NC073258, Knowe of Milk
Bainneach, bainniche	adj.	*BANyuch*	abounding in milk, milk-producing	Càrn Luig Bainn(e)iche, Glen Lednock, NN782267, Milky Pass Cairn
Brochan, brochain	m	*BROchan*	porridge, gruel	Poll Bhrochain, Seil, NM774195, Porridge Pool
Buaile, buailtean	f	*BOOiluh*	fold for sheep or cattle	Buaile nam Biorach, Edinbane, Skye, NG338537, Fold of the Heifers or Colts?
Buntàta	m	*BUNtahtuh*	Potato	Cnoc a' Bhuntàta, North Harris, NB207127, Knowe of the Potatoes
Càbag, càbaig, càbagan	f	*CAApak*	cheese	Druim Càbaig, Mull, NM412523, Cheese Ridge

Cachaileith, cachailei-the, cachaileithean	f	*CACHulay*	field gate, hurdle	Cachaileith Liath, Glen Artney, NN698169, Grey Hurdle (**Plate 17**)
Caipleach, caiplich	f	*KEHPluch*	place of horses	Loch Mòr na Caiplich, Skye, NG475311, Big Loch of the Horse Place
Càise, càisean	m	*CAHshuh*	cheese	Sgiath a' Chàise, Strathyre, NN584169, Wing-Shaped Hill of the Cheese
Ceapach, ceapaich, ceapaich	m / f	*KEHpoch*	tillage plot	Ceapach, Strathyre, NN586134, Tilled Land
Cirean, cirein, cìreanan	m	*KEErahn*	honeycomb	Crean Geardail, Point of Stoer, Assynt, NC010347, The Honeycomb of the Short Valley?
Clas, claise	f	*clash*	furrow	Lochan na Claise, Assynt, NC134138, Little Loch of the Ditch
Cluain, cluaine, cluain-tean / cluainean	f	*CLOOylin*	meadow, lawn	Allt Cluain Àirighe, Knoydart, NG753056, Meadow Shieling Stream
Coileach, coilich, coilich	m	*CAWLuch*	cockerel	Tom nan Coileach, Tomintoul, NJ135194, Hillock of the Cockerels
Coirce	m	*CAWirkuh*	oats	Achadh a' Choirce, Skye, NG477459. Field of the Oat
Crò, crotha / crothadh. cròithtean	m	*crow*	sheep pen, fold	Àird a' Chrotha, Mull, NM737315, Height of the Sheep Pen
Croit, croite, croitean	f	*CRAWtch*	croft	Allt na Croite, Moidart, NM718697, Stream of the Croft
Cuidhe / cuithe, cuidhe / cuithe	f	*COOyuh*	enclosure, cattle fold, pen	Loch na Cuithe Mòire, South Uist, NF737234, Loch of the Cattle Fold
Dail, dalach, dailean	f	*dahl*	haugh, level field by river	Cnoc Dail Chàirn, Strath of Kildonan, NC856283, Hillock of the Cairn Haugh

Table 16 (cont.)

Name	Gender	Sound	Meaning	Example
Dìg, dìge, dìgean	f	*jeek*	ditch, wall of lose stones	Meall na Dìge, Balquidder, NN451226, Rounded Hill of the Ditch
Eachraidh	m	*EHCHree*	stud of horses	Blàr an Each(d)raidh, Strathyre, NN558153, Plain of the Stud
Eòrna	m	*YAWRnuh*	barley	Tom an Eòrna, Braeleny, NN634114, Hillock of the Barley
Faing, faing / fainge, faingean	m/f	*fang*	sheep pen, fank	Cnoc na Faing, Loch Shiel, NM736692, Knowe of the Fank
Feannag, feannaige, feannag	f	*FYEHnak*	lazybed - ridge of raised ground used for growing potatoes	Allt na Feannaig, Diabaig, Torridon, NG803610, Stream of the Lazybed
Fearann, Fearainn	m	*FEHrown*	land, estate, farm, earth, land (as distinct to sea)	Loch an Fhearainn Duibh, Loch Ailort, NM713822, Loch of the Black Land
Feur, feòir	m	*FEEar*	grass, hay	Feur-loch, Assynt, NC270135, Grass Loch
Fiodhan, fiodhain, fiodhanan	m	*FEEahm*	cheese vat or press	Meall an Fhiodhain, Balquidder, NN548248, Hill of the Cheese Press (**Plate 28**)
Gàrradh, gàrraidh, gàrraidhean	m	*GAAHrugh*	wall, dyke, garden, enclosure	Gàrradh Cruaidh, Glen Artney, NN708159, Hard Garden
Gart, gairt	m	*garsht*	field, cornfield	Seann Ghairt, Islay, NR383676, Old Field
Gead, gid, geadan	f	*geht*	small plot of arable land, lazy bed	Rubha Gead nam Bràthan, Ardnamurchan, NC545616, Point of the Plot of the Querns
Geàrraidh, geàrraidhean	m	*gyaahree*	green pasture land around a township (see Dwelly)	Geàrraidh Mhurchaidh, Loch Seaforth, NB229025, Murdo's Pasture

Gaelic	Gender	Pronunciation	Meaning	Examples
Goirtean, goirtein, goirteanan	m	GAWRsh-tahn	small patch of enclosed arable land, park	Goirtean Beag, Iona, NM264246, Little Park.
Greigh, greighe, greighean	f	gray	herd, flock, stud of horses	Meall Greigh, Loch Tayside, NN678438, Rounded Hill of a Stud (**Plate 27**)
Ìm, ime	m	eem	butter	Loch Glac an Ime, Scalpay, Skye, NG597304, Loch of the Hollow of Butter
Innis, innse, innsean / innseachean	f	EENish	field for grazing cattle, pasture or resting-place for cattle, haugh, riverside / meadow (see Dwelly)	Loch na h-Innis Fraoich, Assynt, NC163263 Loch of the Heather Meadow (**Plate 26**)
Machair, machaire / machrach, machrai-chean	m/f	MACHehr	large, low-lying fertile plain, often on the coast e.g. long ranges of sandy plains fringing the Atlantic coast of the Outer Hebrides	A' Mhachair, Iona, NM267237, The Machair
Peighinn, peighinne, peighinnean	f	PAYin	pennyland	Bruach na Seann Pheighinne, Mull, NM361527, Bank of the Old Pennyland
Pòr, pòir, pòran	m	pawr	crops in general	Caochan nam Pòran, Strathnairn, NH648342, Little Stream of the Crops
Raon, raoin, raontan / raointean	f	roeun	field, plain, meadow, agricultural holding	Raon na Ceàrdaich, Assynt, NC093254, Meadow of the Smithy
Rèidh, rèidhean	m	ray	smooth, level ground, plain, meadow	Rèidh an Daraich, Knoydart, NG? Meadow Plain of the Oak

Table 16 (cont.)

Name	Gender	Sound	Meaning	Example
Roinn, roinne, roin-nean	f	*royn*	share, division	Roinn Mhòr, Strathyre, NN562154, Big Divide
Ruighe, ruighean	m / f	*ROOeeyuh*	shieling, hill slope	Ruighe an Fhraoich, Rannoch, NN652541, Shieling of the Heather
Seagal, seagail	m	*SHEkul*	rye	Cnoc an t-Seaga(i)l, Assynt, NC244136, Knowe of the Rye
Sop, suip, sopan	m	*sawp*	wisp, loose bundle of hay or straw	Àth nan Sop, Comrie, NN769219, Ford of the Straws
Stapag, stapaig, sta-pagan	f	*STAHpak*	mixture of oatmeal and water or cream	Lòn na Stapaig, Greshornish, Skye, NG335540, Marshy Stream of the Stapag. (Duthaich nan Stapag is one name given to Trotternish)
Todhar, todhair, tod-haran	m	*TOHuhr*	field manured by penning cattle in it	Todhar Dubh, Mull, NM414518, Black Dung Field.
Uisge-Beatha	m	*OOSHkuh BEHuh*	whisky, water of life	Cnoc Bothain Uisge Beathain, Strathnaver, NC744432, Hillock of the Whisky Hut (though Beathan may be a personal name).

148

Plate 30: Balquidder - Leum an Èirionna(i)ch is on the right of the picture (also in colour section)

Royal hunting forests, they would have been used for carrying game, especially deer from the hill, just as the garron, or Highland pony, is used today on large shooting estates. *Gearran* is the Gaelic, but it is rare in place-names when compared with *each*. The Trossachs OS Explorer sheet 365 covers some of the Scottish monarchy's hunting forests of Glen Artney and Glen Finglas, and includes *Blàr an Each(d) raidh - Plain of the Stud* (NN558153), *Beinn Each - Horse Mountain* (NN602158) and two instances of *Bealach nan Searrach - Pass of the Foals* (NN577124 and 597129), all within a few miles of each other in Strathyre. Horse culture was once widespread in the Highlands.

The popular assumption that the Highlanders did not keep pigs must be challenged by the numerous records of that animal in place-names, though some of these may be references to the wild animal, where the qualifying adjective wild (*allaidh*) has been dropped or lost. According to Fraser Darling and Morton Boyd, writing in 1969: 'the conversion of the people to an extreme type of Presbyterianism engendered a Judaic attitude to the pig, and numbers fell away rapidly after the nineteenth century conversions.'

Table17: Domestic and Farm Animals

Name	Gender	Sound	Meaning	Example
Agh, aighe, aighean	m/f	*ugh*	heifer	Cnoc nan Aighean, Rannoch, NN734558, Knowe of the Little Heifers
Bò, bà, bà	f	*boh*	cow	Bealach nam Bò, Trossachs NN481075, Pass of the Cows (**Plate 5**)
Caora, caorach, caoraich	f	*COEUruh*	sheep	Beinn Chaorach, Rannoch Moor, NN294550, Mountain of Sheep
Capall / capull, capaill / capuill, capaill / capuill	m	*CAHpowl*	horse, mare	Beinn nan Capull, Skye, NG499354, Mountain of the Horses
Cearc, circe, cearcan	f	*Cyerk / cyark*	hen	Bioran na Circe, Strathyre, NN558118, Little Spike of the Hen
Coileach, coilich, coilich	m	*CAWLyuch*	cock	Tom a' Choilich, Ross of Mull, NM509254, Hillock of the Cockerel.
Crodh, cruidh	m	*crow*	cattle	Allt a' Mheanbh-c(h)ruidh, Rannoch, NN504545, Stream of the Little Cattle.
Cù, coin, coin	m	*coo*	dog	Linne a' Choin Duibh, Rannoch Moor, NN348448, Pool of the Black Dog
Each, eich, eich	m	*ech*	horse	Beinn Each, Strathyre NN602158, Mountain of Horses
Èireannach, éireannaich	m	*EHryuhmuch*	wether / wedder (castrated) goat	Leum an Èireannaich, Balquidder, NN518246, Leap of the Wedder Goat, (**Plate 30**)
Gamhainn, gaimhne / gamhna, gaimhne / gamhna	m	*GAwin*	stirk	Eilean a' G(h)amhna, NC206334, Island of the Stirk
Gearran, gearrain	m	*GYAHran*	gelding, horse, hack, 'garron'	Sròn a' Ghearrain, Blackmount, Glen Orchy, NN217457, Nose-shaped Hill of the Garron.

150

Gaelic	m/f	Pronunciation	Meaning	Example
Gobhar / gabhar, gobhair / goibhre, gobhair / goibhrean	m/f	*GOWer*	goat	Creagan nan Gabhar, Glen Ample, Loch Earnside, NN607198, Rocks (or Little Rock) of the Goats
Làir / làire, làireadh / làrach / làiridhean	f	*LAAihr*	mare	Allt Làire, Glen Spean, NN324767, Mare Stream
Laogh, laoigh, laoigh / laoghan	m	*loeugh*	calf	Cnapan nan Laogh, Atholl, NN955850, Little Lumpy Hill of the Calves
Leth-chù	m	*LEH-choo*	Lurcher (literally: half dog)	Bac an Leth-choin, Gairloch, NG777882, Hollow of the Lurcher
Madadh, madaidh, madaidh / madaidhean	m	*MAHTugh*	dog, mastiff	Lùban Fèith a' Mhadaidh, Rannoch, NN517532, Bends of the Dog's Bog Stream (**Plate 23**)
Meann, minn, minn	m	*myown*	kid	Gleann nam Meann, Trossachs NN524130, Glen of the Kids
Muc, muice, mucan	f	*moochk*	pig, sow	Sgiath nam Mucan Dubha, Trossachs NN498074, Wing-shaped Hill of the Little Black Pigs
Searrach, searraich, searraich	m	*SHEHruch*	foal, colt, filly	Bealach nan Searrach, Strathyre, NN597128, Pass of the Foals
Sprèidh, sprèidhe	f	*spray*	cattle, livestock	Tìr na(n) Sprèidh, Ross of Mull, NM403197, Land of the Cattle
Tarbh, tairbh, tairbh	m	*TAHrav*	bull	Stiol nan Tarbh, Glen Artney, NN633159, String of Bulls
Tunnag, tunnaig, tunnagan	f	*TOOnak*	duck	Loch Tunnaig, Loch Aweside, NS915015, Duck Loch
Uan, uain, uain	m	*OOahn*	lamb	Lochan nan Uan, Loch Tayside NN648427, Little Loch of the Lambs

9: CLIMATE, SEASON, SOUND AND TIME

A few years before the Battle of Culloden, in which he played a part on the rebel side, Alasdair Mac Mhaighstir Alasdair (Alexander MacDonald) wrote a long song to summer (*Òran an t-Samhraidh*). The classical reference in the lines below shows that he was not the kind of untutored Gael depicted in 17th century Scottish Government edicts. Indeed, he was a teacher in an SPCK school.

> 'S moch bhios Phèbus ag òradh
> *Phoebus early turns yellow*
> Ceap nam mòr-chruach 's nam beann,
> *the cap of mountain and peak,*
>
> (extract from Thomson, 1993, 23)

A little later, he penned a matching Song to Winter (*Òran a' Gheamhraidh*).

> Theid a' ghrian air a thuras mun cuairt
> Do thropaic Chapricorn ghruamaich gun stad,
>
> *The sun proceeds on its course*
> *to grim Capricorn's tropic, in haste,*
>
> (in Thomson, 1993, 29)

The full gamut of the wet, cloudy, cold and windy Gàidhealtachd climate, sometimes with an abundance of snow, is also expressed in place-names. In recognition of the rapidly changing weather of the Highlands, bright and sunny places are also recorded. Sometimes these have been anglicised. Across the Firth of Clyde for example, Greenock comes from *Grianaig* - a sunny knoll. In Glen Etive there is another hillock called *An Grianan* (NN192506), which has the same meaning. This hill may be a reference to *Taigh Grianach*, the house of Deirdre of the Sorrows, who, with the sons of Uisneach, sought refuge there from the unwanted suit of the King of Ulster. Further down Loch Etive is *Eilean Uisneachan* (NN053368), where there are remains of a structure in which Deirdre and her companions may also have dwelt.

Although many glens do not now hear the human voice, many places remain recorded in a Gaelic soundscape, usually connected with water. *Uamh an Tartair* (NC276206) in Assynt has been carved from Ordovician Durness limestone by a tributary burn of the River Traligill. Perhaps the clamour the water makes as it tumbles into the cavern below prompted the Norse name, Troll Ravine. Trallval, Troll Mountain on the Isle of Rum (NB377952), is thought to be named after the cries of Manx Shearwaters who fly into their nest burrows on the summit during the night.

The bellowing of stags during the rut in October, *An Damhair* – thought to derive from *daimh-dhàir* – *the stag rutting*, is recorded by the noun *Bùirich*. So loud is the speech of the Lawers Burn - *Allt Labhair* (NN683397), as it cascades over beds of slate, schist and quartzite, that it has given its name, by a process of back formation, to a large mountain, a village and a parish. *Uisge Labhair* (NN414702) in Lochaber, with the same meaning, flows into the River Ossian *(Abhainn Oisein)* on Rannoch Moor.

Bealach Gliogarsnaich (NN638190), to the South of Loch Earn, means Tinkling Pass. This name may refer to the sound of *Allt a' Bhealaich Gliogarsnaiche* to the south and over the watershed. As the word seems to be onomatopoeic and resonates more with a dry than a wet sound, it may relate to the slipping sounds of the fine screes on the cone of Ben Vorlich to its west as they shift after frost, snowmelt or in the heat of summer. *Gliogadaich*, describing the sound loose change makes in the pocket, is very similar. In its definition of *sgàirneach* - a continuous heap of loose stones covering a hillside, Dwelly's Dictionary notes another dry sound - the sound of such stones falling along a steep and rocky hillside.

More directly there is *Loch Èigheach - Shouting Loch* (NN447573), to the West of Loch Rannoch. The slower rhythm of the seasons is usually connected with transhumance and place-names refer to winter, summer or the Feast of Samhain, which broadly equates to a Harvest Festival and the beginning of the darker part of the year. *Meall na Samhna - Rounded Hill of Hallowtide* (NN492326), north of Glen Dochart, rises adjacent to shielings in *Coire Lobhaidh - The Rotting or Stinking Corrie.*

Table 18: Climate, Season, Sound and Time

Name	Gender	Sound	Meaning	Example
Àileach	adj	*AAHLyuch*	airy, windy, breezy	Sròn Àileach, Glen Artney, NN676152, Breezy Nose (**Plate 17**)
Braon, braoin, braonan	m	*broeun*	drizzle, shower	Leacann nam Braonan, Rannoch Moor, NN287566, Slabby Place of the Showers
Braonach	adj	*BROEUnuch*	showery, drizzly, rainy, dewy	A' Bhraonaich, Glen Artney, NN660159, The Drizzly Place
Bùirich, bùiriche, bùirichean	f	*BOOireech*	bellowing	Meall Bhùirich, Blackmount, Bridge of Orchy, NC251503, Rounded Hill of the Bellowing
Ceòthach	adj	*CYAWuch*	cloudy	Coire Ceòthach, Balquidder, NN489141, Cloudy Corrie
Fionnar	adj	*FYOOnar*	cool, fresh	Rubha Fionnar, Crinan, NM794963, Cool Point
Fionnarachd	f	*FYOOnarachd*	cool, coolness	Coire na Fionnarachd, Glen Artney, NN696128, Corrie of the Coolness (**Plate 6**)
Fliuch	adj	*flooch*	wet	Àirigh Fhliuch, Glen Lochy, Tyndrum, NN283387, Wet Shieling
Foghar, foghair	m	*FUHvur*	Autumn, harvest time	Leathad a' Bhaile Fhoghair, Assynt, NC053283, Slope of the Autumn Township
Fuaim, fuaime, fuaimean	m/f	*FOOym*	noise, echo	Fuaim Fuaran, Trossachs, NN558096, Noise Spring
Fuar	adj	*FOOuhr*	cold	Fuar-Bheinn, Kingairloch, NM854564, Cold Mountain
Galanach	adj or noun (f)	*GAHlanuch*	noisy, tumultuous	Allt na Gallanaich, St Fillans, NN688237, Stream of the Noisy One
Gaoth, gaoithe, gaothan	f	*goeu*	wind	Dùn Dà Ghaoithe, Mull, NM673363, Fort of the Two Winds

Table 18 (cont.)

Name	Gender	Sound	Meaning	Example
Gaothach	adj	GOEUuch	windy	Meall Gaothach, Trossachs, NN458136, Rounded Windy Hill
Geamhradh, geamhraidh, geamhraidhean	m	GYOWrugh	winter	Baile Geamhradh, Mull, NM632429, Winter Township
Grianan, grianain	m	GREEuhman	sunny spot or eminence, sunny place where peats are dried	Grianan Beag, Glen Tilt, NN925745, Little Sunny Place
Gliogarsnaich	adj	GLEE-gursneech	tinkling	Bealach Gliogarsnaich, Loch Earnside, NN638190, Tinkling Pass
Labhar	adj	LAVuhr	loud (common in stream names)	Uisge Labhair, Lochaber, NN447713, Loud Water
Oidhche, oidhche, oidhcheannan	f	OYchuh	night, evening, darkness	Loch Airigh na h-Aon Oidhche, South Uist, NF796257, Loch of the One Night Shieling
Samhradh, samhraidh, samhraidhean	m	SOWrugh	summer	Mullach an t-Samhraidh, Strathyre, NN523159, Summer Summit
Samhain, samhna	f	SAHvin	the feast of All Souls, Hallowtide	Meall na Samhna, Glen Dochart, NN492326, Rounded Hill of Hallowtide
Sèid, sèide, sèidean	f	shaytch	blowing of the wind	Meall na Sèide, Glen Turret, NN779286, Rounded Hill of the Blowing

156

Sileadh, silidh, silidhean	m	*SHEElugh*	the act of raining, dropping or dripping	Creag Dhubh an t-Silidh, Glen Turret NN773307, Black Rock of the Dripping
Sior	adj	*SHEEur*	continual, long, perpetual	Carraig an t-Sior Shruith, Mull, NM697287, Fishing Rock of the Continual Current
Sneachd(a), sneachda	m	*shnyechk*	snow	Bealach an t-Sneachda, Balquidder, NN495226, Pass of the Snow
Soilleir	adj	*SAWLyehr*	light, shining, clear	Creagan Soilleir, Loch Snizort, Skye, NG375535, Little Shining Rock
Tartar, tartair, tartaran	m	*TAHRstur*	noise, swelling sound, clamour, noise of trampling	Uamh an Tartair, Assynt NC276206, Cave of the Clamour
Tiormachd	adj	*CHEEru-machd*	dryness, drought	Lochan Tior(a)machd NC762648, Bettyhill, Little Drought Loch

10: THE CULTURAL LANDSCAPE

10.1: Buildings, Settlements and Structures

Baile is the default Gaelic word for a settlement, but it also applies at the scale of the Scots fermtoun. It has been commonly anglicised to *bal, ball, balle, bali, balli* or *bally*. It is the most comprehensively distributed toponymic marker for where Gaelic is, or was, spoken throughout the whole of Scotland. *Baile* prevails more in the eastern Highlands, Easter Ross and north-east of the Great Glen than in the western Highlands. Since the name implies permanent settlement, its use was favoured on good agricultural land, which is more widespread in the east.

At the scale of the individual building, apart from some dramatic coastal sites of medieval castles and duns, the influence of architecture or other structures on the Highland landscape cannot be said to be of any great visual significance at the time of Ordnance Survey mapping. The houses, barns, mills, shieling huts and agricultural buildings used by most people were made of materials which came from the landscape and which were easily reclaimed by it. The meaning of *clachan* is related to, *clachan* meaning stones, but there is a subtle difference in their pronunciation. Meaning village the last syllable is voiced as *–an*, meaning stones, it is *–un*. Two Gaelic words for ruin and site, *tobhta* and *làrach*, are perhaps indicative of the ephemeral nature of settlement in the Highlands. Even an external structure such as a bridge, *drochaid*, is rare in place-names in comparison to what preceded it, the ford, or *àth*. Some words like *cabhsair* and *staidhrichean*, meaning pavement and stairs should not be taken too literally. The first is on the side of a remote unnamed hill in Strathdearn and the second is 950m high on the south ridge of *Stob Innein*

- Anvil Stump (mapped as Stob Binnein) in the Braes of Balquidder. These places are not actually pavements or staircases, but merely resemble them.

The word for a house, *taigh* or *tigh*, has generated many place-names across the Highlands. It is anglicised to *ty, ti* or *tay*. A geographically significant example is *Taigh an Droma* or Tyndrum, the House of the Ridge, at NN327305. The settlement lies close to the watershed between the Tay catchment and Lorne and was once the boundary between the Scots and Pictland or *Bràghaid Albann*, Breadalbane - the Ridge of Scotland. Watson argues that Angus, son of King Fergus, defeated the Picts under Nechtan, to the West of Tyndrum, near *Lochan na Bì - Lochan of the Pitch Pine* (NN308312). In support of this story, he cites *Sròn nan Colann - the Nose of the Bodies or Carcases* (NN314304), rising above the loch to the South.

Bothies are common in remote Highland places. They may once have been the sites of old shieling huts, which have been taken over by shepherds and built upon more substantially. Now they provide welcome shelter to climbers and walkers. The Gaelic word is *bothan*, where the *th* is pronounced as *h*, serving merely to separate the two syllables with a puff of breath.

Ceàrdach, (Plate 16), meaning smithy is very common throughout the Gàidhealtachd and testifies to the great demand for horse and cow shoes, cow and goat fetters (*Tom na(n) Spearraichean*, Inveroran, NN267417), pots (*Lag nam Poiteachan*, Strathyre, NN563185), ploughshares and of course weaponry, before the Disarming Acts of 1747. Smithies are sometimes close to 'bloomery mounds,' where waste slag from the smelting of bog iron was dumped.

10.2: Church and Chapel

In contrast to the distribution of *baile, cill,* which is cognate with the Latin *cella*, and means cell or church, occurs primarily in the south-west Highlands. It gives us the anglicised prefix *Kil* or *Cil*, which together with *sliabh* and *carraig* is one of the oldest Gaelic place-name generics. Like them, as a naming element, it quickly went out of fashion as the Gaelic-speaking settlement of Scotland expanded east and north over almost the entire country. *Cil* is frequently associated with the personal names of Saints. Nicolaisen notes that

Table 19: Buildings, Settlements and Structures

Name	Gender	Sound	Meaning	Example
Baile, bailtean	m	*BAHluh*	farm, hamlet, homestead, township	Baile Mòr, Iona, NM285243, The Big Township
Barpa, barpannan	m	*BAHRpuh*	chambered cairn	Dùn (a') Bharpa, Barra, NF672018, Chambered Cairn Fort
Bàthaich, bàthaich / bàthcha, bathaichean	m/f	*BAAeech*	byre, cowshed	Allt a' Bhàthaich, Cowal, NS023810, Stream of the Byre
Both, botha, bothan	m	*bawh*	cottage, hut, bothie	Bothan Gleann Ghòithean, St Fillans, NN681204, Couch Grass Glen Hut
Bùth / bùtha, bùthan / bùithtean	m	*boo*	booth, hut, cottage	Cnoc a' Bhùithean, Scourie, NC159442, Knowe of the Little Shop
Cabhsair, cabhsair, cabhsairean	m	*COWshehr*	causeway, pavement, paved path	An Cabhsair, Strathdearn, NH755165, The Paved Path
Caisteal, caisteil, caistealan	m	*CAHshtyal*	stone wall, stone fort, castle or castle-like landform	Port an t-Sean(n) Chaisteal, Sound of Kerrera, NM823258, Port of the Old Castle
Cathair, cathrach, cathraichean	m	*CAHer*	seat, bench, fortified place	Cathair Mhic Dhiarmaid, Ardnamurchan, NM513694, MacDiarmid's Seat
Ceàrdach, ceàrdaich, ceàrdaichean	f	*CYARduch*	smithy, forge	Sròn na Ceàrdaich, Ardtalnaig, NN704380, Nose of the Smithy (**Plate 16**)
Clachan, clachain	m	*CLAHchan*	village	Sròn a' Chlachain, Killin, NN563331, Nose of the Village
Drochaid, drochaide, drochaidean	f	*DRAWchetch*	bridge	Gleann Àird na Drochaide, Mull, NM735310, Glen of the Height of the Bridge

160

Gaelic	Gender	Pronunciation	Meaning	Example
Dùn, dùin, dùn	m	*doon*	fortress, castle, fortress-like heap	Dùn an (na) Garbh Shròine, Lorne NM802090, Fort of the Rough Nose-shaped Hill
Eileach, eilich, eili-chean	m	*EHluch*	stony place, mill dam or lade, weir, mound, islet, bank of stones to guide fish into a bag net	Eileach Mhic 'Ille Riabhaich, Gruinard, NG933835, Stoney Place of the Son of the Brindled Boy
Fasgadh, fasgaidh, fàsgadhean	m	*FASkagh*	shelter, refuge, fold for cattle	Port an Fhasgaidh, Staffa, NM324355, Port of the Shelter
Geata, geataichean, geatachan	m	*GEHtah*	gate	Creag a' Gheata, Strathyre, NN584148, Rock of the Gate
Làrach, làraich, làirichean	f	*LAAruch*	site of a building, ruin	Bealach Beag Laraich, Glen Artney, NN642156, Little Pass of a Ruin
Puball, pubaill, pubaillean	m	*POOpul*	tent	Meall (a') Phuball, Upper Glenlyon, NN447429, Rounded Hill of a Tent
Ràth	m / f	*raah*	fort, fortress, residence, artificial mound or barrow	Loch nan Ràth, Loch Etive, NM920354, Loch of the Fortress
Rathad, rathaid / rothaid, ròidean	m	*RAAhut*	road, way, path, track	Rathad an t-Seilich, Trotternish, NG386704, Road of the Willow
Sabhal, sabhail sabhalan	m	*SOWul*	barn, granary	Eilean an t-Sabhail, Shieldaig, NG802733, Island of the Barn
Saidh, saidhe, said-hean	f	*sye*	upright beam or post, prow of ship	Sgeir nan Saidhean, Firth of Lorne, NM703116, Skerry of the Beams
Sràid, sràide, sràidean	f	*SRAAhtch*	road, street, lane	Sràid Stac na Mòine, The Oa, Islay, NR28847s, Street of the Stack of Peat (natural dyke)

Table 19 (cont.)

Name	Gender	Sound	Meaning	Example
Staidhir, staidhreach, staidhrichean	f	*STYuhr*	stair, steps	Na Staidhrichean, Balquidder, NN438215, the Stairs
Taigh / tigh, taighe / tighe, taighean / tighean	m	*toy*	house	Port T(a)igh an Àirigh, Lunga, Sound of Luing, NM713087, Port of the Shieling House
Teine, teine teintean	m	*TCHEHnyuh*	fire, beacon	Allt Dail Teine, Strathy, Sutherland, NC823634, Stream of the Fire Meadow
Tobar, tobair / to-brach, tobraichean	m / f	*TOAHpur*	well, spring, fountain	Allt Tobar Sneachda, South Loch Earnside, NN653199, Snow Well Stream
Tobhta, tobhtaichean	m	*TOHtuh*	walls of house, ruin with walls standing	Tobhta nan Druid(head), Trotternish, NG520588, Ruin of the Starlings.

there are fifteen known place-name instances of *Brenainn*, fifteen of *Bride*, sixteen of *Faolan*, thirty of *Cronan* and 208 of *Colman*. Such large numbers and the known lifespans of the individuals concerned suggest that Saints were not necessarily directly connected with the founding of each church, but may instead just have been commemorated in their establishment. As a member of a collective, a saint is remembered at *Àird an Naoimh* (NR293749) in northern Islay.

Annaid is the Old Irish term for early or mother church. The word is well distributed throughout the Highlands and sometimes occurs in remote and obscure places, and so this original meaning may not hold true in Scotiish Gaelic. There is little sign of the *annaid*, tucked behind Beinn Dòbhrain apart from an old burial ground, which gives its name to the honey tasting stream of *Allt na h-Annaid* (NN343385). As mentioned in the section on hydronymy, this burn appears in Duncan Ban MacIntyre's poem in praise of the mountain.

Suidhe, literally seat, is included in the table on hill name generics. It is widely distributed and usually linked to a saint's name. *Saint Blane's Seat - Suidhe Bhlà(tha)in* (NS096527) and *Saint Cattan's Seat - Suidhe Chatain* (NS097547) are two kilometres apart on the Isle of Bute, near Kilchattan. Both provide expansive vantage points for contemplating the green pastures of Ayrshire to the east and the contrasting serrated profile of Arran to the west.

Tobar Loch Shianta - the well of the enchanted, holy or magical loch (Loch Sheanta NG472698), near Staffin in Skye - is qualified by a general word for religious association. The same word applies to the Shiant Islands (NG418978) and two mountains in Ardnamurchan and Jura, Ben Hiant (NM537633) and Beinn Shiantaidh (NR513747). On the Shiants, *Eilean Mhuire* has the ruined chapel of St Mary at NR432986 and *Àirighean na h-Annaid* is on *Garbh-Eilean* at NG412984. To the south-west of Ben Hiant lies *Cladh Chiara(i)n - Ciaran's cemetery* (NM561618) with a cross slab and a little to the east is St Columba's well. To the south of the well, there is another ancient burial ground on *Rubha Àird Shlignich* (NM563610). In contrast, there are no mapped Christian sites near Beinn Shiantaidh on Jura. It is said that the summit of the mountain was used for observing the winter solstice. *Sianta* can also therefore apply to pre-Christian beliefs which have persisted as superstitions like those observed by Martin Martin at *Tobar Loch Shianta* (see hydronomy section). Of course, churches and chapels were often built close to, or even upon pre-Christian sites. There is a chambered cairn next to the cemetery of *Cladh Chiara(i)n* on Ardnamurchan.

Coffin routes often led to cemeteries from places so remote that they had no church. *Làirig nan Lunn - Pass of the Bier Poles* (NN450387), running between Glen Lyon, through Glen Lochay to the graveyard at Killin is an example. *Àth nam Marbh - Ford of the Dead* (NR506647) in south-east Jura may have formed part of such a route or it may refer to pre-Christian beliefs about passage to the underworld.

10.3: Culture - artefacts

Many references to artefacts concern processes associated with the growing, transporting and processing of crops for subsistence. We have vessels for milking, churning, mashing and kneading. *Losaid* is a kneading trough and commonly anglicised to lossit. Ian Fraser believes the word is applied to the most fertile part of a land holding. When exploring shieling sites, once a source of fresh water has been found, it is worth trying to find the large flat topped stone on which a churn would have been placed, *Leac na Muidhe*, whilst butter was being churned. After the Massacre of Glencoe, some of the survivors made their way through to Appin through *Gleann Leac na Muidhe* (NN114553), where MacIain, their chief had his summer shieling.

Brà or *bràdh*, meaning quern or handmill, can be a useful word for reading the landscape, since the location of the word can tell us something more about its context. *Alltan na Bràdhan*, near *Clach Toll*, Assynt, powered a horizontal mill whose ruins can still be seen and was abandoned as late as the early twentieth century. Further east in Assynt, lies another Stream of the Querns, *Allt na Bràdhan* (NC2272887). This watercourse flows parallel to *Druim na (h-)Uamha Mòire - Ridge of the Big Cave*, which defines a band of quartzite running parallel to the Moine Thrust fault. Did this rock provide hard stone suitable for the querns? Below the Quiraing ridge in Trotternish on Skye there is *Loch Leum nam Bràdh - Loch of the Jump of the Querns* (NG459701), so named, because Lord

Table 20: Culture - Church and Chapel

Name	Gender	Sound	Meaning	Example
Annaid, annaid(e)	f	*ANNetch*	early or mother church	Tòrr na h-Annaid, Ross of Mull, NM365220, Tower of the Mother Church
Caibeal, caibeil, caibealan	m	*CEHpuhl*	chapel	Port a' Chaibeil, Scarba, NM720057, Port of the Chapel
Cill, cille, cillean / cilltean	f	*keel*	church, chapel, burial place	Eilean na Cille, Crinan, NR752970, Island of the Chapel
Ciste	f	*CEEshtuh*	coffin, chest	Bealach na Ciste, Harris, NB158051, Pass of the Coffin
Cladh, claidh / cladha, cladhan	m	*clugh*	burial place	Cladh nan Sassunach, Ardeonaig, NN683358, Cemetery of the Englishmen
Crois, croise, croisean	f	*crawsh*	cross	Port na Croise, Mull, NM426264, Port of the Cross
Eaglais, eaglaise, eaglaisean	f	*EHKleesh*	church	Rubha na h-Eaglaise, Morvern, NM599584, Point of the Church
Rèilig, rèilige, rèiligean	f	*REHlik*	grave, burying place, church	Fèith Rèilig, Loch Hope, Sutherland, NC503592, Marsh Grave
Teampall, teampaill, teampaill	m	*TEHMpull*	church, temple	Sgeir an Teampuill, Lismore, NM795390, Skerry of the Church

MacDonald used to roll the confiscated hand querns of his tenants into the loch to compel them to use only his mill. In Lochaber, there is *Lochan Lunn Dà Bhrà - Little Loch of Two Querns* (NN087660). Just as coffins were borne across *Làirig nan Lunn* between Glen Lyon and Glen Lochay, were poles used in the same way for carrying quern stones from the quarry to the mill?

References should not be taken too literally. *Plaide Mhòr - Big Blanket* (NR349922) in Colonsay describes the ribbed or knitted texture of a rocky foreshore, where different rock types have eroded at different rates. Similarly, *Cìr Mhòr - Big Comb* on Arran (Plate 7) is not literally a comb, but a serrated ridge with a comb-like, toothed appearance. This is quite different to the usage of the Scots *kaim* in place-names. Here the attribute is to do with a curving length, like an old horn comb. The word is applied to long meandering drumlins, like that found at Kaimend, near Carnwath in Lanarkshire.

10.4: People and Occupations

Contrary to some past perceptions, made by outsiders, of the Highlands as irredeemably barbaric and lawless, the place-name evidence presents a diverse and structured society with several references to the law and its enforcement. Evidence of a subsistence society perpetually destitute is not supported by the characters connected with the governance and administration of justice. There are, of course, also some places named after thieves or where they hid. *Cnoc a' Mhèirlich – Hillock of the Thief* (cover plate) in Trotternish, Skye, must have made an ideal lair, whence to prey upon travellers journeying on the steep, winding and misty pass that crosses the peninsula. If thieves were caught they would be hanged on one of the many Hangman's or Hanging Hillocks: *Cnoc a' Chrochaire* or *Tom na Croiche*. These are usually near a castle or grand house whence such baronial justice would be administered.

At Loch Finlaggan at the heart of the Lordship of the Isles there is a Council Island, *Eilean na Comhairle* (NR387680). The Council advised the Lord of the Isles and made laws and legal decisions. In Loch Leven, Glen Coe, property disputes were discussed on the Island of Conversation - *Eilean a' Chòmhraidh* (NN087594). If resolution were achieved, then all parties rowed to the Island of

Table 21: Culture – artefacts

Name	Gender	Sound	Meaning	Example
Airgead, airgid	m	*EHRegut*	silver, money, riches	Sidhean an Airgid, Parks, Lewis, NB254135, Fairy Hill of the Money
Bachall, bachaill, bachallan	m	*BAchul*	crozier, staff, shepherd's crook	Bachuil. Lismore, NM863437, Crozier
Balg, builg, builg	m	*BAlak*	leather bag, wallet	Creag Bhalg, Glen Lednock, NN775249, Bag Rock Topgraphically, Balg can also mean a bulge or bag-like protrusion.
Bàta, bàtaichean	m	*BAAHtuh*	boat	Geò (à) Bhàta, Benbecula, NF738458, Boat Ravine
Brà / bràdh, bràdhan / brathan, bràdhntan / bràthntan	f	*braah*	quern, handmill	Port Alltan na Bràdhan, Clach Toll, Assynt, NC047263, Port of the Little Stream of the Quern
Bròg, bròige, brògan	f	*brawk*	shoe	Cnoc na Bròige, Assynt, NC113314, Knowe of the Shoe
Cìr	f	*ceer*	Comb, honeycomb, crest of a cock	Cìr Mhòr, Isle of Arran,NR973432, The Big Comb, **(Plate 8)**
Claidheamh, claidheimh, claidhnean	m	*CLAYoo*	sword	Lochan a' Chlaidheimh, Rannoch, NN408603, Little Loch of the Sword
Corran, corrain, corrain	m	*CAWran*	sickle, reaping-hook, sickle-shaped point of land	An Corran, Staffin, Trotternish, NG490687, The Sickle-shaped Point, **(Plate 21)**
Crann, crainn / croinn, crainn / croinn	m	*crown*	Plough, mast, tree	Tòrran nan Cram, Loch Leven, Lochaber, NN150605, Little Tower of the Masts
Croich, croiche, croichean	f	*CROYch*	Gallows, gibbet	Tom na Croiche, Blair Atholl, NN873667, Hillock of the Gallows
Crudh / crudha, cruidhe, cruidhean	m	*croo*	horseshoe	Crudh an Eich, Loch Shiel, NM746681, The Horseshoe

Table 21 (cont.)

Name	Gender	Sound	Meaning	Example
Cuinneag, cuinneige, cuinneagan	f	*COONyak*	small pail, milking pail, churn	A' Chuinneag, Assynt, NC163263 The Milking Pail (**Plates 2 and 26**)
Curach, curaich, curaichean	f	*COOruch*	Coracle, skin covered boat	Port na Curaich, Iona, NM263216, Port of the Coracle
Dabhach, dabhaich, dabhcha / dabhaichean	f	*DAHvuch*	Vat, large tub, mash tun, land divison	Cnoc Dabhaich, Lochinver, Assynt, NC080233, Vat Hillock
Diollaid, diollaide, diollaidean	f	*JEEoleetch*	saddle	Rubha na Diollaide, Ulva, NM383390, Point of the Saddle
Èileag, èilige, èileagan	f	*EHLyag*	deer trap, V-shaped structure wide at one end narrower at the other into which deer were driven and shot with arrows as they came out	Allt Eileag, Assynt, NC294064, Deer Trap Stream
Innean, innein, inneanan	m	*EENyan*	smith's anvil, anvil-shaped hill	Meall Innein, Glen Artney, NN693191, Anvil Hill
Leaba / leabaidh, leapa, leapannan	f	*LEHpuh*	bed, lair, channel of river	Leaba Dhonnacha Dhuibh a' Mhonaidh, Rannoch, NN487553, The Bed of Black Duncan of the Moor
Lìon, lìn, liontan	m	*LEEuhn*	net	Loch nan Lion, Assynt NO097274, Loch of the Nets
Long, luinge, longan	f	*lowng*	ship	Port Luinge Mhic Dhùghaill, Loch Etive, NN038344, Ship Port of MacDougal
Losaid, losaide, losaidean	m/f	*LAWsitch*	Kneading-trough	Rubh' an Losaid, Leverburgh, Harris, NF009866, Point of the Kneading Trough.

Gaelic forms	m/f	Pronunciation	Meaning	Example
Muidhe, muidhean, muidheachan	m	*MOOyuh*	churn	Allt na Muidhe, Glencoe, NN107548, Stream of the Churn
Òrd, ùird, òrdan / ùird	m	*awrsht*	hammer	Beinn nan Òrd, Ardnamurchan, NM444647, Mountain of Hammers
Plaide, plaidean	f	*PLAHtchuh*	blanket	Ruigh nam Plaidean, Glen Tromie, NN780894, Shieling of the Blankets
Poit, poite, poiteachan	f	*pohtch*	pot	Lag nam Poiteachan, Strathyre, NN563185, Hollow of the Pots
Ràmh, ràimh, ràimh	m	*raahv*	oar	Bidein Druim nan Ràmh, Cuillins, Skye, NG457239, Pointed Peak of the Ridge of Oars.
Sac / saic, saic, sacan	m	*sachk*	sack, bag, burden, load, horse-load	Druim nan Sac, Strath Canaird, NC185014, Ridge of the Sacks
Saighead, saighde, saighdean	f	*SYut*	arrow, dart, stitch	Coire nan Saighead, Braeleny, NN606157, Corrie of Arrows
Sgian, sgeine / sgine, sgeinean / sgineachan	f	*SKEEun*	knife	Sgurr na Sgine, Glen Shiel, NG946113, Pointed Peak of the Knife.
Snaoisean, snaoisein	m	*SNOEUshen*	snuff, powder	Tom an t-Snaoisein, Bridge of Orchy, NN297411, Hillock of the Snuff
Snàthad, snàthaid, snàthadan	f	*SNAAhat*	needle, earmark on sheep	Loch Shnàthaid, South Uist, NF827426, Needle Loch. This loch is not needle-shaped, so if the name is correct, it may apply to some other attribute.
Spearrach, spearraich, spearraichean	f	*SPEHruch*	cow, sheep or goat fetter	Tom na(n) Spearraichean, Inveroran, NN267417, Hillock of the Cow Fetters
Ulaidh, ulaidhe, ulaidhean	f	*OOlye*	treasure	Tom na h-Ulaidhe, Strathyre, NN588116, Hillock of the Treasure.

*Plate 11: Suilven – Ùidh Fheàrna, Caisteal Liath, Meall
Meadhonach and Meall Beag (Ùidh Fheàrna is to the left of
centre below the dome of Suilven) (also in colour section)*

Fairness, *Eilean na Bàine* (NN159619), near Kinlochleven, where
matters were documented and ratified. Elsewhere similar functions
were exercised at *Clach a' Mhòid - Stone of the Court or Meeting.*
These are usually found by castles, whose lairds administered justice
in what was a feudal society. This is the same word as the modern
Gaelic Mòd, though justice at these events is confined to the award
of medals for singing, reciting and dancing.

The evidence portrays a society which, though it included many
a herdsman, *buachaille* (Plate 3), also had sufficient surplus resources
to support the arts, poetry and music. References to bards, pipers,
fiddlers and clarsach players are common in place-names. This was
a society where people could also enjoy the products of specialised
artisans, such as tailors, smiths and weavers. Mention of saints, priests,
bishops and monks must be pre-Reformation, whilst names referring
to ministers must of course be post-Reformation, dating from from
the end of the sixteenth century or later. Since the Reformation
discouraged music and dancing, it is likely that references to these
pleasures can be dated earlier than the mid-sixteenth century.

More generic characters are remembered by the many references
to old men and old women. There are nine instances alone of hills

Plate 31: Amulree – Cnoc an Dannsaidh is in the right middle ground

called *Am Bodach* and fifteen called *A' Chailleach*. Sometimes these words can be paired across an intervening valley, like hillocks named after king and queen. *Cailleach* can also refer to a witch or hag, and reference has already been made to the witch's step on Arran, *Ceum na Caillich* (NR974443). On the west coast of Jura, there is a rock scar which runs north-west to south-east for about 2.5k, from 33m to 420m above sea level up the slopes of *Beinn an Òir*. It is called *Sgrìob na Caillich* and has the names *Loch na Sgrìoba* (NR464772) and *Cnoc na Sgrìoba* (NN482759) associated with it. The Old Woman's scrape or scratch is said to have been made by the Goddess of Thunder, *Beithir,* as she flew past the island. There is also a *Beinn a' Bheithir* near Ballachulish at NN045554.

Perhaps the most famous Old Man is that close to the Storr on Trotternish , on Skye (Plate 32), although this may be a respectable form of *Bod an Stòrr,* the Penis of Storr, (NG503538). 'Old man' is north English slang for the same thing. In making their lighting installation on the Storr, the art company nva mapped more names amongst these dramatic landslips. There is another anthromorph, *Creag na Lùdaig - Rock of the Little Finger* or Pinkie in Scots, and two zoomorphs, *Ite Bheag* and *Ite Mhòr - Little and Large Fins,* so close together, it is as if the the latter spawned the former. Interestingly, the ring or fourth finger in Gaelic is *màthair na lùdaig.*

The idea of progenitor and offspring can also be seen at *Mac is Màthair - Son and Mother* (NH068868) near Dundonnell in Wester Ross. The hill has a very small summit arising from a much larger mass beneath. In a more abstract sense *Mac an Talla* or *Mac-Talla,*

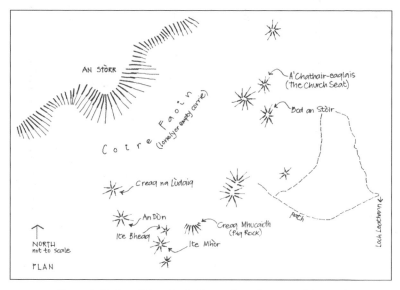

Figure 9: Bod an Stòir - Rock Names (not shown on OS maps)

literally son of the rock, means echo in Gaelic. Similarly, to the west of Glen Ogle in Perthshire we can also find *Creag Mac Rànaich - Rock of the Roaring, Shrieking or Bellowing Son* (NN546255). Mother can also mean source and *Lochan Màthair Èite* on Rannoch Moor at NN288544 is the source of the River Etive. There appears to be no use of the word for father, *athair*, in Gaelic place-naming.

*Plate 32: Bod an Stòir - A' Chathair-eaglais is
the low pinnacle to the right of Bod an Stòir*

Table 22: Culture - People and Occupations

Name	Gender	Sound	Meaning	Example
Amadan, amadain	m	*AHmuhtan*	fool, simpleton	Sgeirean an Amadain, Loch Maree, NG946705, Sker-ries of the Fool
Baintighearna	f	*BEHNtyuhrnuh*	lady, ladyship, proprietor's lady	Ceann na Baintighearna, Balquidder, NN474177, The Lady's Headland
Banrigh, banrighe, banrighean	f	*BAAHnree / BONree*	queen	Sròn na Banrigh, Glenfeshie, NN877883, The Queen's Nose
Bàrd, bàird, bàird	m	*BAAHrsht*	bard, poet, rhymer	Àirigh a' Bhàird, Reay Forest, NC285456, The Poet's Shieling
Bean, mnà, mnathan	f	*ben*	woman, female, wife	Lochan na Mnà, South Loch Earnside, NN647208, Little Loch of the Woman
Bodach, bodaich, bodaich	m	*BAWtuch*	old or churlish man, rustic, countryman	Am Bodach, Strathbraan, NN876342, The Old Man
Bràthair, bràthar, bràithrean	m	*BRAAHer*	brother	Rubha nam Bràth(ai)rean, Trotternish, Skye NG528629, Point of the Brothers
Breabadair	m	*BREHputehr*	weaver	Coire Riabhach a' Bhreabadair, Glenfeshie, NN837865, Brindled Corrie of the Weaver
Buachaille, buachaille, buachaillean	m	*BOOuchylyuh*	cowherd, shepherd, youth	Tom a' Bhuachaille, Ardeonaig, NN654332, Hillock of the Shepherd, (**Plate 3**)
Cailleach, cailliche, cailleachan	f	*CAHLyuch*	old woman or witch	Ceum na Caillich(e), Isle of Arran, NR974444, The Witch's Step (**Plate 8**)

173

Table 22 (cont.)

Name	Gender	Sound	Meaning	Example
Ceàrd, ceàird, ceàr-dan	f	*cyaard*	smith, craftsman,	Creag nan Ceàrd, Atholl, NN893656, Rock of the Smiths or Tinkers
Clàrsair, clarsair, clàrsairean	m	*CLAAHRsehr*	harper, minstrel	Uchd a' Chlàrsair, Atholl, NN813818, The Breast-shaped Hill of the Harper
Clèireach, clèirich, clèirich	m	*CLEHruch*	cleric, clergyman	Sròn a' Chlèirich, Atholl, NN7784768, The Nose of the Cleric.
Crochaire, crochairean	m	*CRAWchehruh*	villain, rogue, hangman, one who has been hanged	Cnoc a' Chrochaire, Kinlochewe, NH026624, The Hangman's Knowe.
Crùbach, crùbaich	m	*CROOpuch*	lame person	Cnoc a' Chrùbaich Bhig, Strath Ullie, Sutherland, NC865179, Hillock of the Small Lame Person
Duine, duine, daoine	m	*DUNyuh*	man, person, body; people	Dùn 'n Aon Duine, St Fillans, NN675233, The Fort of the One Man, **(Plate 10)**
Easbaig, easbaigean	m	*EHSpik*	bishop	Achadh an Easbuig, Kilmahog, NN598092, The Bishop's Field
Fàidh, fàidhe, fàidhean	m	*FAAee*	prophet, seer, soothsayer	Coire an Fhàidhe, Glen Artney, NN653148, The Cor-rie of the Seer
Fear, fir, fir	m	*fehr*	man, husband, male	Tom a' Mhòr-fhir, Rannoch, NN708533, The Hillock of the Big Man
Feòladair, feòladairean	m	*FYAWludehr*	butcher, flesher	Clach an Fheòladair, Arran, NR907278, The Butcher's Stone

Gaelic	Gender	Pronunciation	Meaning	Examples
Fidhlear, fidhleir, fidhlearan	m	*FEElehr*	fiddler	Càrn an Fhidhleir, Lorgaidh, Glenfeshie, NN856876, The Fiddler's Cairn
Figheadair, fighead-airean	m	*FEEuhtehr*	weaver, knitter	Tom an Fhigheadair, Inveroran, NN259415, The Weaver's Hillock
Forsair, forsairean	m	*FAWRsehr*	forester, one who watches a deer forest	Stùc an Fhorsair, Glen Artney, NN668197, The Jutting Hill of the Forester (**Plate 18**)
Gall, goill	m	*gowl*	foreigner, stranger	Rubha nan Gall, Tobermory, NM507571, Point of the Strangers
Gille, gillean	m	*GEELyuh*	boy, lad, youth, servant man	Sgurr nan Gillean, Cuillins, NG473254, Peak of the Boys
Gobha, gobhann / gobhainn, goibhnean	m	*GOWuh*	blacksmith	Eas Gobhainn, Callander, NN612075, Blacksmith Waterfall
Iasgair, iasgairean	m	*EEusgehr*	fisher, fisherman, angler	Creag Iasgair, Balquidder, NN513214, Fisher Rock
Mac, mic	m	*machk*	son	Mac is Màthair, Dundonnell, Wester Ross, NH068868, Son and Mother
Maighdean, maigh-dinn	f	*MYjun*	maid, maiden, maid servant	Cìoch na Maighdean, Ardtalnaig, NN736364, Maiden's Pap (**Plate 34**)
Manach, manaich, manaich	m	*MAHnuch*	monk, friar	Beinn Mhanach, Upper Glenlyon, NN374412, Mountain of Monks (**Plate 15**)
Maor, maoir	m	*moeur*	constable, bailiff, officer of justice, messenger	Coille Baile a' Mhaoir, Glen Ample, NN602212 Wood Town of the Bailiff
Marbh, mairbh	m	*MAHrav*	dead person, the dead	Tom nam Marbh, Strath Avon, NJ136212, Hillock of the Dead

Table 22 (cont.)

Name	Gender	Sound	Meaning	Example
Màthair, màthar, màthrichan	f	*MAAhehr*	mother, cause, source	Lochan Màthair Èite, Rannoch Moor, NN288544, Little Loch of Etive's Source
Mèirleach, mèirlich, mèirlich	m	*MEHRluch*	thief, robber	Cnoc a' Mhèirlich, Trotternish, Skye, NG445684 Thief's Knowe (**Cover plate**)
Ministear, ministeir, ministearan	m	*MEEnishcher*	minister	Leabaidh a' Mhinisteir, Eye, Lewis, NB499294, The Minister's Bed
Morair, morairean	m	*MAWrehr*	lord, earl, nobleman	Meall a' Mhorair, Atholl, NN840633, Rounded Hill of the Lord
Naomh, naoimh	m	*noeuv*	saint	Eileach an Naoimh, Garvellachs, NM643100, Rough Island of the Saint
Nighean, nighinn, nigheanan	f	*NEEuhn*	daughter, maiden, unmarried woman	Cruach nan Nighean, Glen Orchy, NN206318, Heap of the Girls
Pìobaire, pìobaire, pìobairean	m	*PEEpuruh*	piper	Sgiath a' Phìobaire, Glen Vorlich, NN634209, Wing-Shaped Hill of the Piper
Rìgh, rìgh, rìghrean	m	*ree*	king	Tom an Rìgh, Trossachs, NN493128, The King's Hillock
Sagart, sagairt, sagartan	m	*SAHkursht*	priest, churchman	Bealach an t-Sagairt, St Fillans, NN709232, The Priest's Pass (**Plate 7**)
Saighdear, saighdeir, saighdearan	m	*SYjur*	soldier	Meall nan Saighdearan, South Loch Earnside, NN673207, Rounded Hill of the Soldiers

176

Saor, saoir, saoir	m	*soeur*	carpenter, joiner, wright	Lùb an t-Saoir, Glen Gour, Ardgour, NM937644, Bend of the Joiner
Sasannach, Sasannaich	m	*SAHsunnuch*	Englishman	Creag an t-Sasunnaich, Glen Dochart, NN474273, Englishman's Rock
Sealgair, sealgairean	m	*SHEHLgehr*	hunter, fowler, gamekeeper	Tom an t-Sealgair, Strath Avon, NJ137293, Hunter's Hillock
Tàillear, tàilleir, tàillearan	m	*TAAHlehr*	tailor	Maol an Tàilleir, Loch Ard Forest, NS483987, The Bald Hill of the Tailor

10.5: the Gaelic Anatomy

Human anatomy has been thoroughly externalised in the Gaelic landscape. Sometimes walking amongst gigantic, anthropomorphic features is like existing in an out of body experience. This is too literal. For when we say, in English *'Turn left at the brow of the road,'* we are not directly seeing the road as a skull with a forehead. When we climb the shoulder of the hill, we do not see the land in literal human form. Nor do we see the body laid out in plan when we conceive of the head of the loch, or the mouth of the glen. This is true in both English and Gaelic conversation and writing. What could be more natural when trying to understand the landscape through naming than to use the structured vocabulary of something most familiar to us, our body. There are exceptions to such habitual usage in the abstract. *Claigeann Mòr* (NF08690), St Kilda, is a sea cliff which resembles a large skull. In comparison to Gaelic, modern English has lost much of its anthropomorphic toponymy in its mapped record of place-names.

Such a difference between the two languages can make attempts to translate exactly seem rather awkward. The nose-shaped promontory of the rounded hill hardly runs off the tongue. Different words do show different levels of abstraction. Baldness (*maol*) can equally apply to man or land bereft of hair or trees. A nose *(sròn)* can be seen as a smaller projection from the larger form of the head or from a hill. *Sròn Mhòr Mhic Laurainn*, near St Fillans at NN688229, may not literally be a comparison

Plate 7: St Fillans - Dùn Dùirn (Dundurn) - in the middle ground and Bealach an t-Sagairt to the left of Dùn Dùirn amongst the trees (also in colour section)

of landform to MacLaren's Big Nose. Instead it may simply refer to a large promontory on land associated with someone called MacLaren. *Meur,* finger, shows a greater level of abstraction. It can be applied to glens and more commonly watercourses. It is the notion of the palm of the hand branching into fingers which informs its role in place-naming. As has been discussed in the hydronymy section, many water name generics have become so semantically fluid that they have lost their primary meanings.

A word commonly encountered in the Highlands is *achlais,* meaning oxter or armpit. It is applied where a cupped shape typifies both lochs and landforms, or just directly to an oxter spot, or *bad* in Gaelic. *Am Bile - The Lip* (NG504446) in Skye denotes a curved and steepening slope of a basalt formation, which culminates in a plateau dipping to the west, just to the east of Portree. Such layered flows of basalt are known as 'trap' landscapes, after the Scandanavian word for stair or step, '*trappa.*' Coshieville in Glenlyon, Perthshire, a small village, which nestles beneath a brae near the mouth of the glen is a French-sounding corruption of *Cois a' Bhile, Close to the Lip* (NN777493). *Bile* as a word is not confined to trap landscapes. However, the word *sròn,* given its habitual position and form as a steep-sided outlier at the end of a ridge, seems a good equivalent to a spur truncated by glacial flow. *Cnoc, dùn* and *tom* appear to be typical of moraine landscapes. It would be an interesting exercise to relate Gaelic landform terminology more closely to the academic vocabulary of physical geography.

Table 21: the Gaelic Anatomy

Name	Gender	Sound	Meaning	Example
Achlais, achlaise, achlaisean	f	*ACHleesh*	armpit or oxter	Loch na h-Achlaise, Rannoch Moor NN312482, Loch of the Oxter
Aghaidh, aighnean / aghaidhean	f	*UHee*	face, visage, countenance,	Aghaidh an Laoigh, Assynt, NC163098, The Calf's Face
Amhach, amhaiche, amhaichean	f	*AHvuch*	neck	Loch nan Amhaichean, Easter Ross, NH418762, Loch of the Necks
Aodann, aodainn, aodainnean	m	*OEUtown*	face,	Braigh an Aodainn Bhain (Edinbane), Skye, NG354513, The Brae of the White Face
Beul, beòil, beòil	m	*BEEal*	mouth	Camas a' Mhòr-bheòil, Skye, NG530354, Bay of the Big Mouth
Bile, bile, bilean	f	*BEELuh*	lip	Bile B(h)uidhe, Forest of Abernethy, NJ074117, Yellow Lip
Bonn, buinn, buinn / bonnan	m	*bown*	heel/sole	Allt Bhuinne, Glen Lyon, NN633485, Stream of a Heel
Ceann, cinn, cinn	m	*cyown*	head	Tràigh Ceann a' Chaolais, Strath Canaird, NH117995, Head of the Narrows Beach
Cioch, ciche, ciochan	f	*CEEoch*	breast	Cioch na Maighdean (Maighdinn), Ardtalnaig, NN736364, Maiden's Pap (Plate 34)
Claigeann, claiginn.	m	*CLEH-kown*	skull	Claigeann an T(a)igh-Faire, St Kilda, NF083994, Skull of the Watch House
Dòrn, dùirn, dùirn	m	*dawrn*	fist	Allt Dòrnach, Arran, NR994473, Fistlike Burn
Druim, droma, dromannan	m	*DROYeem*	back	Druim Àirigh nan Seileach, Trotternish, Skye, NG475608, Ridge of the Shieling of Willows
Feusag, feusaige, feusagan	f	*FEEusak*	beard	Creag Feusag, Glen Cannich, NH215331, Beard Crag
Fiacail, fiacla, fiaclan	f	*FEEachkil*	tooth	Fiacail Dhubh, Glen Garry NN718713, Black Tooth

Fiaclach	adj	FEEach-kluch	toothed, jagged, pronged, serrated	Sgeir Fhiaclach, Scourie, NC148453, Toothed Skerry
Gob, guib	m	gohp	bill, beak, mouth	Allt Dà Ghob, Glen Lyon, NN695454, Two Beaks Burn
Gualann, gualainn / guailne, guailnean / guaillean	f	GOOuluhn	shoulder	Gualann Sheileach, Glen Garry, Atholl, NN617653, Willow Shoulder
Màm, màim, màman	m/f	mahm	breast	Màm a' Phobuill, Cuillins, NO513260, Breast-shaped hill of the People or of the Tent
Maol, maoil, maoil	m	moeuhl	bald head, hill	Maol an Uillt Mhòir, Applecross, NG754470, The Bald Hill of the Big Stream
Meur, meòir, meòir / meuran	m	MEEar	finger, toe, branch of a river, knot in wood	Meur Luachaireach, Strath Avon, NJ178113, Rushy Finger
Òrdag, òrdaig, òrdagan	f	AWRtak	thumb, great toe (lit: little hammer)	Sgeir nan Òrdag, Lunga, NM703094, Skerry of the Thumbs
Sàil, sàl / sàile / sàlach, sàilean / sàiltean	f	saahl	heel	Sàil Gharbh, Assynt, NO209292, Rough Heel (Plate 2)
Sròn, sròine, srònan	f	strawn	nose	Sròn Mhòr Mhic La(u)rainn, St Fillans, NN688229, MacLaren's Big Nose (Plate 29)
Sùil, sùl / sùla, sùilean	f	SOOeel	eye	Toba(i)r na Sùl, Luing, NM753116, The Well of the Eye. Sùil can also describe the issue of a spring in a barren heather moor.
Teanga, teangaidh, teangan / teangannan	f	CHUNH-guh	tongue	Teanga Mhòr, Sligeachan, Skye NG512288, Big Tongue
Tòn, tòine, tònan / tòinean	f	tawn	fundament, bottom	Tòn Eich, Glen Turret, NN81294, Horse Bottom
Uchd, uchda, uchdan	m	oochk	breast	Uchd a' Bhlàir, Muck, NM423798, Breast-shaped Hill of the Plain.

10.6: Events

This section moves from discussions listing some unmapped memories, recalled in recent times on the very edge of the Gàidhealtachd, to those which record local episodes relating to wider, recorded national history, often associated with the several Jacobite risings or the earlier Wars of Independence.

Many events remembered in Highland place-names refer to violent ocurrences. Between 1965 and 1971, Máirtín Ó Murchú of the Dublin Institute of Advanced Studies interviewed Mary Stewart at her home at Croftmore *(Croit Mhòr)* in Glen Fender *(Gleann Fionndair - White Stream Glen)*, Blair Atholl *(Blàr an Athall)*. She was one of the last native speakers of Gaelic in the Highlands of Eastern Perthshire. Amongst many recorded conversations, several refer to stories connected with place-names. What follows are direct quotes, where the language is slightly different in spelling and grammar to the mainstream Gaelic, which is spoken today.

> *Bha thu ag innseadh dhomh mu dheidhinn Loch nan Ceann,*
> *ciamar a fhuair e an t-ainm a th' air?*
>
> **You were telling me about Loch nan Ceann,**
> **how did it receive the name which it has?**

> *Och, is e sgeul a th' annsein, cuideachd. Bha am fear a bha a'*
> *fuireach ann Leòid Bheag, bha teans gun do mharbh e, no fhuair*
> *e dusan ceann, is chor e ann … as loch uthard air mullach a'*
> *mhonadh annsein iad, is fhuair e an t-ainm Lochan nan Ceann.*
>
> **Och, that is just a story, also, The man who had been living in**
> **Little Lude was … perhaps he killed, or just obtained a dozen**
> **heads, and put them in the lake above on top of the mountain**
> **there, and it got the name Lochan nan Ceann.**
>
> (Ó Murchú 1989, 150).

> *Agus ainm eile a th' ann Gleann Teilt - Pull*
> *an Tè - dè' n sgeul a' dol air sin?*
>
> **And another name which is found in Glen Tilt - Pull an Tè (the**
> **woman's Pool) - what is the story there?**

> *Ó, bha 'n duine aice a' goid crodh a Gleann Fionndair, is chuile*
> *tarruing a bha iad uthard astaigh annsan fhang, bha i gan leigeil*

as; is bha e an comhnaidh cho fiadhaich is cho mosach rithe. Is an
tarruing mu dheireadh a rinne e sein, leig i as iad, agus bha e cho
fiadhaich rithe gun deachaidh i amach agus bhàth i i fhein annsa
… pull, annsan abhainn aig … Gleann Teilt.

Oh, her husband was stealing cattle from Glen Fender, and every
time they were above the pen, she used to let them out; and he was
always so vicious and nasty to her. And the last time he did that,
she let them out, and he was so vicious to her that she went out
and she drowned herself in the pool, in the river at … up Glen Tilt.

(Ó Murchú 1989,151).

Agus bha thu ag innseadh dhomh cuideachd mu dheidhinn na
cuirn air Achadh an Ruidhe, dè 'n sgeul a th' annsein?

And you were telling me about the cairns on Achadh an Ruidhe
(Field of the Shieling) - what was the story about them?

Bha seachd mic aig an tè bh' annan Achadh an Ruidhe is
chaidh iad amach air sealg. Is thubhairt i gun robh i an dòchas
gum biodh na sia Mhic aice sàbhailte air son tighinn air ais.
Is thubhairt banaltrach - thog ise aon leanabh - is thubhairt i
gun robh i an dòchas gum biodh am mac a thog ise sàbhailte
air son tighinn air ais. Bha iad a' pleighe am measg a chèile, is
mharbh iad a chèile, is bha iad uile marbh ach am mac a thog am
banaltrach is … is thog iad … chaidh cairn mór a thogail.

The woman who was in Achadh an Ruidhe had seven sons
and they went out hunting. And she said that she hoped that
her six sons would be safe for (their) return. And a nurse
said - she reared one child - and she said that she hoped
that the son whom she reared would be safe for (his) return.
They were fighting among one another, and they killed one
another, and they were all dead except the son whom the
nurse reared and … they built … a great cairn was built.

(Ó Murchú 1989, 152).

The names Mary Stewart talks about obviously predate her own time in Glen Fender. The violent and lawless acts she spoke about hark back to the period of clan feuds and cattle raiding, and thus before the Disarming Act of 1747. The quotes are included in full, not only because they are in a lost dialect of Gaelic, and not just because they employ the correct Gaelic rendering of Glen Tilt

(Gleann Teilt) and Glen Fender *(Gleann Fionndair)* or because of the sheer reach of her inherited memory. They are also included because Mary Stewart's stories relate to places which are not now recorded on OS 1:25,000 maps. Perhaps those who passed on the names to her were not employed as informants by Ordnance Survey map makers, or, if they were, their knowledge was mistranslated, lost or not used. Given the absence of Gaelic speakers in Atholl, it would now be very hard to find when and where these events actually occurred.

In 1896, Mrs Carnegie of Stronvar collected 231 names from her gamekeeper, Duncan Lamont, and other old people in the parish of Balquidder. Of these, 131 are not shown on OS maps. Charles Maclean has collected over 750 unmapped names from informants on the Island of Mull alone. Given these two sets of figures from different areas and established 100 years apart, the quantity of unrecorded and probably now irretrievable names once current in the Highlands must be considerable.

There are a number of stories about clan conflict, which can be dated and related to mapped place-names. In the late fifteenth century near Dunan, to the west of Loch Rannoch, a Stewart of Appin was robbed and murdered by *Clann Iain Bhuidhe* (yellow-haired Iain). The Stewarts took their revenge in due course and routed the culprits at *Caochan na Fola* (NN478578). It must have been a thorough job, as the name means The Streamlet or Rill of Blood. One hundred years later, *Lochan na Mnà* (NN647207) to the South of Loch Earn and above Ardvorlich is associated with another gruesome tale. The Lady of Ardvorlich, whose father was Drummond of Drummond Eireanach and the Royal Forestor of Glen Artney, welcomed a party of MacGregors. While she was away preparing food for the visitors they put the blood-stained head of her father, whom they had killed earlier, upon the meal table. She fled into the hills in grief. Some days later women in the shielings wondered why their cows were yielding so little milk. They discovered that the lady of the house had been sheltering by a lochan and milking their cows at night. It has been known as the Lochan of the Woman, *Lochan na Mnà,* ever since.

Several associations with well known historical events have also been mapped. Some relate to the Jacobite Risings, many of them remembering the flight of Charles Edward Stuart after Culloden. One of the most striking names is *Coirean nan Spàinteach* (NN992134) in Glen Sheil *(Gleann Seile)*, where Spanish troops were defeated in the short-lived rising of 1719. The Prince of course landed on Eriskay at *Coilleag a' Phrionnsa* (NF786107) - the Cockle Beach of the Prince. (*Coilleag* is also used for a bowl-shaped depression in sand where marram grass grows). Less well known, but precisely locatable, is *Leaba Dhonnacha Dhuibh a' Mhonaidh* (NN 487553) or the Bed of Black Duncan of the Moor, which lies on the eastern flank of Meall Chomraidh at the western end of Loch Rannoch *(Raineach)*. Here Black Duncan Cameron, also a fugitive from Culloden, hid on a rocky shelf which conveniently afforded an excellent vantage point over the nearby Hanoverian barracks at Bridge of Gaur *(Drochaid Ghamhair)*. Also in Rannoch, at the eastern end of the Loch, is *Clach Sgoilte* (NN682576), said to have split from top to bottom on the same day that the Battle of Culloden was lost. In Torridon, legend has it that folk fled up the hill with portable provisions to escape a Government warship, which had dropped anchor in the Loch, to *Glac Dhubh a' Chàise - the Black Hollow of the Cheese.*

Rannoch also posseses earlier place-names linked with Robert Bruce and the Wars of Independence. Once a party of MacDougalls and English soldiers came through *Gleann Sassun* (Glen of the English) at NN657545 but were defeated by the Robertsons at Dalchosnie - *Dail Chosnaidh - the Haugh of Winning* (NN676577).

The victory was signalled from a beacon on Lassintullich - *Lasadh an Tullaich - Flame of the Hillock* (NN694577), a few miles to the east. At the other end of Loch Rannoch, and in the same period, another MacDougall escaped in a boat from imprisonment on *Eilean nam Faoileag - Island of Seagulls* (NN531577) and landed by *Creagan MhicDhùghaill* (NN524574) on the southern shore. Bruce himself and his party, after a defeat by the MacDougalls near Tyndrum at Dalrigh - *Dail an Rìgh - the King's Meadow* (NN342292), threw their arms into *Lochan (n)an Arm – The Little Loch of the Weapons* (NN3392878) in order to speed their escape from the field of battle.

Lochs seem to have a habit of attracting unwanted weapons. After a brief stand-off between their clansmen, the 'Sheep of Atholl' and the 'Dogs of Lochaber,' the Earl of Atholl and the Chief of Clan Cameron settled their dispute over grazing rights at the boundary of their estates by throwing their swords into an hitherto nameless lochan, which became known thereafter as *Lochan a' Chlaidheimh – The Little Loch of the Sword* (NN408603). Even in those days the wastes of Rannoch Moor were clearly not really worth fighting over. Several other waterbodies with the same description exist in the Highlands and there may have been similar stories behind these names. The full tale told by Duncan MacInnes of Glencoe was recorded by the School of Scottish Studies in 1959 and can be listened to at the website below.

http://www.tobarandualchais.co.uk/fullrecord/68131/1

Disputes were not always resolved so peacefully. In 1663, two sons of the chief of the Glen Garry MacDonalds were murdered during a quarrel with an uncle and his six sons. The deaths were avenged by sixty clansmen who arrived at the uncle's house to carry out the executions. The bodies were decapitated and their heads washed in a spring, which flows into Loch Ness, no doubt to make them presentable as a trophy for the Chief at Invergarry. Ever since, the spring has been known as *Tobar nan Ceann,* known in English as The Well of the Seven Heads. In 1360, after another clan fight, severed heads were thrown into the Kinlochewe River, later to be washed up at *Àth nan Ceann - the Ford of the Heads* (NH024627).

10.7: Legend and the Supernatural

Given the importance of rivers to early Celtic peoples and river deities derived from them, it is not surprising that water is the origin of many beliefs about the supernatural. Mythical animals, like the water horse or water bull, dwell in remote mountain lochs such as *Lochan an Tairbh-Uisge – Little Loch of the Water Bull* (NN592397) beneath *Meall nam Tarmachan – Rounded Hill of the Ptarmigan,* in Perthshire. In the early twentieth century Parlan MacFarlane of Brig o' Turk told Professor William Watson: '*Tha tarbh uisge air Loch Ceiteirein: chan fhaca mise an tarbh, ach chunnaic mi an laogh*' - '*There is a water bull in Loch Katrine: I have not seen the bull, but I have seen the calf.*'

The *ùruisgean* were semi-human creatures associated with deep ravines, waterfalls and moorland lochans. Their name means 'on water' *(air uisge).* William Gillies, who was Minister at Kenmore

Table 22: Culture – Events

Name	Gender	Sound	Meaning	Example
Bruadar, bruadair, bruadaran	m	*BROOutur*	dream, reverie, vision	Coire nam Bruadaran, Cuillins, NG520251, Corrie of Dreams
Cath / catha, cathan, cathannan	m	*cah*	battle, fight, struggle, contest	Creag Chath-bhoc, Glen Finglas, NN548103, Rock of the Roe-buck Battle
Comhairle, comhairlean	f	*CAWihrlyuh*	advice, counsel, council	Eilean na Comhairle, Loch Finlaggan, Islay, NR388680, Island of the Council
Còmhradh, còmhraidh, còmhraidh	m	*CAWragh*	conversation, dialogue	Eilean a' Chòmhraidh, Loch Leven, Glen Coe, NN087594
Cràbhadh / cràbhachd, cràbhaidh / cràbhachd	m	*CRAAvugh*	worship, devotion, piety	Tom na Cràbhachd, Glen Lednock, NN749265, Hillock of the Devotion (**Plate 20**)
Dannsadh, dannsaidh	m	*DOWNsugh*	dancing	Tom an Dannsaidh, Strathbraan, NN918383, Hillock of the Dancing (**Plate 31**)
Imrich, imriche, imrichean	f	*EEMreech*	flitting, change of residence	Bealach na h-Imriche, Trossachs, NN466056, Pass of the Flitting
Ìobairt, ìobairte, ìobairtean	f	*EEPuhrsht*	offering, sacrifice	Clach na h-Ìobairt, Blair Atholl, NN875653, Stone of the Offering
Leum, lèim / leuma, leuman / leumannan	m/f	*LAYum*	leap, bound, spring, frisk, start, shake.	Allt Leum Nèill, Assynt, NC222286, Burn of Neill's Leap
Loisgte	adj	*LAWshk-chuh*	burnt, scorched, scalded, parched	Cnoc Loisgte, Harris, NB184055, Burnt Knowe
Mòd, mòid, mòdan	m	*mawt*	court, trial, assembly, meeting	Clach a' Mhòid, Strathbraan, NN973403, Hill of the Court
Òran, òrain	m	*AWrahn*	song, poem	Tom Òrain, Glen Quaich, NN865368, Song Hilllock
Sealg, seilg, sealgan	f	*SHEHlak*	hunt, chase	Dùn Seilg, Glen Tilt, NN888726, Hunt Fort.

between 1912 and 1938, cites a Gaelic rhyme (my translation), which lists 12 *ùruisgean* in Breadalbane alone.

'*Peallaidh an Spuit*
'**Peallaidh of the spout**

Is Brunaidh an Easain,
And Brunaidh of the little waterfall.

Babaidh an Lochain
Babaidh of the little loch

Is Brunaidh an Eilein;
And Brunaidh of the island;

Paderlan a Feàrnan,
Paderlan from Fearnan,

Peadragan, Patragan.
Peadragan, Patragan,

Triubhas-dubh a Fartairchall,
Black Breeks from Fortingall,

Fuath Coire Ghamhnain,
The Spectre of Stirk Corrie,

Cas-luath Leitir,
Swift Foot of the Slope,

Amhlagan-dubh
Black Amhlagan

Is Catan Ceann-liath,
And Catan Grey Head,

Is Ùruisg dubh more Eas-amhlagan.'
And the Big, Black Uruisg.'
of Amhlagan's waterfall.'

(in Gillies 1938, 341)

The most famous was *Peallaidh* of the Spout, the King of the *ùruisgean* who stayed near the Falls of Moness, Aberfeldy, and was known for his shaggy pelt and hoof-like footprint. *Peallaidh* gave his name to the town *Obar Pheallaidh* (OHpuhr FAYlee) and had a shieling at *Ruighe Pheallaidh* (NN633483) in Glenlyon. Whilst near Acharn on Loch Tay, another *ùruisg* gave its name to a corrie and a burn below *Meall Greigh – Rounded Hill of the Herd or Stud: Coire Phadairlidh*

(NN687437) and *Allt Coire Phadairlidh* (NN693430 respectively. The *ùruisgean* would meet annually at *Coire na(n) Ùruisgean* (NN483077) in the Trossachs below Ben Venue by Loch Katrine.

Plate 5: Loch Katrine: Bealach nam Bò, Coire na(n) Ùruisgean and Eilean Molach. (Bealach nam Bò is the break of slope in the left background below the rock face, Coire na(n) Ùruisgean is above the steamboat and Eilean Molach is at the bottom right) (also in colour section)

Further west, the original Gaelic name for Glen Etive and Loch Etive is *Èite* where *Èiteag*, the horrid little one, stayed to the north of Ardchattan, in *Gleann Salach - the Dirty Glen* at NM976386. The source of the River Etive is *Loch Màthair Èite*, literally the *Loch of Èite's Mother* (NN287544). It is thought that the name may have arisen because of the wild and unpredictable squalls, which prevail there, and which may have been whipped up by Èiteag. Perhaps the name also owes something to the famous tidal waterfall of the Falls of Lora, near the mouth of the loch at Connel. Given that there are thirteen mapped fairy hills - *sìthean* in Perthshire alone and at least as many *Cnoc na Sìthe* (Plate 19) in the county, there is no doubt that the fairies were a powerful force in the naming of the landscape. References to the other world are common in Strathyre. Here, within a few kilometres of each other can be found *Sìdhean Dubh - Black Fairy Hill* (NN538159), *Beinn an t-Sìdhein - Mountain of the Fairy*

Hill (NN547178), *An Sìdhean - the Fairy Hill* (NN548172), *Bruach an Tannaisg - Bank of the Spectre* (NN562177), *Cnoc an t-Sìdhein - Hillock of the Fairy Hill* (NN563173) and *Sìdheag - Female Fairy* (NN558167). Sleepless in Strathyre might result. Perhaps the strangest supernatural creature to have appeared was a three-headed cat in the district of Oa in Islay, which inspired the corrupted name of the township of Ballychatrigan (NR324419), or, in Gaelic, *Baile Chat nan Trì Ceann.*

Giants also appear in the Gaelic landscape, or rather giant features or impressive landforms, such as the sea stacks at *Na Famhairean* (NG525582), off the east coast of Trotternish. Mythical giants are often associated with the stories of the Fianna, a band of independent warriors led by Fionn Mac Cumail or Fingal, which feature in early Irish and Scottish folk tales. Places associated with these stories can be found all over the Highlands associated with different types of landform, at *Sgòrr nam Fiannaidh - The Peak of the Fianna* (NN141583) at the western end of the *Aonach Eagach* ridge in Glen Coe, *Bealach nam Fiann - the Pass of the Fianna* (NC272382) near Kylesku and possibly at *Leac na Fionn - the Slab of the Fianna* (NG454704) on the Trotternish peninsula in Skye.

*Plate 33: Trotternish, Skye - Leac na(n) Fionn, just
to the right of centre (also in colour section)*

Fionn himself is said to have been buried at Killin, *Cill Fhinn* (NN572330) and his grave is marked by Fingal's stone; though the village name could also mean The White Church. There is a tradition that Ossian or in Gaelic *Oisean*, who was Fionn's poet son, was interred long ago beneath *Clach Oisein* in the Sma' Glen, which is shown on the OS map as Ossian's Grave (NN895906). When the stone was moved by General Wade's road-makers, human remains were indeed revealed beneath it. Such was the strength of Fingalian belief that the bones were borne away with much ceremony and pipe music by sixty local men to be reinterred on a now unknown summit somewhere in Glen Almond *(Gleann Amain).*

When Fionn was alive in Loch Tayside he was so large that he could stand with one foot on *Cìoch na Maighdean - the Maiden's Breast* (NN736364) near Ardtalnaig and with the other on *Ciste Buille a' Chlaidheimh - the Chest of the Sword Blow* (NN729352), wash his hands in *Lochan nan Làmh – Little Loch of the Hands,* possibly above Glen Lednock, and then turn around to drink from Loch Tay (*Loch Tatha). Lochan nan Làmh* cannot be traced with certainty on the maps, but from the above description it could well be the unnamed water at NN741308, which is roughly equidistant with Loch Tay, from Fionn's standpoint astride *Gleann a' Chilleine – The Glen of Concealment*, to the south-east of Ardtalnaig.

*Plate 34: Ardtalnaig - Cìoch na Maighdean (to the left)
and Ciste Buille a' Chlaidheimh (to the right) either side of
Gleann a' Chilleine, which Fionn straddled*

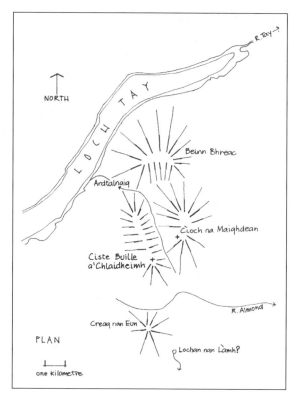

Figure 10: Plan showing Cìoch na Maighdean and Ciste Buille a' Chlaidheimh in relation to Loch Tay and the possible location of Lochan nan Làmh

Plate 35: Ardtalnaig - Buille a' Chlaidheimh

Explorer sheet 378 wrongly shows *Ciste Buille a' Chlaidheimh* as *Ciste Buide a' Chlaidheimh* and the 1:50,000 OS map substitutes this name with The Shee of Ardtalnaig. Shee is a corruption of *sìth* meaning fairy and is also found in the glen of that name further east. **Plate 35** shows what seems to be a large cut in the rounded flank of the hill. William Gillies, a Gaelic speaker from Barra, quotes the correct name, which he gathered in the district in the 1920s. This unusual landform is coincident with an igneous intrusion into the surrounding quartzite. Differential erosion, or erosion at the junction between the two rock types, may account for the appearance of a Fingalian-sized sword blow.

Duncan Bàn MacIntyre stayed for a time near the paired fairy hills of *Sìdhean Mòr* (NN351389) and *Sìdhean Beag* (NN354391), behind Beinn Dòbhrain. Curiously, he makes no mention of fairies or Fingalians anywhere in his work.

Plate 14: Trotternish, Skye – Baca Ruadh, Coire an t – Seasgaich and Sgùrr à Mhadaidh Ruadh to the right of the picture (also in colour section)

Table 23: Culture - Legend and the Supernatural

Name	Gender	Sound	Meaning	Example
Bèist, bèiste, bèistean	f	*baysht*	beast, beast of prey, monster, wretch	Loch na Bèiste, Wiay, Benbecula, NF873457, Loch of the Beast
Famhair, famhairean	m	*FAHvir*	giant, champion, mole-catcher – derived from the supernatural Fomoire of Irish myth	Na Famhairean, Trotternish, Skye, NG524581, The Giants.
Fiann, Fèinne	m/f	*FEEuhn*	giant, warrior, Fingalian, Fianna	Leac na(n) Fionn, Staffin, Trotternish - (NG454704), the Slab of the Fianna (**Plate 33**)
Fuath, fuatha	m	*FOOah*	spectre, apparition, ghost, kelpie	Beinn Fuath, St Fillans, Loch Earn, NN692218, Spectre Mountain
Gaisge	f	*GASHkuh*	heroism, bravery, valour, boldness	Meall na Gaisge, Glen Artney, NN726181, Hill of the Bravery
Sìth, sìthe, sìthean	f	*shee*	Fairy	Cnoc na Sìthe, Glen Lednock, NN758258, Hillock of the Fairy (**Plate 20**)
Tannasg, tannaisg	m	*TOWNusk*	apparition, spectre, ghost	Bruach an Tanna(i)sg, Strathyre, NN562177, Bank of the Spectre
Ùruisg, ùruisge, ùruisgean	m	*OOrishk*	water being, brownie, uruisk	Coire na(n) Ùruisgean, Trossachs, NN483077, Coire of the Uruisks (**Plate 5**)

11: ADJECTIVES

11.1: Colour, Pattern and Texture

Peter Drummond, to whom this section is indebted, has observed that the colour spectrum in Gaelic is more differentiated than in English, and it is not therefore possible to translate it directly into words of exactly equivalent meaning. The Gaelic spectrum, Drummond says, '... *is pastel rather than primary, gentle rather than bold.*' Meanings also seem to overlap, but they are, however, informed and distinguished by their changing landscape context. In particular, blues, greens, greys and whites are more diverse and more differentiated than in English. Hue does not appear to have constancy in its application to landscape. Colour temperature and saturation are more important defining elements than hue alone. Perhaps a pastoral people, reliant on transhumance, needed to have greater precision in the way they described the potential nutritional condition of upland grasses from a distance, before the time-consuming task of moving stock from winter townships in the glen to summer shielings in the hills. The colour of grasses in the high corries would become progressively more saturated with the green colour of chlorophyll as spring advanced. Distinctions based on temperature and saturation might also lend precision to definition, during the short and dark days of winter in the far north, when the grayscale prevails. Language becomes part of the place that it is required to name. In toponymic terms, it becomes specific to, and is modified by, its context. As any specific classification of the world is rooted in a specific indigenous culture, languages do not always map neatly onto one another. Plate 36 shows a Gaelic Colour Chart with variable saturation and several kinds of white and blue (see colour section)

The Gaelic word *gorm,* for example, does not always literally and directly mean the colour blue in the English sense. It also implies a warmer colour temperature. Whereas the Gaelic term *glas* is cooler, implying a paleness or sheen, as the chart tries to demonstrate. So when native speakers ask: *A' bheil am feur gorm fhathast? - Is the grass still blue?* (MacDonald 2000,186), they are referring to a depth in colour, perhaps indicative of an altered condition, rather than a hue. Similarly, *sùil ghorm* refers to an eye of a deep colour rather than merely a blue eye. Homer's repeating motif of wine-dark seas in the *Odyssey* perhaps signifies something similar.

The double axis of classification between hue and temperature also applies to boundaries between white and yellow; red and brown; and brown, blue and black. Such distinctions also exist in Welsh. As a result, places can be named and described with a precision, which accommodates the possibility of change. In both Welsh and Gaelic such complex distinctions are unfortunately being lost amongst contemporary speakers. The grass is now much more likely to be *uaine*, or just plain green.

Colour Summary

In summary, there are three kinds of white: pale, lilac, bright and cold *(fionn)*; pale, light, wan and fair *(bàn);* and clear, radiant and glistening *(geal). Fionn* is mostly found in the bright, sharp light of the north-west Highlands and Skye. It can be confused with the Gaelic for wine, *fìon,* or *Fionn* the Fingalian hero. *Bàn* is typically present in the west Highlands and the Inner Isles. It can be applied to fair-haired people and gives the surname Bane, Bayne or Bain. *Geal* is applied to hill names in the neighbouring valleys of the Laggan and Spey. It may apply to summits which retain a late covering of snow. *Geal* is never applied to people.

There are three words in the blue-green wavelength - *gorm, glas* and *uaine*. All three are common in place-names, with *glas* being the most frequent and *uaine* the least. *Gorm* can signify an azure blue or a verdant green. Its most well known application is the Cairngorms, collectively named after one of its major peaks *An Càrn Gorm - The Blue Cairn.* The Gaelic name for the range is *Am Monadh Ruadh,* which has quite different meaning of The Ruddy Moor. These two names may have arisen because the close-up appearance of the hills is different to the long distance view. There is a Gaelic saying: *Is gorm na cnuic a tha fada bhuainn – the hillocks far away from us are blue*– which reflects the fact that blue wavelengths travel further than red ones, which are absorbed by dust in the atmosphere. (Interestingly the same proverb in Irish uses *glas* instead of *gorm).* The contrasting descriptions could reflect two perceptions, one local and the other regional. *Glas* means grey, pale, ashy or sallow. It can be applied to unripe corn or the growth of new shoots of grass in Spring. However, *liath,* meaning grey, shares this meaning with glas. The secondary meaning of *liath,* mouldy, supports this grey-green, penicillin-like interpretation. The perception of grey greenness may arise from grass growing amongst scree. *Uaine* suggests a greener and more livid green. It is often applied to lochs and lochans and may indicate the colour of algal or weedy growth.

There are two reds in Gaelic. *Ruadh* is similar to the English ruddy and can be applied to people with red hair, which is the origin of the tag-name or surname Roy. The word also seems to be associated with the warm colour of Old Red Sandstone. *Dearg* denotes a brighter blood red or crimson or sometimes the colouration of rocks made by the setting sun. It can apply to granite and Torridonian sandstone, but never to people. Yellow in Gaelic, *buidhe* can describe individuals and gives the surname Bowie. In the landscape, it is not a bright colour. It describes hills, which are distinguished by their covering of white grasses such as *Nardus stricta* (Matt Grass) and *Deschampsia flexuosa* (Wavy Hair Grass), so called because of the bleached look of their dead growth in winter. Both *dubh* and *donn* can also apply to the appearance of vegetation in winter, but in this case they describe heather, which darkens hillsides when its green growth turns brown after flowering. *Dubh* is more common than *donn* and can apply to places, which are dark because of their outlook or sense of enclosure. *Donn* is cognate with the English dun, and gives the surname Dunn. *Odhar* is another drab colour like khaki, which lies somewhere between *buidhe* and *donn*. It is more frequent than the latter and seems to apply to peaty places and rounded hills or hillocks. It is the origin of the surname Orr. When Edmund Burt, a colleague of General Wade, wrote about the Highland hills in the early eighteenth century as 'monstrous Excresences' with drab colours 'a dismal gloomy Brown drawing on a dirty Purple' (Burt, 1754, Vol 2, 32), even in his self-evident distaste he could not have described the *donn* of heather hills in early winter any better.

Pattern

It is hard to establish where pattern ends and texture begins. *Breac* and *riabhach* do seem to be more about the former, however. *Breac* also means a trout and refers to the patterns of red, black or yellow spots which adorn the flanks of the fish. Whatever the colour of these marks, pattern is the defining characteristic of the species, rather than in English, where it is merely and somewhat inaccurately, just plain brown. Spotted mountains are distinguished by their patches of heather, blaeberry or white grasses mixed in with scree. Landforms, which are *riabhach,* meaning brindled, have a more striped pattern. *Cnoc Riabhach* (NN705237) near St Fillans is distinguished by long patches of rough grass or bracken alternating with long patches of bare rock. Perhaps the most famous example of *riabhach* is the anglicised *Braeriach, Am Bràigh Riabhach,* in the Cairngorms. Other corruptions of the two words give the surnames Reoch and Breck. The Devil is known as *An Riabhach Mòr!*

Texture

Garbh, leacach and *creagach* are the most common landscape textures, particularly *garbh. Mìn,* meaning smooth is quite rare, which is perhaps indicative of the overall rugged character of the Highlands, although *An Slìos Mìn - The Smooth Side* was once the name given to an extensive tract of country to the North of Loch Rannoch. Inexplicably, given the many written references to this name in history and oral tradition, it is not present on Ordnance Survey maps of the area.

11.2: Adjectives and Adjectival Nouns - Form, Size and Position

Gaelic adjectives for size, form and texture, which have been applied to a variety of landscapes can usually be read directly from the map, where such names have retained their correct spelling. The range of vocabulary is surprisingly similar to the kinds of word, which today's landscape architects are advised to use when making assessments of

Table 24: Colour, Pattern and Texture

Name	Gender	Sound	Meaning	Example
Bàn	adj	*baahn*	fair, white, pale, light in colour, wan	Beinn Bhàn, Strathyre, NN536137, Fair Mountain
Breac	adj	*brehck*	spotted, speckled, chequered, piebald	Beinn Bhreac, Jura, NR534778, Spotted Mountain
Buidhe	adj	*BOOyuh*	yellow	Beinn Bhuidhe, Ardnamurchan, NM438674, Yellow Mountain
Creagach	adj	*CREHkuch*	rocky	Àirigh a' Chinn Chreaga(i)ch, Glen Beich, NN634304, Shieling of the Rocky Head
Dearg	adj	*JEHRrak*	red, crimson	Stob Dearg, Taynuilt, NN063307, Red Stump
Donn	adj	*down*	brown, dun, sable	Beinn Donn, Appin, NM962477, Brown Mountain
Dorch / dorcha	adj	*DAWroch(uh)*	dark, black, dusky	An Àird Dorch, Skye, NG577288, Dark Height
Dubh	adj	*doo*	black, dark	Dùn Dubh, Glen Artney, NN722189, Black Fort
Fionn	adj	*fyoon*	white, fair, pale, blessed, holy	Am Fionn-allt, Torridon, NG847524, The White Burn
Garbh	adj	*GAHRav*	rough, rugged, coarse	Lòn Garbh, Staffin, Syke, NG490687, Rough Marshy Stream, (**Plate 21**)
Geal	adj	*gyahl*	white, clear, bright, radiant, glistening	Rubha Geal, Kylesku, NC264337, White Point
Glas	adj	*glahs*	grey, green (of grass), pale, wan	Beinn Ghlas, Loch Tayside, NN627463, Grey Mountain (**Plates 3 and 19**)
Gòbhlach	adj	*GOHluch*	forked, pronged, divided	A' Bheinn Ghòbhlach, Little Loch Broom, Ullapool, NG056944, The Forked Mountain

199

Table 24 (cont.)

Name	Gender	Sound	Meaning	Example
Gorm	adj	GAWrom	blue, azure, green (of grass)	Càrn Gorm, Glenlyon, NN634502, Blue Cairn.
Leacach	adj	LEHCHkuch	stony, flagged	Creag Leacach, Deeside, NO209817, Slabby Rock.
Liath, lèith / lèithe	adj	LEEuh	grey	Clach Mhòr na h-Àirighe Lèithe, Glen Tarken, NN658274, The Big Stone of the Grey Shieling (**Plate 29**)
Min	adj	meen	soft, tender, delicate, smooth, level	Meall Mìn, Ulva, NM445389, Smooth Rounded Hill
Molach	adj	MAWluch	rough, hairy, shaggy	Eilean Molach, Trossachs, NN487084, Shaggy Island (**Plate 5**)
Odhar, uidhir	adj	OHur	drab, dun, sallow, yellowish	Meall Odhar, Ben Ledi, NN565096, Sallow Rounded Hill
Riabhach	adj	REEhvuch	brindled, grizzled, greyish, brown	Cnoc Riabhach, St Fillans, NN705237, Brindled Knowe
Ruadh	adj	ROOugh	red, reddish, brown	Rubha a' Chamais Ruaidh, Loch Torridon, NG743594, Point of the Reddish Bay
Sgroillte	adj	SKRAWLtchuh	peeled, pared	Creag Sgroillte, Glen Finglas, NN516086, Peeled Rock
Sgroilleach, sgroilliche	adj	SKRAWLyuch	peeling, paring	Stob Sgroilleach, Glen Finglas, NN514088, Peeling Stump
Sleamhainn / sleamhuinn, sleamhna	adj	SLAYvin	slippery, smooth	Meall nan Leac Sleamhuinn, Arran, NR915478, Rounded Hill of the Slippery Slabs
Uaine	adj	OOynyuh	green, pallid, wan	Lochan Uaine, Glen Turret, NN785309, Little Green Loch

landscape character. The following table is taken from Landscape Character Assessment Guidance (2002) published by Scottish Natural Heritage (SNH).

Table 25: Checklist of Aesthetic and Perceptual Qualities in the Landscape

Aesthetic Qualities				
scale	intimate	small	large	vast
enclosure	tight	enclosed	open	exposed
diversity	uniform	simple	diverse	complex
texture	smooth	textured	rough	very rough
form	vertical	sloping	rolling	flat
line	straight	angular	curved	sinuous
colour	monochrome	muted	colourful	garish
balance	harmonious	balanced	discordant	chaotic
movement	dead	still	calm	busy
pattern	random	organised	regular	formal
Perceptions / Impressions				
rarity	ordinary	unusual	rare	unique
security	comfortable	safe	unsettling	threatening
wildness	domestic	managed	natural	wild
beauty	boring	interesting	attractive	inspiring
familiarity	ordinary	familiar	unusual	striking
management	derelict	disturbed	tended	manicured
productivity	barren	sparse	productive	lush

This list is clear enough. Yet it is unusual to see such a lucid and understandable expression of vocabulary applied to landscape amongst English place-names. In Scottish Gaelic many of SNH's guide words have a reasonable and readable equivalent in the language, which can be directly linked to many place-name qualifiers. Diverse attributes of landscape, which together generate its character seem to be embedded in Gaelic vocabulary. It would be interesting for a Gaelic-speaking landscape architect to make an assessment of the character of a specific landscape using the vocabulary of the language. In so doing, as has been found with colour terms, a set of words particular to Gaelic, and its need to find ways of describing specific forms, sizes, textures and atmospheres indigenous to the Highland landscape might emerge as a useful and specific tool. Languages, after all, have their own individual lens for perceiving the world.

The Gaelic word *tana is* perhaps an example of this. It means thin. Several lochs in South Lewis share this description, but they are no thinner than any other of the many lochs nearby: some are plumply ovoid, *Loch Tana* at NB275281, NB299344 and NB335297 being examples. One can only conclude that thin in these instances may mean shallow rather than narrow, which is after all an equivalent to thinness in the vertical dimension.

Generally, the opposites *beag* and *mòr, leathan* and *caol* are the most common adjectives of form on the map. *Caol* originally described the Sma' Glen in Perthshire, with the emphatic word order of *An Caol-ghleann,* which is also in the Scots form. *Reamhar* is more common in the Perthshire Highlands, often qualifying *meall or cnoc,* which is perhaps a reflection of the rounded nature of the hills in the county.

Just as *gòbhlan* is powerful in the naming of birds, *gòbhlach,* meaning forked, is widely used for a variety of differing features. *Allt Gòbhlach* in Arran at NR886439 has no fewer than twelve tributary forks along its length. *A' Bheinn Ghòbhlach* to the west of Loch Broom, Ullapool, at NH056943 is blessed with twin summits. Ten miles to the south, *Cadha Gòbhlach* forks up the north-east face of *Sàil Liath,* the grey heel, on the *An Teallach* range, the hearth or forge.

Form, Size and Position - Position

Àrd, bun and *eadar* are the most frequent words describing position. *Eadar,* between, is commonly anglicised to *edder* or *edra. Tarsainn* (formerly *tarsuinn*) is also common, though it does not have an accurate equivalent in English. It refers to something, usually a hill, which crosses the path obliquely or transversely. *Uachdar* is common in anglicised form as *auchter* or *ochter* and gives Ochtertyre (*Uachdar Thìre* - upper land) and Auchtermuchty (*Uachdar Mucaidh - upper pig area*). The North Fife pronunciation of that village is *Uchtermuchty,* which is much closer to Gaelic. Drumochter (NN626770), or *Bealach Dhruim Uachdair,* where *druim* means a ridge, is the high pass through which the A9 now goes, separating the catchments of the Rivers Tay and Spey. *Uachdar* can mean cream - literally, the top of the milk. The height of higherness, *Àird Uachdarachd* (NA103005) on St Kilda is a peninsula lying immediately to the east of Conachair, the highest sea cliff in the UK.

Deas, which is cognate with the Latin *dexter*, and *tuath* are represented in *Uibhist a Deas* and *Uibhist a Tuath* in *Na Eileanan An Iar*, North and South Uist in the Western Isles. In some dialects of Gaelic you go up south, *suas gu deas*, and *sios gu tuath*, down north. Walking sunwise or clockwise is *deiseil*, which has overtones of rectitude, at least in the northern hemisphere.

Table 26: Form, Size and Position

Name	Gender	Sound	Meaning	Example
Àrd	adj	*aarsht*	high, lofty	Caisteal Àrd, Harris, NB188094, High Castle
Beag	adj	*bake*	little, short, diminutive	Dùn Beag, Trotternish, Isle of Skye, NG459687, Little Fort-like Hill (**Plate 21**)
Bho / fo dheas	adj	*vo / fo yehs*	southern, right hand side	Mulla fo (bho) Dheas, Harris, NB143077, South Top
Bho / fo thuath	adj	*vo / fo HOOah*	northern	Mulla fo (bho) Thuath, Harris, NB144084, North Top
Bun, buin / buna, buin / bunan	m	*boon*	base, foot, foundation	Loch Bun Abhainn Eadarra, Harris, NB125035, Loch at the Foot of the River Between
Cam	adj	*cam*	crooked, distorted, curved, bent	Cam-loch, Assynt, NC213136, Crooked Loch
Caol	adj	*coeuhl*	narrow, slender, thin	Creagan a' Chaol-achaidh, Glen Spean, NN283801, Little Rock of the Narrow Field
Carach	adj	*CAHruch*	winding, meandering, turning	Cnoc Carach, Fiunary Forest, Morvern, NM658476, Winding Hillock
Cas	adj	*cas*	steep	Allt Cas-leac, Glen Etive, NN148453, Steep Stone Burn
Cearcall, cearcaill, cearcallan	m	*CYEHRcull*	circle	Coire a' Chearcaill, Glen Quaich, NN834358, Corrie of the Circle (**Plate 12**)
Claon	adj	*cloeun*	sloping	Claonairigh, Inveraray, Loch Fyne, NN058047, Sloping Shieling
Còig	num	*CAWik*	five	Còig na Peighinnean, Ness, Lewis NB530649, The Five Pennylands
Corr / corra	adj	*cawr*	pointed	Corr-sgeir, Islay, NR433458, Pointed Skerry

204

Corrach	adj	CORuch	steep, precipitious	Caisteal Corrach, Braeleny, NN643121, Steep Castle
Crìoch, crìche, crìochan	f	CREEuch	boundary, frontier, end, limit, march	Sròn na Crìche, Ardeonaig, NN664334, Nose of the Boundary
Cròcach	adj	CRAWCHkuch	branched, antlered	Loch Cròcach, Kylesku, NC197395, Branched Loch
Crom	adj	crowm	crooked, bent, curved	Sgiath Chrom, Glen Dochart, NN464314, Crooked Wing (**Plate 13**)
Cumhang / cumhann	adj	COOan	narrow	An Caolas Cumhann, Kylesku, NC227339, The Narrow Straits
Dà	num	daah	two	Sròn Dhà Mhurchaidh, Ben Lawers, NN407393, Nose of the Two Murdos
Deas	adj	jehs	south	Caochan Deas, Strath Avon, NJ145134, South Rill
Domhainn / dom-hann	adj	DAWeen	deep, hollow	Allt Eas Domhain(n), Glen Tarken, NN664288, Stream of the Deep Waterfall
Eadar	prep	EHter	between	Maol Eadar a' Chinn, Braeleny, NN623133, Bald Hill between the Head
Eagach	adj	EHkuch	notched, indented, jagged	Aonach Eagach, Glen Coe, NN156584, Notched Ridge
Ear	adj	ehr	east	An Tràigh Ear, North Uist, NF827765, The West Beach
Fada	adj	FAHtuh	long, distant	Beinn Fhada, Glen Coe, NN163543, Long Mountain
Frith	adj	frih	small, little	Frith-sgeirean, Colonsay, NR346878, Small Skerries
Geàrr	adj	gyahr	short	Geàrr-aonach, Glen Coe, NN159555, Short Ridge
Gòbhlach	adj	GAWluch	forked, pronged	Creag Gòbhlach, Strathyre, NN575109, Forked Rock
Goirid	adj	GUHritch	short	Dùn Goirid, Loch Snizort, Skye, NG413515, Short Fort

Table 26 (cont.)

Name	Gender	Sound	Meaning	Example
Iar / siar	adj	*EEuhr / SHEEuhr*	west	An Tràigh Iar, South Harris, NF036967, The West Beach
Ìochdar(ach)	adj	*EEuchkur(uch)*	lower part, the bottom of something	Bealach Ìochdarach, Trotternish, Isle of Skye, NG410733, Lower Pass
Ìosal	adj	*EEusul*	lower part, the bottom of something	Sgeir na Seamraig Ìosal, Kentra, NM637689, Lower Skerry of the Clover
Leathan / leathann	adj	*LEHuhn*	broad, spacious	Bàgh Leathann, Eddrachillis, NC163386, Broad Bay
Leth	adj	*lay*	half	An Leth-allt, Loch Duich, NG943247, The Half-stream
Meanbh	adj	*MEHnev*	little, small, diminutive	Cadha a' Mheanbh-Chruidh, NH007634, Narrow Pass of the Small Cattle
Meadhan / meadhon, meadhain / meadhoin, meadhanan / meadhonan	m	*MEEun*	middle	Càrn Mheadhoin, Braes of Abernethy, NJ066149, Middle Cairn
Mòr	adj	*more*	large, great	Dùn Mòr, Trotternish, Isle of Skye, NG459687, Large Fort-like Hill (**Plate 21**)
Reamhar, reamhra	adj	*REHvur/ RAHvur*	fat, plump, fleshy	Lochan nam Breac Reamhar, Rannoch Moor, NN246587, Loch of the Plump Trout
Seachd	adj	*shechk*	seven	Eilean nan Seachd Seisrichean, Ardnamurchan, NM424638, Island of the Seven Ploughing Teams

Tana	adj	*TAHnuh*	thin, slender, slim, lean, shallow	Loch Tana, Lewis, NB293555, Shallow Loch. Waterbodies so named often dry up completely in summer
Tarsainn / tarsuinn	adj	*TAHrsing*	across, oblique, transverse, lateral	Beinn Tharsuinn, Harris, NB204006, Transverse Mountain
Uachdar(ach)	adj	*OOuchkur*	top, upper part, summit	Bealach Uachdarach, Trotternish, Isle of Skye, NG415731, Upper Pass

12: READING THE LANDSCAPE THROUGH PLACE-NAMES

What is meant by reading the Gaelic landscape? At a fundamental level, landscape is composed of physical, biological and cultural elements. These interact and influence one another and can be read as vertical layers, with geology, geomorphology and hydrology at the bottom and culture at the surface, sandwiching landcover and associated flora and fauna in the middle. Landscape is also partly imaginary, and so its qualities are shaped in part by our perception and the values prevailing in society and cultures at the time. One has only to contrast the change in attitude towards Highland landscape shown by the lexicographer Dr Johnson in the late eighteenth century with that of William Wordsworth in the early nineteenth century, to see how perception can change diametrically in less than forty years. Writing in 1765 in his *A Journey to the Western Islands of Scotland*, Johnson remarks:

> '... an eye accustomed to flowery pastures and waving harvests is astonished and repelled by this wide extent of hopeless sterility. The appearance is that of matter incapable of form or usefulness ...'
>
> (Johnson 1775, 29)

William Wordsworth, in contrast, on the tour he made with his sister Dorothy in 1803, celebrates *The Highland Girl of Inversneyde - Inbhir Snàthaid -* Needle Confluence (NN336088) on the east shore of Loch Lomond:

> '... a very shower
> of beauty is thy earthly dower! ...
>
> ... This little bay, a quiet road
> That holds in shelter thy abode ...

In truth together ye do seem
Like something fashion'd in a dream ...

(in Wordsworth 1997, 112)

In the twentieth century we seem to have come full circle again in T. S. Eliot's poem 'Rannoch by Glencoe,' 'where: ... *the crow starves, and the patient stag breeds for the rifle and substance crumbles in the thin air*' (in Dunn 1979, 74). This resonates with Fraser Darling's neo-Johnsonian perception of the Highlands in 1955 as a wet desert. It is inevitable that any reading of the landscape will be partly skewed by cultural context and individual preference. Mapmakers and place-namers are not immune to such influences.

In the living and non-living layers, matters are less skewed by perception. This book has argued that the Gaelic vocabulary which describes landform, seascape and colour possesses a diversity of differentiation which English lacks. Over 600 generic name words in the mapped Gaelic vocabulary have been listed and categorised from all over the Highlands. Whilst this survey may not be complete, comprehensive map searches suggest it must approach completion. Relative numbers of generic words in each category are shown in the table below. Name words which relate to colour, pattern and texture; form, size and position; and the Gaelic anatomy do not really fit the model of abiotic, biotic and cultural layers. They have been excluded from percentage calculations relating to the three layers, but included in overall percentages relating to all name types. No attempt has been made to quantify the actual numbers of specific and locatable names, which would be an enormous task.

Table 29: Frequency of Generic Name Words in Place-names

Category	Number	%	Layer	Number	%
Landform – Mountains, Hills	43	8			
Landform – Hollows, Valleys, Passes	37	7	**Abiotic**	179	35
The Gaelic Waterscape, Hydronymy	71	14			
Climate, Season, Sound and Time	28	6			
Landcover and Ecology	20	4			
Flora	51	10	**Biotic**	122	24
Fauna	51	10			

Category	Number	%	Layer	Number	%
Agriculture and Crops	53	10			
Domestic and Farm Animals	23	4			
Buildings and Settlements	27	5	Cultural	210	41
Church and Chapel	9	2			
Cultural Artefacts	31	6			
People and Occupations	46	9			
Events	13	3			
Legend and the Supernatural	8	2			
Sub-total	511				
Colour, Pattern and Texture	24	4			
Form, Size and Position	42	7	n/a	n/a	n/a
The Gaelic Anatomy	27	4			
TOTAL	8				

In terms of toponymic utility, generic words in the cultural layer are the most diverse in place-names, at over 40%, followed by those in the abiotic layer at 35%, and least of all by words in the biotic layer, which are present in 24% of place-names. This is a vocabulary developed to describe a landscape which has been intensely named and differentiated to reflect its human activities and associated land practices. In the highly modified environment of the Highlands, ecology and landcover have the least influence in naming distinctions, whilst the form and characteristics of the land and the coast continued, at the time of mapping, to be significant in naming despite a dominant overlay of cultural influences. Place-name evidence supports the view that woodland habitats were widely fragmented by the time the Gaelic landscape was named. The dominance of the cultural toponymic layer counters the romantic perception of the wild Highlander as a kind of noble savage at one with the wild landscape and its grandeur. The realities of subsistence farming in a difficult climate, the gathering of fuel and the continual tending of stock in an unenclosed landscape paints a more pragmatic picture.

Overall the most common terms are those related to hydronymy (12%), whether describing fresh or salt water or coastal features. (Indeed Gaelic water terminology is common to both marine and inland situations). This is not surprising given the complexity of the west coast of Scotland and its mountainous hinterland with its high levels of precipitation. Understanding drainage patterns would have been vital for the success of subsistence farming in marginal areas. Before the great road building projects of the eighteenth century, communication was more efficient by sea and freshwater loch. Understanding winds, tides, currents and how they affect harbours and anchorages would have been essential to successful navigation. Naming distinctions within the abiotic layer have proved most resistant to landscape change and so have the most relevance to our use and enjoyment of the landscape today. Time has wrought more significant changes to ecology and culture in the Gàidhealtachd, and especially to the Highland way of life. Often what remains of winter and summer towns are a few humps and bumps amongst impoverished grassland and heath.

Reading landscape in the field is not just a question of looking and recording what is physically present. It is also about finding trace evidence, which indicates what has happened and what is likely to happen, when things changed and what caused them to change. It is possible to identify four processes, which occur in the landscape: erasure, origination, transformation and migration. When reading the Gaelic landscape through its place-names we can identify some examples of these processes. The landscape of transhumance and shieling pastures has been erased by large scale sheep farming and the consolidation of small scale agricultural holdings. Sometimes the origination of this process can be dated to a documented clearance event, often because forced measures were involved. Subsequently, when sheep farming proved less lucrative, it was erased, in many cases by the establishment of shooting estates. These transformations can be seen in the shift away from names like àirigh (aahree) meaning shieling and imrich (imreech) meaning flitting (moving house) to English and Scots names like sheepfold, fank and bothy, and later to butts, for grouse shooting.

Similarly, where Gaelic names have been heavily anglicised in the Angus Glens, it is reasonable to conclude from the prevalence of Scots names that language loss or language <u>migration</u> <u>originated</u> before the Ordnance Survey mapmakers undertook their work in the late nineteenth century. In some cases, bilingualism appears to have been recorded in place-names of equivalent meaning, existing at the time of mapping lying within a few 100 metres of one another. <u>Migration</u> of species from the landscape can also be registered in the <u>erasure</u> of different woodland types and associated fauna. The named record preserves these as tree types, whose regeneration has been prevented by sustained and intensive grazing pressure from prehistoric times. A woodland landscape has been <u>transformed</u> to moor and heath. It is not always possible to establish the <u>origins</u> of these events exactly just from the mapped record, as the date of <u>origination</u> of a name is likely to be different to the date it was documented. If indeed arguments made in the text are correct about a much earlier <u>erasure</u> of woodland from the Highlands, it becomes difficult to make general conclusions about the dates of tree names and the moorland species which have <u>migrated</u> into the spaces left behind them.

We can make some general conclusions about the cultural layer. Names which mention priests, saints and perhaps the domestic pig are likely to be pre-Reformation. Those which refer to poets and musicians are likely to be of the same period, since these activities were discouraged by the Statutes of Iona in 1609 and the Reformation. The influence of the literary tradition in Ireland was also waning. Those names citing ministers can be assumed to be post Reformation, whilst those referring to clan conflict can also be dated no later than the middle of the eighteenth century and probably earlier, when the Highlands were becoming more peaceable, notwithstanding Jacobite insurgence. In general, we can relate trends and patterns in toponymy to the character, constituents and inhabitants of the landscape that has been named, albeit with the caveat that the named layer is not a temporally homogeneous overlay. A reference to a hangman's hill may pre-date, and its function have ceased to be contemporary with the date of a sheiling name. The wood that once hid a wolf's den, may have gone long before that species also disappeared.

Reading place-names on the mapped record is rather like reading a book written by several authors over different periods of time. Sometimes their writing has been intermittent, executed in great bursts separated by long periods of silence. At other times it has accumulated steadily. The resultant manuscript we hold in our hands today has been transcribed many times over by others sometimes unfamiliar with the original writers, and sometimes unfamiliar with the language of the text. Mistakes and misinterpretations have multiplied and some pages of the original document have gone missing. Sometimes the text has become blurred. W. G. Hoskins likened landscapes subject to such continual reworking to palimpsests – manuscripts or engravings which has been erased and overwritten or re-engraved by successive texts or images. In a sense Ordnance Survey records resemble the oldest books on earth, still in use but subject to different perceptions and interpretations. Like ancient texts, for all their ineluctable imperfections, Ordnance Survey maps are perhaps the best available record we possess, and certainly carry deep social significance in how and what they have named in their cartographic record. Their imperfect genesis contributes to, and is a reflection of, the people and societies who played both minor or major roles in their creation.

It has been argued that the toponymic landscape of the Highlands is frozen in time, which might imply that everything frozen has been frozen at the same time. What has been mapped however, is not just what was present at any one time or continuously present. It also prompts memories of what was once or what might have been present, or imagined as a mythical overlay transferred from another imaginary locality. OS mapping can be dated accurately and is, therefore, an <u>origination</u>. It is an <u>origination</u> in a landscape whose names have been frozen, thawed and refrozen over several eras. The Highlands have been subject to such great changes, so that the landscape place-names once recorded has often become invisible over large areas, and remains, indicated only in the surface toponymic layer. Those named places, which still bear some resemblance to their original representation, are more likely to be found in the abiotic layer, representing landform and water. Given significant changes in Highland ecology and society, 'ground truthing' in the biotic and cultural layers is less likely to find present conditions sharing any equivalence with past conditions.

Walking through Highland toponymic landscape can be like travelling in the kind of fragmented dream world portrayed in 'Hallaig,' though without MacLean's poetic purpose to compose our journey. We pass the site of a clan battle whose participants, no doubt sprited enough at the time, have long been forgotten, together with their cause. We skirt a rock once concealing the den of a pine marten, and once covered in scrub. We ford a burn once stirred up each year by the feet of people and their beasts as they travelled together each summer to the breezy sheiling in the hills. This experience escapes us, if place-names merely serve to blacken the map with their print. This book intends a semantic recapture not only of a lost landscape, but also of a landscape which has been lost to us. By trying to explain Highland landscape through the lens of the language that evolved to describe and interpret its individual domain, and in so doing was shaped by that territory, another perception of the Gàidhealtachd can be revealed. We will develop the ability to see landform, seascape and colours in ways different to those possible in English. We will begin to see the landscape through the eyes of those who named it over several hundreds of years. Our appreciation of place and its provenance will deepen as a result.

FURTHER READING

Peter Drummond calls Watson's *The Celtic Place-names of Scotland*'
and Nicolaisen's *Scottish Place-names* originally published fifty
years apart in the 1920s and 1970s, the Old and New Testaments
of toponymic study. They remain essential, though sometimes
difficult reading for enthusiasts. Nicolaisen covers place-names in
all of Scotland's current and former languages. Watson primarily
deals with Celtic names. He also grounds his book in the influence
of legend and tradition: in particular, on the early Celtic church and
its saints. Place-name analysis is often supported by comparative
etymology across many Indo-European languages. Watson was also
fortunate in being able to use the knowledge of many more Gaelic-
speaking informants from across the Gàidhealtachd than exist today.

Nicolaisen's book is led by the then emerging theory of toponymy.
He relates different distributions of place-names to the settlement
history of different colonising cultures. There are several useful maps
to illustrate the points he makes. He begins to explore the relationship
between names and what they name. What do words actually mean
when applied to the landscape they describe?

In her book *Place-names in the Landscape - the geographical
roots of Britain's place-names,* Margaret Gelling pursues this line
of investigation in an English context, where the topographic
vocabulary of Anglo-Saxon settlers was highly refined when applied
to landform and its potential for settlement and land use. Most of this
subtle terminology has gone from modern English, so Gelling uses
images of the landscape gathered in the field to illustrate toponymic
distinctions. She argues that the essence of place-name studies lies in
its link with a topographically based language.

Several contemporary and specific guides to regional place-names produced by Scottish Natural Heritage follow this approach, but extend it, to consider selected aspects of ecology and landscape history. These are available on line, as is Ordnance Survey's *Guide to Gaelic origins of place names in Britain,* which this book has categorised and expanded. Less physically accessible is the work of Ian Fraser, formerly of the School of Scottish Studies in Edinburgh, which are spread across a range of academic journals and, as the papers of Nicolaisen and Watson have been, deserve to be collated. Fraser's two part exploration of the toponymy of agriculture, published in the *Transactions of the Gaelic Society of Inverness,* is essential to an understanding of the agricultural history of the Highlands and how it has been expressed through naming.

For hillwalkers, Peter Drummond's book *Scottish Hill Names* is informative, readable and well illustrated with maps and sketches and with good sections on folklore and colour in the Gaelic landscape and the history of mapping. Chris Smout's work on the history of Scottish woodlands places ecological history in the context of maps and place-naming. Anne Lorne Gillies's book on Gaelic song is deep and detailed, and yet is accessible to the newcomer to the language. Her background notes about how and for whom songs were composed are particularly useful. The history of mapping in Scotland is sumptuously and comprehensively covered in *Scotland: Mapping the Nation* by Fleet, Wilkes and Withers. Further detail about Timothy Pont can be found in *The Nation Survey'd* edited by Ian Cunningham. The stories leading to Roy's 'magnificent sketch' are elegantly related by Rachel Hewitt in *Map of the Nation.*

SELECTED BIBLIOGRAPHY

Academic Sources

Bil, A (1990) *The Shieling 1600 – 1840: The Case of the Scottish Central Highlands.* John Donald Publishers Ltd: Edinburgh.

Cathcart, Alison. *The Statutes of Iona: The Archipelagic Context.* Journal of British Studies Jan. 2010, Vol. 49, No. 1, pp 4-27.

Coates, R (1990) *The Place-names of St Kilda, Nomina Hirtensia.* Celtic Studies 1.

Edlin, H, L (1959) *Place-names as a Guide to Former Forest Cover in the Grampians.* Scottish Forestry 13, pp 63-67.

Fleet, C, Wilkes, M, and Withers, C W J (2011) *Scotland: Mapping the Nation.* Birlinn: Edinburgh.

Fraser, I A (1989) *Place-name opposites in Scotland.* Shadow 6, pp 17-21.

Fraser, I A (1992 & 1994) *The Agricultural Element in Scottish Gaelic Place-names.* Transactions of the Gaelic Society of Inverness 57 & 58, pp 203-223 & 223-246.

Harley, J B (1988) *Maps, Knowledge and Power.* In *The Iconography of Landscape* Cosgrove, D and Daniels, S. (eds.). Cambridge University Press.

Hewitt, R (2010) *Map of a Nation.* Granta: London.

Hoskins, W G (1988) *The Making of the English Landscape.* Hodder and Stoughton: London.

Hough, M (1990) *Out of Place: restoring identity to the regional landscape.* Yale University Press: Newhaven.

King, J (2008) *Analytical Tools for Toponymy: Their Application to Scottish Hydronymy.* Unpublished PhD thesis, University of Edinburgh.

MacDonald, S (2000) *A' bheil am feur gorm fhathast? – Some Problems concerning Language and Cultural Shift.* Scottish Studies 33, pp 186-197. School of Scottish Studies, University of Edinburgh.

McNiven, P E (2011) *Gaelic Place-names and the Social History of Gaelic Speakers in Medieval Menteith.* Unpublished PhD thesis, University of Glasgow.

Meek, D (1998) *Place-names and Literature: Evidence from the Gaelic Ballads.* In The Use of Place-names. Taylor S. (ed.), pp 147-168. Scottish Cultural Press. Edinburgh.

Newton, M (2006) *Dùthchas nan Gàidheal - Selected Essays of John MacInnes.* Birlinn: Edinburgh.

Nicolaisen, W F H (1961) *The Distribution of Certain Gaelic Mountain-Names.* Transactions of the Gaelic Society of Inverness Vol. 45, pp 113-128.

Nicolaisen, W F H (2001) *Scottish Place-names.* John Donald: Edinburgh.

Ó Murchú, M (1989) *East Perthshire Gaelic.* Dublin Institute for Advanced Studies: Dublin.

Ross, R J & Hendry, J (1986) *Sorley MacLean - Critical Essays.* Scottish Academic Press: Edinburgh.

Smout, T, C (1997) *Scottish Woodland History.* Scottish Cultural Press.

Smout, T, C, MacDonald, A, R & Watson, F (2005) *A History of the Native Woodlands of Scotland, 1500 - 1920.* Edinburgh University Press.

Smout, T, C (2006) *Woodland in the Maps of Pont,* in *The Nation Survey'd.* Cunningham, I. C. (ed.), pp77-92. John Donald: Edinburgh.

Stuart-Murray, J (2006) *Differentiating the Gaelic Landscape of the Perthshire Highlands.* Scottish Studies 34, pp159-177. School of Scottish Studies, University of Edinburgh.

Taylor, I (2011) *Place-names of Scotland.* Birlinn, Edinburgh.

Taylor, S (1998) *The Use of Place-names.* Scottish Cultural Press: Edinburgh.

Taylor, S & Wentworth, R (2006) *Pont and Place Names,* in *The Nation Survey'd.* Cunningham, I. C. (ed.), pp55-76. John Donald: Edinburgh.

Watson, W. J. (1990) *The History of The Celtic Place-names of Scotland.* Birlinn: Edinburgh.

Watson, W. J. (1928) *The Place-names of Breadalbane.* Transactions of the Gaelic Society of Inverness Vol. 34, pp248-279.

Whittow, J (1992) *Geology and Scenery in Britain.* London: Chapman Hall.

Withers, C (1984) *Gaelic in Scotland.* John Donald: Edinburgh.

Withers, C (2000) *Authorising Landscape: 'Authority,' Naming and the Ordnance Survey's Mapping of the Scottish Highlands in the Nineteenth Century.* Journal of Historical Geography, issue 26, Vol. 4, pp 532-554. Academic Press.

Literary Sources

Burt, W (1754) *Letters from the North of Scotland Volumes 1 & 2.* Facsimile edition (1974) John Donald: Edinburgh

Carmichael, A (1992) *Carmina Gadelica.* Collected Edition: Lindisfarne Books.

Dunn, D (1979) *The Poetry of Scotland.* B. T. Batsford Ltd: London.

Gunn, N M (1976) *Young Art and Old Hector.* Souvenir Press: London

Johnson, S (1775) *A Journey to the Western Isles of Scotland.* Penguin Classics (1978 edition).

Lorne Gillies, A (2005) *Songs of Gaelic Scotland.* Birlinn: Edinburgh.

MacLean, S / MacGill-Eain, S (1989) *O Choille gu Bearradh - From Wood to Ridge.* Carcanet: Manchester.

MacLeoid, A, Macleod, A (1978) *Orain Dhonnchaidh Bhàin - The Songs of Duncan Ban Macintyre.* Scottish Academic Press: Edinburgh

MacPherson, D (1868) *An Duanaire – A New Collection of Gaelic Songs and Poems.* MacLachlan and Stewart: Edinburgh.

Martin Martin, (1716) *A Description of the Western Islands of Scotland.* Birlinn: Edinburgh (1999).

Pennant, T (1774) *A Tour in Scotland and Voyage to the Hebrides.* Melven Press: Perth.

Thomson, D, S (1993) *Gaelic Poetry in the Eighteenth Century.* ASLS: Aberdeen.

Wordsworth, D (1803) *Recollections of a Tour made in Scotland.* Yale University Press (1997).

General Publications

Carnegie, Mrs (1896) *Place-names of Balquidder.* The Scottish Geographical Magasine. Vol. 12. Edinburgh.

Cunningham, I, C, (2006) *The Nation Survey'd.* John Donald: Edinburgh.

Drummond, P (2007) *Scottish Hill Names their Origin and Meaning.* Scottish Mountaineering Trust Publications Ltd.

Dwelly, E (1988) *Faclair Gàidhlig gu Beurla / The Illustrated Gaelic - English Dictionary.* Gairm: Glasgow.

Farquhar, A (2005) *The Storr - Unfolding Landscape.* Luath Press Ltd: Edinburgh.

Fenton, A (1976) *Scottish Country Life.* Tuckwell Press: Edinburgh.

Fenton, A (1980) *The Traditional Pastoral Economy.* in Parry, M, L & Slater, T R The Making of the Scottish Countryside: London.

Flanagan, D and Flanagan, L (2002) *Irish Place-names.* Gill and Macmillan: Dublin.

Fraser, D (1978) *Highland Perthshire.* Standard Press: Montrose.

Fraser, I A (1999) *Place-names* in The Perthshire Book. Omand, D. (ed.), pp 199-210. Birlinn: Edinburgh.

Fraser, I A (1999) *The Place-names of Arran.* The Arran Society of Glasgow.

Fraser, I A (2004) *The Place-names of Argyll in The Argyll Book.* Omand, D. (ed.), pp 243-254. Birlinn: Edinburgh.

Fraser Darling, F (1955) *West Highland Survey.* Oxford University Press

Fraser Darling, F & Morton Boyd, J (1969) *The Highland and Islands.* Collins Fontana.

Gelling, M (1984) *Place-names in the Landscape - The Geographical Roots of Britain's Place-names.* Phoenix Press: London.

Gordon, Seton (1935) *Highways and Byways in the West Highlands.* MacMillan: London

Gordon, Seton (1948) *Highways and Byways in the Central Highlands.* MacMillan: London

Grimble Ian (1980) *Highland Man.* HIDB: Inverness.

Hull, R (2007) *Scottish Mammals.* Birlinn: Edinburgh.

Hutchinson, R (2005) *A Waxing Moon: The Modern Gaelic Revival.* Mainstream: Edinburgh.

Hutchinson, R (2006) *Calum's Road.* Birlinn: Edinburgh.

Jedrej, C and Nuttall, M. (1996) *White Settlers.* Luxembourg

King, J and Cotter, M (2011) *Ainmean-àite ann an Ìle agus Diùra - Place-names in Islay and Jura.* Dualchas Nàdair na h-Alba, Peart. Scottish Natural Heritage: Perth.

Macaulay, D (1982) *Place Names in The Sutherland Book.* In Omand, D. (ed.), The Northern Times Ltd: Golspie.

MacCulloch, J (1824) *The Highland and Western Islands of Scotland.* London.

MacGregor, A and Cameron, D (1886) *A Gaelic Topography of Balquidder Parish.* Edinburgh University Press.

Mackenzie, O H, (1924) *A Hundred Years in the Highlands.* Geoffrey Bles: London.

MacKinnon, K (1991) *Gaelic - A Past and Future Prospect.* Saltire Society: Edinburgh.

Maclean, C (1997) *The Isle of Mull: Place-names, Meanings and Stories.* Maclean Publications: Dumfries.

Maclean, R (2004) *The Gaelic Place-names and Heritage of Inverness.* Culcabock Publishing: Inverness.

MacIlleathain, R, Maclean, R (2010) *A' Ghàidhlig air aghaidh na tìre Ainmean-àite ann an Iar-thuath na Gàidhealtachd - Gaelic in the Landscape Place names in the North West Highlands*. Dualchas Nàdair na h-Alba, Peart. Scottish Natural Heritage: Perth.

MacIlleathain, R, Maclean, R (2010) *A' Ghàidhlig is Lochlannais air Aghaidh na Tìre Ainmean-àite ann an Gallaibh, Cataibh is Dùthaich MhicAoidh - Gaelic and Norse in the Landscape Place names in Caithness and Sutherland*. Dualchas Nàdair na h-Alba, Peart. Scottish Natural Heritage: Perth.

MacIlleathain, R (2010) *Gaelic on Signs and Maps in Scotland - Why it Matters*. The Islands Book Trust: Lewis.

McLennan, G (2009) *A Gaelic Alphabet - a guide to pronunciation*. Argyll Publishing: Glendaruel.

MacLeod, F (1989) *Togail Tìr - Marking Time - the Map of the Western Isles*. Acair: Stornoway.

Milliken, W & Bridgewater, S (2007) *Flora Celtica - Plants and People in Scotland*. Birlinn: Edinburgh.

Nicolson, A (2002) *Sea Room*. Harper Collins: London.

Ordnance Survey (2005) *Guide to Gaelic origins of place names in Britain*.

Waugh, D (1989). *Place Names*. In The New Caithness Book Omand, D. (ed.), pp 141-155. North of Scotland Newspapers: Wick.

Websites

http://www.ambaile.org.uk/

http://www.gaelicplace-names.org/index.php

http://www.jimwillsher.co.uk/Site/Runrig/Lyrics/

http://www.ordnancesurvey.co.uk/oswebsite/freefun/didyouknow/place-names/docs/gaelic_guide.pdf

http://www.ordnancesurvey.co.uk/oswebsite/freefun/didyouknow/place-names/docs/gaelicorthographyextent.pdf

http://www.scottish.parliament.uk/Gaelic/place-namesA-B.pdf

http://www.skyecomuseum.co.uk

http://www.smo.uhi.ac.uk/index_gd.html

http://www.snh.org.uk/pdfs/publications/gaelic/GaelicNorseintheLandscape.pdf

http://www.snh.org.uk/pdfs/publications/gaelic/Gaelic%20in%twentiethe%20landscape.pdf

http://www.snh.org.uk/pdfs/publications/gaelic/islay%20jura%20book.pdf

http://theses.gla.ac.uk/2685/01/2011mcnivenphd.pdf

http://lac-repo-live7.is.ed.ac.uk/handle/1842/3020

INDEX OF GENERIC NOUNS

Generic nouns are listed in modern Gaelic.

Generic noun	Page	Gender	Definite article - nominative & genitive
bealaidh	115	m	am bealaidh, a' bhealaidh
bean	173	f	a' bhean, na mnà
beannan	64	m	am beannan, a' bheannain
beàrn	74	m/f	Am beàrn / a' bheàrn, a' bheàirn / na beàirn / na bèirn
beinn	64	f	a' bheinn, na beinne
bèiste	194	f	à bhèiste, na bèiste
beithe	115	f	a' bheithe, na beithe
beum	92	m	am beum, a' bheuma
bidean	64	m	am bidean, a' bhidein
binnean	64	m	am binnean, a' bhinnein
biod	64	m	am biod, a' bhioda
biolair	115	f	a' bhiolair, na biolaire
bioran	64	m	am bioran, a' bhiorain
blàr	74	m	am blàr, a' bhlàir
bò	150	f	a' bhò, na bà
boc	127	m	am boc, a' bhuic
bodach	173	m	am bodach, a' bhodaich
bodha	92	m	am bodha, a' bhodha
bogach	105	m/f	am bogach / a' bhogach, a' bhogaich / na bogaich
boglach	105	m/f	am boglach / a' bhoglach, a' bhoglaich / na boglaich
borrach	105	m	am borrach, a' bhorraich
bota	92	m	am bota, a' bhota
brà	167	f	a' bhrà, na bràdhan/bràthan
bradan	127	m	am bradan, a' bhradain
bràigh	64	m	am bràigh, a' bhràighe / a' bhràghad
braon	155	m	am braon, a' bhraoin
bràthair	173	m	am bràthair, a' bhràthar
breabadair	173	m	am breabadair, a' bhreabadair
breac	127	m	am breac, a' bhric
bròg	167	f	a' bhròg, na broige
broighleag	115	f	a' bhroighleag, na broighleig
broc	127	m	am broc, a' bhruic
brochan	144	m	am brochan. a' bhrochain
bruach	64	f	a' bhruach, na bruaich
bruthach	64	m/f	am bruthach / a' bhruthaich, a' bhruthach / na bruthaich
buachaille	173	m	am buachaille, a' bhuachaille
buaile	144	f	a' bhuaile, na buaile
bùirich	155	f	a' bhùirich, na bùirich
buntàta	144	m	am buntàta, a' bhuntàta
bùrn	92	m	am bùrn, a' bhùirn
càbag	144	f	a' chàbag, na càbaig
cabhsair	160	m	an cabhsair, a' chabhsair
cachaileith	145	f	a' chachaileith, na cachaileithe
cadha	74	m	an cadha, a' chadha
caibeal	165	m	an caibeal, a' chaibeil
caigeann	74	m/f	an caigeann / a' chaigeann, a' chaiginn / na caiginn
cailleach	173	f	a' chailleach, na cailliche
caipleach	145	f	a' chapleach, na caiplich
cairidh	93	f	a' chairidh, na cairidh
caise	93	f	a' chàise, na càise
càise	145	m	an càise, a' chàise

Generic noun	Page	Gender	Definite article - nominative & genitive
caisteal	65	m	an caisteal, a' chaisteil
calltainn/	115	m	an calltainn, a' challtainne
calltuinn			
calman	127	m	an calman, a' chalmain
camas/camus	93	m	an camas / camus, a' chamais
canach	115	m/f	an canach / a' chanach, a' chanaich / na canaich
caochan	93	m	an caochan, a' chaochain
caolas	93	m	an caolas, a' chaolais
caora	150	f	a' chaora, na caorach
caorann	115	m/f	an caorann / a' chaorann, a' chaorainn / na chaorainn
capall/capull	150	m	an capall / an capull, a' chapaill / a' chapuill
càrn	65	m	an càrn, a' chàirn / a' chuirn
càrnach	105	m/f	an càrnach / a' chàrnach, a' chàrnaich / na càrnaich
carraig	93	f	a' charraig, na carraige
cat	127	m	an cat, a' chait
cath	187	m	an cath, a' chatha
cathair	160	f	a' chathair, na cathrach
càthar	105	m	an càthar, a' chàthair
ceann	93	m	an ceann, a' chinn
ceapach	145	m/f	an ceapach / a' cheapach, a' cheapaich / na ceapaich
cearc	150	f	a' chearc, na circe
cearcall	204	m	an cearcall, a' chearcaill
cearc-fhraoich	127	f	a' chearc-fhraoich, na circe-fhraoiche
ceàrd	174	f	a' cheàrd, na ceàird
ceàrdach	160	f	a' cheàrdach, na ceàrdaich
cill	165	f	a' chill, na cille
cìoch	180	f	a' chìoch, na cìche
cìr	167	f	a' chìr, na cìre
cìrean	145	m	an cìrean, a' chìrein
ciste	165	f	a' chiste, na ciste
clachan	160	m	an clachan, a' chlachain
cladach	93	m	an cladach, a' chladaich
cladh	165	m	an cladh, a' chlaidh / a' chladha
claidheamh	167	m	an claidheamh, a' chlaidheimh
claigeann	180	m	an claigeann, a' chlaiginn
clamhan	127	m	an clamhan, a' chlamhain
clàrsair	174	m	an clàrsair, a' chlàrsair
clas	145	f	a' chlais, na claise
clèireach	174	m	an clèireach, a' chlèirich
cleit/cleite	65	f	a' chleit / a' chleite, na cleite
cleiteadh	93	m	an cleiteadh, a' chleitidh
cluain	145	f	a' chluain, na cluaine
cnap	65	m	an cnap, a' chnaip
cnaimhseag	115	f	a' chnaimhseag, na cnaimhseig
cnoc	65	m	an cnoc, a' chnoic / a' chnuic
coileach	145, 150	m	an coileach, a' choilich
coille	105	f	a' choille, na coille
coirce	145	m	an coirce, a' choirce
coire	74	m	an coire, a' choire
comhairle	187	f	a' chomhairle, na comhairle
còmhradh	187	m	an còmhradh, a' chòmhraidh

Generic noun	Page	Gender	Definite article - nominative & genitive
coinean	127	m	an coinean, a' choinein
còinneach	115	f	a' chòinneach, na còinnich
comar	93	m	an comar, a' chomair
corra	127	f	a' chorra, na corra
corran	93, 167	m	an corran, a' chorrain
cràbhachd	187	m	an cràbhachd, a' chràbhaidh
crann	167	m	an crann, a' chrainn / a' chroinn
crannag	94	f	a' chrannag, na crannaig
craobh	116	f	a' chraobh, na craoibhe
crasg	74	f	a' chrasg, na craisge
creag	65	f	a' chreag, na creige
creachann	65	m	an creachann, a' chreachainn
creamh	116	m	an creamh, a' chreamh
crìoch	205	f	a' chrìoch, na crìche
critheann	116	m	an critheann, a' chrithinn
crò	145	m	an crò, a' chrodha / a' chrothadh
crochaire	174	m	an crochaire, a' chrochaire
crodh	150	m	an crodh, a' chruidh
croich	167	f	a' chroich, na croiche
crois	165	f	a' chrois, na croise
croit	145	f	a' chroit, na croite
cruach	65	f	a' chruach, na cruaiche
crùbach	174	m	an crùbach, a' chrùbaich
crudh/crudha	167	m	an crudh / crudha, a' chruidhe / a' chrudha
cù	150	m	an cù, a' choin
cuan	94	m	an cuan, a' chuain
cudaig	127	f	a' chudaig, na cudaige
cuidhe / cuithe	145	f	a' chuidhe / a' chuithe, na cuidhe / na cuithe
cuileag	128	f	a' chuileag, na cuileige
cuilc	116	f	a' chuilc, na cuilce
cuileann	116	m	an cuileann, a' chuilinn
cuing	94	f	a' chuing, na cuinge
cuinneag	168	f	a' chuinneag, na cuinneige
cuiseag	116	f	a' chuiseag, na cuiseige
cuithe	74	f	a' chuithe, na cuithe
cumhang	74	m	an cumhang, a' chumhaing
cunglach	75	m	an cunglach, a' chunglaich
curach	168	f	a' churach, na curaich
cuthag/cubhag	128	f	a' chuthag, na cuthaige
dabhach	168	f	an dabhach, na dabhaich
dail	145	f	an dail, na dalach
damh	128	m	an damh, an daimh
dannsadh	187	m	an dannsadh, an dannsaidh
darach	116	m	an darach, an daraich
dearcag	116	f	an dearcag, na dearcaig
dìg	75, 145	f	an dìg, na dìge
dìollaid	75, 168	f	an dìollaid, na dìollaide
dìthreabh	105	f	an dìthreabh, na dìthreibh
dòbhran	128	m	an dòbhran, an dòbhrain
dòirlinn	94	f	an dòirlinn, na dòirlinne
doire	105	m/f	an doire, an doire / na doire

Generic noun	Page	Gender	Definite article - nominative & genitive
dòrn	180	m	an dòrn, an dùirn
dris	117	f	an dris, na drise
drochaid	160	f	an drochaid, na drochaide
droigheann	117	m	an droigheann, an droighinn
druid	128	m	an druid, an druide
druim	180	m	an druim, an droma
duileasg	117	m	an duileasg, an duilisg
duine	174	m	an duine, an duine
dùn	65	m	an dùn, an dùin
each	150	m	an t-each, an eich
eachraidh	146	m	an t-eachraidh, an eachraidh
eag	75	f	an eag, na h-eige
eaglais	165	f	an eaglais, na h-eaglaise
eala	128	f	an eala, na h-eala / na h-ealaidh
earb	128	f	an earb, na h-earba
easbaig	174	m	an t-easbaig, an easbaig
eas	94	m	an t-eas, an easa
easg	105, 75	m/f	an t-easg / an easg, an easga / na h-easga
eidheann	117	f	an eidheann, na h-eidhne
eileach	161	m	an t-eileach, an eilich
èileag	168	f	an èileag, na h-èileige
eilean	94	m	an t-eilean, an eilein
eilid	128	f	an eilid, na h-eilid
èirionnach	150	m	an t-èirionnach, an èirionnaich
eòrna	146	m	an t-eòrna, an eòrna
eun	128	m	an t-eun, an eòin
fadhail	94	f	an fhadhail, na fadhlach
fàidh	174	m	am fàidh, an fhàidhe
famhair	194	m	am famhair, an fhamhair
fang/faing	146	m/f	am fang / an fhaing, an fhaing / na fainge
faochag	128	f	an fhaochag, na faochaige
faoileag	128	f	an fhaoileag, na faoileige
faoileann	129	f	an fhaoileann, na faoilinn
fàsach	105	m/f	am fàsach / an fhàsach, an fhàsaich / na fàsaich
fasgadh	161	m	am fasgadh, an fhasgaidh
fathan	117	m	am fathan, an fhathain
feadag	129	f	an fheadag, na feadaige
feadan	95	m	am feadan, an fheadain
feannag	129	f	an fheannag, na feannaige
fear	174	m	am fear, an fhir
fearann	146	m	am fearann, an fhearainn
feàrna	117	f	an fheàrna, na feàrna
fèith	95	f	an fhèith, na fèithe
feòladair	174	m	am feòladair, an fheòladair
feur	117, 146	m	am feur, an fheòir
feusag	180	f	an fheusag, na feusaige
fiacail	129	f	an fhiacail, na fiacla
fiadh	129	m	am fiadh, an fhèidh
fiann	194	m	am fiann, an fhèinne
fiantag	117	f	an fhiantag, na fiantaige

Generic noun	Page	Gender	Definite article - nominative & genitive
fìdhlear	175	m	am fìdhleir, an fhìdleir
figheadair	175	m	am figheadair, an fhigheadair
fiodhag	117	f	an fhiodhag, na fiodhaige
fiodhan	146	m	am fiodhan, an fhiodhain
fireach	65	m	am fireach, an fhirich
fitheach	129	m	am fitheach, an fhithich
foghar	155	m	am foghar, an fhoghair
forsair	175	m	am forsair, an fhorsair
fraoch	117	m	am fraoch, an fhraoich
freumh	117	m	am freumh, an fhreumha
frìth	105	f	an fhrìth, na frìthe
fuaim	155	f	an fhuaim, na fuaime
fuaran	95	m	am fuaran, an fhuarain
fuath	194	m	am fuath, an fhuatha
gamhainn	150	m	an gamhainn, a' ghamhna / ghaimhne
gaineamh	95	f	a' ghaineamh, na gaineimh
gaisge	194	f	a' ghaisge, na gaisge
gall	175	m	an gall, a' ghoill
gaoth	155	f	a' ghaoth, na gaoithe
gàrradh	146	m	an gàrradh, a' ghàrraidh
gart	146	m	an gart, a' ghairt
gead	146	f	a' ghead, na gid
geàdh	129	m/f	an geàdh / a' gheàdh, a' gheòidh / na geòidh
geamhradh	156	m	an geamhradh, a' gheamhraidh
geàrraidh	146	m	an geàrraidh, a' gheàrraidh
geata	161	m	an geata, a' gheata
geodha	95	m	an geodha, a' gheodha
gil	95	f	a' ghil, na gile
gille	175	m	an gille, a' ghille
giuthas	117	m	an giuthas, a' ghiuthais
glac	75	f	a' ghlac, na glaic(e)
gleann	75	m	an gleann, a' ghlinne
glumag	95	f	a' ghlumag, na glumaig
gob	171	m	an gob, a' ghuib
gobha	175	m	an gobha, a' ghobhann / a' ghobhainn
gobhar	151	m/f	an gobhar / a' ghobhar, a' ghobhair / na gobhair, a' ghoibhre / na goibhre
gòinean	118	m	an gòinean, a' ghòinein
goirtean	147	m	an goirtean, a' ghoirtein
greigh	147	f	a' ghreigh, na greighe
grianan	156	m	an grianan, a' ghrianain
gualann	181	f	a' ghualann, na gualainn / na guailne
guilbneach	129	f	a' ghuilbneach, na guilbnich
iasgair	175	m	an t-iasgair, an iasgair
ìm	147	m	an t-ìm, an ime
imrich	187	f	an imrich, na h-imriche
inbhir	95	m	an t-inbhir, an inbhir
innean	168	m	an t-innean, an innein
innis	147	f	an innis, na h-innse
ìobairt	187	f	an ìobairt, na h-ìobairt

Generic noun	Page	Gender	Definite article - nominative & genitive
iola	96	f	an iola, na h-iola
Iolair(e)	129	f	an iolair(e), na h-iolaire
iubhar	118	m	an t-iubhar, an iubhair
lach	129	f	an lach, na lacha
lag	75	m/f	an lag, an laig / na laig, an luig / na luig
laimrig/làimrig	96	f	an laimrig, na laimrige
làir/làire	151	f	an làir, na làireadh / làrach
làirig	75	f	an làirig, na làirige
laogh	151	m	an laogh, an laoigh
làrach	161	f	an làrach, na làraich
leaba/leabaidh	168	f	an leaba / leabaidh, na leapa
leamhan	118	m	an leamhan, an leamhain
lèana	75	f	an lèana, na lèana
lèanag/lianag	75	f	an lèanag, na lèanaig
leathad	75	m	an leathad, an leathaid / leothaid
lèig	106	f	an lèig, na lèige
leitir	75	f	an leitir, na leitire / leitreach
leum, lèim	187	f	an leum, na lèim
linn	96	f	an linn, na linne
lìon	168	m	an lìon, an lìn
loch	96	m/f	an loch, an locha / na luich
lochan	96	m	an lochan, an lochain
lòn	106, 75	m	an lòn, an lòin
long	168	f	an long, na luinge
losaid	168	m/f	an losaid, an / na losaide
losgann	129	m	an losgann, an losgainn
luachair	106	f	an luachair, na luachair / luachrach
lùb/lùib	96	f	an lùb / lùib, na lùib / lùibe
lus	118	m	an lus, an luis
mac	175	m	am mac, a' mhic
machair	76, 106, 147	m/f	am machair / a' mhachair, a' mhachaire / a' mha chrach / na machrach
madadh	151	m	am madadh, a' mhadaidh
magh	76	m/f	am magh / a' mhagh, a' mhagha / na magha
maighdean	175	f	a' mhaighdean, na maighdinn
maigheach	130	f	a' mhaigheach, na maighiche
màm	181	m/f	am màm / a' mhàm, a' mhàim / na màim
manach	175	m	am manach, a' mhanaich
mang	130	f	a' mhang, na maing
maol	65	m	am maol, a' mhaoil
maor	175	m	am maor, a' mhaoir
marbh	175	m	am marbh, a' mhairbh
màthair	176	f	a' mhàthair, na màthar
meacan	118	m	am meacan, a' mheacain
meadhan/ meadhon	206	m	am meadhan / meadhon, a' mheadhain / mheadhoin
meall	66	m	am meall, a' mhill
meann	151	m	am meann, a' mhinn
mèirleach	176	m	am mèirleach, a' mhèirlich
meur	181	m/f	am meur / a' mheur, a' mheòir / na meòir
ministear	176	m	am ministear, a' mhinisteir

Generic noun	Page	Gender	Definite article - nominative & genitive
mòd	187	m	am mòd, a' mhòid
mòinteach	106	f	a' mhòinteach, na mòintich
mol	96	m	am mol, a' mhoil / mhuil / mhola
monadh	66	m	am monadh, a' mhonaidh
morair	176	m	am morair, a' mhorair
morbhach	96	f	a' mhorbhach, na morbhaich
morghan	96	m	am morghan, a' mhorghain
muc	151	f	a' mhuc, na muice
muidhe	169	m/f	am muidhe / a' mhuidhe, a' mhuidhe / na muidhe
muir	91	m/f	am muir / a' mhuir, na mara
mullach	66	m	am mullach, a' mhullaich
muran	118	m	am muran, a' mhurain
nathair	130	f	an nathair, na nathrach
naomh	176	m	an naomh, an naoimh
òb	97	m	an t-òb, an òib
oidhche	156	f	an oidhche, na h-oidhche
oighreag	118	f	an oighreag, na h-oighreig
oitir	97	f	an oitir, na h-oitire / oitreach
òran	187	m	an t-òran, an òrain
òrd	66, 169	m	an t-òrd, an ùird
òrdag	181	f	an òrdag, na h-òrdaig
òs	97	m	an t-òs, an òsa
partan	130	m	am partan, a' phartain
peighinn	147	f	a' pheighinn, na peighinne
pìobair(e)	176	m	am pìobair(e), a' phìobaire
plaide	169	f	a' phlaide, na plaide
poit	169	f	a' phoit, na poite
poll	97	m	am poll, a' phuill
pòr	147	m	am pòr, a' phòir
port	97	m	am port, a' phuirt
preas	118	m	am preas, a' phris
puball	161	m	am puball, a' phubaill
raineach	118	f	an raineach, na rainich
ràmh	169	m	an ràmh, an ràimh
raon	147	m/f	an raon, an raon / na raoin
ràth	161	m	an ràth, an ràth
rathad	161	m	an rathad, an rathaid
rèidh	76, 147	m	an rèidh, an rèidh
rèilig	165	f	an rèilig, na rèilige
riasg	106, 76	m	an riasg, an rèisg
rìgh	176	m	an rìgh, an rìgh
rinn	97	f	an rinn, na rinne
rodh	97	m	an rodh, an rodha
roid	118	f	an roid, na roide
roinn	148	f	an roinn, na roinne
ròn	130	m	an ròn, an ròin
ros	97	m	an ros, an rois
rubha	97	m	an rubha, an rubha
ruighe	148	m/f	an ruighe, an / na ruighe
sabhal	161	m	an sabhal, an t-sabhail

Generic noun	Page	Gender	Definite article - nominative & genitive
sac / saic	169	m	an sac / saic, an t-saic
sagart	176	m	an sagart, an t-sagairt
saidh	161	f	an t-saidh, na saidhe
saighdear	176	m	an saighdear, an t-saighdeir
saighead	169	f	an t-saighead, na saighde
sàil	181	f	an t-sàil, na sàl / sàile / sàlach
sàilean	98	m	an sàilean, an t-sailein
samhradh	156	m	an samhradh, an t-samhraidh
Samhainn	156	f	an t-Samhainn, na Samhna
saor	177	m	an saor, an t-saoir
Sasannach	177	m	an Sasannach, an t-Sasanaich
seabhag	130	m/f	an seabhag / an t-seabhag, an t-seabhaig / na seab haig
seagal	148	m	an seagal, an t-seagail
seilach	119	m	an seileach, an t-seilich
sealg	187	f	an t-sealg, na seilg
sealgair	177	m	an sealgair, an t-sealgair
seamrag	118	f	an t-seamrag, na seamraig
seangan	131	m	an seangan, an t-seangain
searrach	151	m	an searrach, an t-searraich
seasg	119	m/f	an seasg / an t-seasg, an t-seasga / na seasga
sèid	156	f	an t-sèid, na sèide
seileastair	119	m	an seileastair, an t-seileasdair
sgadan	131	m	an sgadan, an sgadain
sgàirneach	66	m	an sgàirneach, an sgàirnaich
sgarbh	131	m	an sgarbh, an sgairbh
sgeir	98	f	an sgeir, na sgeire
sgian	169	f	an sgian, na sgeine / sgine
sgiath	66	f	an sgiath, na sgèithe
sgitheach	119	m	an sgitheach, an sgithich
sgòrr/sgùrr	66	m	an sgòrr / sgùrr, an sgòirr / sgùrra
sileadh	157	m	an sileadh, an t-silidh
sionnach	131	m	an sionnach, an t-sionnaich
sìth	194	f	an t-sìth, na sìthe
sìthean	66	m	an sìthean, an t-sìthein
sliabh	66	m	an sliabh, an t-slèibh(e)
slios	67	m	an slios, an t-sliosa
sloc	76	m	an sloc, an t-sluic
slugaid	76	f	an t-slugaid, na slugaide
snaoisean	169	m	an snaoisean, an t-snaoisein
snàthad	169	f	an t-snàthad, na snàthaid
sneachd(a)	157	m	an sneachd(a), an t-sneachda
sop	148	m	an sop, an t-suip
spàrdan	67	m	an spàrdan, an spàrdain
spearrach	169	f	an spearrach, na spearraich
speireag	131	f	an speireag, na speireig
spidean	67	m	an spidean, an spidein
sprèidh	151	f	an sprèidh, na sprèidhe
sràid	161	f	an t-sràid, na sràide
srath	76	m	an srath, an t-sratha
sròn	67	f	an t- sròn, na sròine

Generic noun	Page	Gender	Definite article - nominative & genitive
sruth	98	m	an sruth, an t-sruith / an t-strutha
stac	67	m	an stac, an staca / staic
staidhir	162	f	an staidhir, na staide
stalla	98	m	an stalla, an stalla
stapag	148	f	an stapag, na stapaig
steall	98	f	an steall, na stèill
stob	67	m	an stob, an stuib
stùc	67	m	an stùc, an stùic
sùbh	119	m	an sùbh, an t-sùibh
suidhe	67	m	an suidhe, an t-suidhe
sùil	181	f	an t-sùil, na sùl / sùla
taghan	131	m	an taghan, an taghain
taigh	162	m	an taigh, an taighe
tàillear	177	m	an tàillear, an tàilleir
tairbeart	98	m/f	an tairbeart, an tairbeirt / na tairbeirt
talamh	76	m/f	an talamh, an talaimh / na talmhainn
tannasg	194	m	an tannasg, an tannaisg
tarbh	151	m	an tarbh, an tairbh
tartar	157	m	an tartar, an tartair
teampall	165	m	an teampall, an teampaill
teanga	181	f	an teanga, na teanga(i)dh
teine	162	m	an teine, an teine
tìr	76	f	an tìr, na tìre
tobar	98	m/f	an tobar, an tobair / an tobair / na tobrach
tobhta	162	f	an tobhta, na tobhta
todhar	148	m	an todhar, an todhair
toll	76	m	an toll, an tuill
tolm	98	m	an tolm, an tuilm
tom	67	m	an tom, an tuim
tòn	181	f	an tòn, na tòine
torc	131	m	an torc, an tuirc
tòrr	67	m	an tòrr, an torra
tràigh	99	f	an tràigh, na tràighe / tràghad
trilleachan	131	m	an trilleachan, an trilleachain
tunnag	151	f	an tunnag, na tunnaig
uamh	76	f	an uamh / uaimh, na h-uaimhe / uamha
uan	151	m	an t-uan, an uain
ubhal	119	m	an t-ubhal, an ubhail
uchd	181	m	an t-uchd, an uchda
ùidh	99	f	an ùidh, na h-ùidhe
ùig	99	f	an ùig, na h-ùige
uinnseann	119	m	an t-uinnseann, an uinnseinn
uisge	99	m	an t-uisge, an uisge
ulaidh	169	f	an ulaidh, na h-ulaidhe
ùruisg	194	m	an t-ùruisg, an ùruisge

INDEX OF ADJECTIVES AND ADJECTIVAL NOUNS

Most adjectives listed below describe attributes of climate, colour, form, position, size and texture. Those beginning with **b, f, m, p** and **s** are lenited after a feminine noun. Where they precede nouns, in order to emphasise the attribute, the noun itself is lenited where possible. Some adjectives, such as *beag* and *mòr*, have plural forms *beaga* and *mòra*. Some adjectives become slender and agree with a noun in the genitive case, e.g. *na beinne bige*. Some words listed below, like *bun* meaning foot, are really nouns but tend to act in an adjectival sense.

Adjective	Page	Adjective	Page		Page
àileach	155	conasgach	116	geal	199
àrd	204	dorch / dorcha	199	labhar	156
bainneach	144	dubh	199	leacach	200
bàn	199	eadar (preposition)	205	leathann	206
beag	204	eagach	205	leth	206
bho / fo dheas	204	ear	205	liath	200
bho / fo thuath	204	fada	205	loisgte	187
braonach	153	fiaclach	181	meanbh	206
breac	199	fionn	199	mìn	200
buidhe	199	fionnar	155	molach	200
bun (adjectival noun)	204	fliuch	155	mòr	206
cam	204	frith	205	odhar	200
caol	204	fuar	155	reamhar	206
carach	204	galanach	155	riabhach	200
ceòthach	155	gaothach	156	ruadh	200
claon	204	garbh	199	sgroillte	200

Adjective	Page	Adjective	Page		Page
sgroilleach	200	donn	199	sìor	157
corr / corra	204	geàrr	205	sleamhainn	200
corrach	205	glas	199	soilleir	157
creagach	199	gliogarsnaich	156	tana	207
cròcach	205	gòbhlach	199	tarsainn	207
crom	205	goirid	205	tiormachd	157
cumhang / cum-hann	205	gorm	200	uaine	200
dearg	199	iar	206	uachdar	207
deas	205	ìochdar(ach)	206		
domhainn / dom-hann	205	ìosal	206		

Biographical note The author was born in the Gold Coast and brought up in Fife and London. Returning to Scotland for family holidays involved many expeditions to the Perthshire Highlands. His father, who knew a little Gaelic, was asked what the hill names meant. He seemed to confuse the words for wife and mountain. After leaving school, when most friends were travelling to the east, the author chose the Western Isles instead. Seasick, homesick, with a broken rucksack frame and leaking tent, he first heard Gaelic on a storm-tossed Barra in 1971 and felt a stranger in his own land. He was one of the first cohorts of students outwith Scotland to sit Gaelic O-grade. He is now Director of Landscape Architecture at the University of Edinburgh, and still discovering the beautiful language and the places it enlivens through naming. The patience of many teachers over the years must be acknowledged: John Dumbreck (Manchester), Callum Ross (Skye), Alasdair MacInnes (Glen Coe), Ewen Maclean (North Uist), John MacKenzie (Lewis), Sheila Kidd (Edinburgh), Gillian Munro (Edinburgh), Ann Paterson (Lewis), Joan MacDonald (Lewis), Rona Wilkie (Mull and Sutherland), Kenneth McManus (Glasgow), Myles Campbell (Staffin) and Neill MacGregor (Edinburgh).